Growing in the Life of Faith

Second Edition

Growing
in the
Life of Faith

SECOND EDITION

Education and Christian Practices

❖

Craig Dykstra

Westminster John Knox Press
LOUISVILLE • LONDON

Scripture quotations marked NRSV are from the New Revised Standard Version of the Bible, copyright © 1989 by the Division of Christian Education of the National Council of the Churches of Christ in the U.S.A., and used by permission.

Scripture quotations marked RSV are from the Revised Standard Version of the Bible, copyright © 1946, 1952, 1971, and 1973 by the Division of Christian Education of the National Council of the Churches of Christ in the U.S.A., and used by permission.

Grateful acknowledgment is made to the following to reproduce previously copyrighted material: Lyric excerpt from "Holy as the Day Is Spent," *The Gathering of Spirits*, by Carrie Newcomer. © 2002 Rounder Records. Used by permission.

Portions of chapter 1 are adapted from "Thinking Faith: A Theological Education for the American Churches," *Living Light* 27 (Fall 1990): 7–16. Copyright © 1990 United States Catholic Conference, Inc., Washington, D.C. Used by permission. All rights reserved.

Chapter 4 contains portions of "Christian Education as a Means to Grace," *Princeton Seminary Bulletin*, July 1992.

Chapter 9 is an adaptation of "Communities of Conviction and the Liberal Arts," *Bulletin of the Council of Societies for the Study of Religion* 19, no. 3 (September 1990): 61–66.

Chapter 10 is an abridgment of "Love's Knowledge: Theological Education in the Future of the Church and Culture," a special publication of the Association of Theological Schools, 1996.

Chapter 11 is an adaptation of "When the Bible Happens," *Alert* 16, no. 2 (August 1986): 9–12.

Chapter 13 is copyright © 1980 Christian Century Foundation. Reprinted by permission from the October 1, 1980, issue of *The Christian Century*. Subscriptions: $49/yr. from P.O. Box 378, Mt. Morris, IL 61054. 1-800-208-4097.

Material on pages 93–94 is copyright © 1986 by *The New York Times*. Reprinted with permission.

Book design by Sharon Adams
Cover design by Dean Nicklas
Cover illustration: THE RIVER © 1987 by John August Swanson Serigraph 30" × 9 ¼"
www.JohnAugustSwanson.com

Second Edition
Published by Westminster John Knox Press
Louisville, Kentucky

This book is printed on acid-free paper that meets the American National Standards Institute Z39.48 standard. ♾

PRINTED IN THE UNITED STATES OF AMERICA

07 08 09 10 11 12 13 14—10 9 8 7 6 5 4 3 2

Library of Congress Cataloging-in-Publication Data is on file at the Library of Congress, Washington, D.C.

ISBN-13: 978-0-664-22758-6
ISBN-10: 0-664-22758-9

To Betsy

Contents

p. 68

PREFACE TO THE SECOND EDITION

"Holy as a Day Is Spent" is the title of a beautiful song in which folksinger/songwriter Carrie Newcomer prays prayers of gratitude for a stream of ordinary encounters in her daily life—including "showerheads and good dry towels" . . . "the busy street / And cars that boom with passion's beat / And the checkout girl, counting change / And the hands that shook my hands today. . . ."[1] She knows somehow that none of this is to be taken for granted—it's all a gift: "Redemption everywhere I look." "It's all a part of a sacrament." And on this matter, the folksinger and the theologian are companions. "Grace and gratitude," Calvin scholar Brian Gerrish makes clear, lie at the very heart and substance of the Christian faith and life.[2]

As Dorothy Bass tells you in her gracious foreword, she and I have been fellow travelers in an ever-growing community of Christian theologians, pastors, and educators who have been trying to articulate more fully and compellingly what the life of Christian faith looks like and feels like—both personally and communally—when understood and lived out in grateful response to God's abundant grace and mercy. I am delighted and honored that Westminster John Knox Press has seen fit to publish a second edition of *Growing in the Life of Faith* and that, in doing so, it has added to it both Dorothy Bass's foreword and Syd Hielema's study guide.

Dorothy's remarks tell the story of the place of this book in the theological movement of which it is a part. I am glad for that, because I have always seen my book to be part of that conversation even though much of it was written quite some time before "Christian practices" became a prominent theme in theological education and church life. The multiple publications on this theme that have been streaming forth in recent years—together with the experiments in education and formation that these works have stimulated—have extended in profoundly encouraging ways the quality and depth of our understanding and practice of faithful Christian living. For Dorothy's leadership and encouragement in all of this—and for the privilege of participating in the community that has emerged in and through shared work—I am deeply grateful.

Syd Hielema's study guide is another kind of gift. Professor Hielema taught *Growing in the Life of Faith* for several years at Dordt College and in his own congregation. A gifted teacher, he recognized that readers would get more out of the book if they could be helped to slow down and unpack for themselves some of the key ideas in it. So he has crafted a superb guide, one that helps readers pause for contemplation at virtually all the most important places and then stimulates just the right kind of reflection on personal and community experience that they will want to bring into conversation with what I have written. I myself learned a lot by working through Syd's guide. I expect you will, too.

In the acknowledgments that follow—written for and unchanged from the first edition—I note my "deep sense of gratitude for pastors, teachers, friends, and family." With regard to pastors and teachers, I did not name any names in the first edition. I wish to mention several here. Among my pastors, two have been most influential: Dr. Bertram deHeus Atwood, who was senior minister at Grosse Pointe Memorial Church when I was a teenager, and Dr. William G. Enright, who has been my pastor for the past decade and has recently retired after twenty-three years of service at Second Presbyterian Church here in Indianapolis. The best part of my formal education came when I was a student in both the M.Div. and Ph.D. programs at Princeton Theological Seminary. I had many wonderful teachers there, but four of them were most prominent in shaping my mind and nurturing my vocation: Professors Diogenes Allen, Freda A. Gardner, James E. Loder, and D. Campbell Wyckoff. As I turn to thank specific friends, I realize that their number has increased in the years since this book's first publication, in part because of the significant expansion that has taken place in the number of colleagues with whom I am now privileged to work on the theme of Christian practices. I do wish to lift up for special thanks for their friendship, collegiality, and support my colleagues in the Religion Division at Lilly Endowment and also Tom Lofton and Clay Robbins, chairman of the board and president, respectively, of the extraordinary charitable foundation in which it has been my privilege to work for fifteen years. I also want to reiterate my gratitude to my dear friend Tom Long, for publishing this book in the first place, and then add my thanks to Janice Catron, a former student of mine at Louisville Seminary, a friend ever since, and now my current editor at Westminster John Knox, for encouraging and guiding the publication of this new edition. With regard to family, the generations have been unfolding and passing since this book was first published. Peter married Janine, so now we have a second lovely daughter-in-law; and Andy and Becky have bestowed on us three beautiful grandchildren: Katie, Charlie, and Maggie. My mother, Pauline Dykstra, died in January 2004, and we grieve her passing while giving thanks for her life. Betsy and I recently celebrated our thirty-sixth wedding anniversary and continue the wondrous life together that began way back in high school days.

If all this seems too personal a note for so public a place as this, well, so be it. This book and those to which it is now a companion are all about a way of life that is abundant in grace and thanksgiving. The grace comes embodied in many particular people, actual places, and daily encounters. All of it is the gift of an exorbitantly generous God who gave so fully as to be Trinity—Father, Son, and Holy Spirit. *Soli deo gloria.*

Craig Dykstra
Indianapolis, Indiana
Pentecost 2005

Notes

1. Carrie Newcomer, *The Gathering of Spirits* (Philo/Rounder Records, 2002).
2. See Brian Gerrish, *Grace and Gratitude: The Eucharistic Theology of John Calvin* (Minneapolis: Fortress, 1993).

Foreword to the Second Edition

Dorothy C. Bass

This is a book that bears many stories. Here you will read of a village in France where a community of Christians practiced hospitality, of a teenager delighted by the declaration that her body is a temple of the Holy Spirit, and of a little boy who made bread with his Sunday school teacher and ate it and found that it was good. And the beautiful image on the front cover, John August Swanson's *The River*, evokes the story of Jesus' baptism, a key moment within the story of God's gracious presence for the world in Jesus Christ, the story from which all the others flow.

As a whole, though, this book is not in narrative form. Rather, it is a work of theology that explains and embodies a way of thinking about the mystery of God and, even more, a way of thinking about the ongoing patterns of shared life in and through which Christian people experience and help one another to receive God's real, but still mysterious, grace. Craig Dykstra calls these patterns "practices."

The story I want to tell here is the story of this remarkable book and the theological movement of which it is a part. Even before its first publication in 1999, the ideas in *Growing in the Life of Faith* were shaping a far-reaching conversation among Christian pastors, educators, and scholars committed to building up God's people in a way of life that reflects and responds to God's grace in Christ, for the sake of the world. Amid the many rich ideas in the book, Craig Dykstra's notion of practices has proven especially intriguing and influential. Today, many Christians in the church, the academy, and daily life have become more articulate about the practices that shape the Christian life, and many are seeking to grow in their participation in Christian practices.

"What does it mean to live the Christian life faithfully and well? And how can we help one another to do so?" I recently heard Craig offer these two questions as a summary of his lifelong interests. As he notes early in

Growing in the Life of Faith, the ongoing forms of Christian living in his family and church were determinative in planting these questions in his mind and shaping his answers to them. Eventually, these questions led him into the ordained ministry of the Presbyterian Church and then to further theological study that equipped him to teach Christian education at the seminary level. After a dozen years of teaching and writing, he became a foundation officer in 1989; from this position, he has been able to encourage ministers, theological educators, and other church members to explore these same questions. Since 1991, I have been privileged to share in this work as director of a foundation-supported project that sponsors books and other resources on Christian practices.

Again and again, I have been struck by how close and generative the connection between these two questions is for Craig—as was clearly also the case during the years when he was in ministry, graduate school, and classroom teaching. Too often it has been assumed that those in Christian education emphasize the "how" of helping one another to live the life of Christian faith while "what does it mean?" becomes the exclusive domain of the theologians. In all of his work, Craig has challenged this facile and ultimately debilitating division. He insists that thinking and doing cannot be separated—and neither can believing and living, education and its content, or theology and the means of sharing it with others. This is where "practices" come in—not at all through a simplistic putting-ideas-into-practice approach but rather by showing how the dualism implied in that cliché disappears when people are actively engaged in the ongoing, thought-filled practices of the Christian life.

Craig Dykstra's understanding of Christian practices, which he developed in a series of lectures and essays in the late 1980s and early 1990s, draws on the work of the moral philosopher Alasdair MacIntyre while also integrating MacIntyre's concepts with theological themes from the Reformed tradition. The most important of this work is published in *Growing in the Life of Faith*, especially in chapters two through five, so I do not repeat it here. MacIntyre's concepts also influenced the work I was doing during those same years, though from a different angle. As a historian whose vocation was to help contemporary Christians find wisdom in the long history of our tradition, I appreciated MacIntyre's notion of a "living tradition" as a "historically extended, socially embodied argument" about the goods at the heart of a tradition. More than through verbal formulations alone or the survival of specific institutions, MacIntyre argued, a living tradition would be extended through the engagement of new generations in practices, a process always characterized by dispute and negotiation.[1]

As we began to discuss our shared interests during the early 1990s, Craig and I saw coming into view a whole way of thinking about the life of Christian faith and how Christian people might help one another to live it. Indeed, we realized, this way of thinking addressed many of the concerns of contemporary Christian leaders as they sought to build up strong and thoughtful communities in a time of rapid social change, including the widespread sense that daily life was losing its coherence and grounding. Thinking about a way of life shaped by a set of Christian practices, we believed, would help people to make connections—between theology and daily life, between the resources of a living tradition and the challenges of the present, with one another, and across other important divisions as well. This perspective, we hoped, would enable contemporary Christians to recognize and reflect on many of the practices that already shape our lives, while also encouraging creativity in strengthening crucial Christian practices within the diverse local contexts where life together actually takes shape.

In 1993, Craig and I invited eleven other theological educators to join us in a seminar on practices.[2] The result was *Practicing Our Faith: A Way of Life for a Searching People*. This book not only sets forth a way of thinking about a way of life but also advocates twelve specific Christian practices: honoring the body, hospitality, household economics, saying yes and saying no, keeping sabbath, testimony, discernment, shaping communities, forgiveness, healing, dying well, and singing our lives to God. Craig and I remain immensely grateful to the friends who collaborated with us in the process of writing this book—a process, indeed, that embodied the Christian community the book commends.

Practicing Our Faith has served groups of readers in congregations, theological schools, and elsewhere as a resource for the very "education in Christian practices" that Craig describes in *Growing in the Life of Faith*. Once *Practicing Our Faith* was in print, Thomas Long (then an editor at Geneva Press) and I realized how crucial it was also to make available the essays and lectures Craig had been writing about education and Christian practices. After Craig made the appropriate revisions and additions, *Growing in the Life of Faith* became available in 1999. I earnestly hope that those who yearn to live the Christian life faithfully and well, and who know that this is a calling for which we need one another's help, will read these two books together, in the context of the shared life of faith.

Practicing Our Faith and *Growing in the Life of Faith*, it has turned out, were starting points for a conversation on the life of Christian faith that continues today. *Way to Live: Christian Practices for Teens* was written to and for (and partly by) students of high school age, encouraging them to ask, "What does it mean to live the Christian life faithfully and well?" while also encouraging them and the adults who care about them to help one another to do so. *Practicing Theology: Beliefs and Practices in Christian Life* drew a dozen theologians into a rich exploration of practices, with special attention to an important claim of *Growing in the Life of Faith* that knowledge of God is available through participation in Christian practices, which become, in Craig's words, "habitations of the Spirit." Craig and I contributed an essay to that book entitled "A Theological Understanding of Christian Practices," which advances our thinking beyond both *Growing in the Life of Faith* and *Practicing Our Faith*. Books on single practices are also emerging to challenge and encourage persons and communities in the participatory, reflective engagement in Christian practices that is essential to growing in the life of faith. And more will come.[3] Watch www.practicingourfaith.org for updates on new publications and other resources on Christian practices.

In the midst of this expanding, ecumenical body of literature on the life of Christian faith and the practices that constitute it, *Growing in the Life of Faith* holds a special place, and not only because it was the first to be conceived and spoken. More important is its dual focus on theology *and* education. While several books explore the question, "What does it mean to live the Christian life faithfully and well?" this one does that, but also much more. The urgent presence of Craig's second question—"How can we help one another to do so?"—and the quality of his response set an agenda for all who care about the church and the world in our time. I especially commend this book to those who hold responsibility for communities within which people can grow in the life of faith—parents and pastors, teachers and caregivers, elders and deacons.

With this second edition, Westminster John Knox makes it possible for this fine book to serve even more of those who care deeply about what it means to live the Christian life and to help others to do so as well. The guide for study and conversation prepared by Professor Syd Hielema of Dordt College will help readers explore and appropriate the rich concepts here set forth. More importantly, it will foster ways of thinking and ways of living through which persons and communities will grow in the life of faith, for the good of the world and to the glory of God.

Dorothy C. Bass
Valparaiso Project on the Education
and Formation of People in Faith
Pentecost 2005

Notes

1. MacIntyre's concepts are in his book *After Virtue*, 2nd ed. (South Bend, IN: University of Notre Dame Press, 1984). My own early use of MacIntyre appears in my essay, "Congregations and the Bearing of Traditions," in *American Congregations*, vol. 2, ed. James P. Wind and James W. Lewis, 169–91 (Chicago: University of Chicago Press, 1994).

2. In addition to Craig Dykstra and myself, the group included Stephanie Paulsell, Ana Maria Pineda, Sharon Daloz Parks, M. Shawn Copeland, Thomas Hoyt Jr., Frank Rogers Jr., Larry Rasmussen, L. Gregory Jones, John Koenig, Amy Plantinga Pauw, and Don E. Saliers.

3. Dorothy C. Bass, ed., *Practicing Our Faith: A Way of Life for a Searching People* (San Francisco: Jossey-Bass, 1997); Dorothy C. Bass, *Receiving the Day: Christian Practices for Opening the Gift of Time* (San Francisco: Jossey-Bass Publishers, 2000); Dorothy C. Bass and Don C. Richter, eds., *Way to Live: Christian Practices for Teens* (Nashville: Upper Room Books, 2002), with related Web site and Leader's Guide at www.waytolive.org; Christine Pohl, *Making Room: Recovering Hospitality as a Christian Tradition* (Grand Rapids: Eerdmans Publishing Company, 1999); Stephanie Paulsell, *Honoring the Body: Meditations on a Christian Practice* (San Francisco: Jossey-Bass Publishers, 2002); Miroslav Volf and Dorothy C. Bass, eds., *Practicing Theology: Beliefs and Practices in Christian Life* (Grand Rapids: Eerdmans, 2002); Thomas G. Long, *Testimony: Talking Ourselves into Being Christian* (San Francisco: Jossey-Bass Publishers, 2004); and Don Saliers and Emily Saliers, *A Song to Sing, A Life to Live: Music as Spiritual Practice* (San Francisco: Jossey-Bass Publishers, 2005).

INTRODUCTION:
MYSTERY AND MANNERS

Flannery O'Connor talks in terms of mystery and manners. She says, "The mystery . . . is the mystery of our position on earth, and the manners are those conventions which . . . reveal that central mystery."[1] O'Connor is discussing mystery and manners to describe what she thinks is the business of fiction writing, namely, "to embody mystery through manners."[2] But there are parallels with the task of educators, the difference being that our turf is not fiction but the real life that goes on in the places where we dwell.

I grew up in a household characterized by order and love. The manners were consistent. Daily my father would come home from work, and he and my mother would talk for an hour or so while my brothers and I played or studied. We never had a dinner not preceded by prayer, and most were followed by reading from the Bible or a Bible storybook. I can still see my father laying out the collection envelopes before we left for church each Sunday. We always went—both to church and to Sunday school. No movies or other commercial forms of recreation were allowed on Sundays. It was a day of rest—unless we were on vacation, when for some odd reason the traditional strictures were let loose a bit.

My grandfather was a minister. He and my grandmother would visit occasionally from their small town in upper New York state. On one such visit, my grandmother broke her hip, so our home became her place of convalescence. While they were with us, my grandfather also got very sick. Even though I was not yet ten, I read the Bible to them and prayed with them. They seemed to find that a great comfort. So did I. My grandfather never recovered from cancer, and when he died my grandmother moved into an apartment of her own nearby. I recall that we spent a lot of time with her, that it seemed very good, and that when she died I felt another loss.

Many other things have happened over the years, though the events are no more extraordinary than these that I have recounted from my childhood. I went to six schools from grade school through my doctoral studies.

I can still see the faces of a dozen or so teachers who opened my eyes to worlds and realities that absorb my attention still, and who opened my life through their friendship. My best teachers have always seemed like friends to me. I am not sure whether they were my best teachers because they became friends or whether they became friends because I thought them my best teachers. Probably both. A number of churches have also been powerfully important in my life. In most, the ministers, too, became friends, and friends turned out to minister. My work has brought friendship as well. Colleagues and students at two seminaries where I taught have become lifelong friends. In recent years the circle has widened even more, through my work as a foundation officer. Above all, I have had the love and friendship of my family. My best friend in high school became my wife, and my wife is my best friend still. We have two sons, adults now, who are friends as well.

My life has also encompassed wars. I was home from college during the summer of 1968 when our city of Detroit went to war in the heat of a racial crisis that still smolders. There were assassinations, each one like a war itself. I was in college and in seminary when people I knew and people I had heard of and thousands more were being killed and torn apart in Vietnam. From young adulthood on, though I have never been harmed, I have never stopped grieving over violence and its ruins.

O'Connor writes that "the fiction writer presents mystery through manners, grace through nature, but when he finishes there always has to be left over that sense of Mystery which cannot be accounted for by any human formula."[3] My life experience is not a fiction, but the sense of mystery coming through the things that have happened—comings and goings, daily prayers, reading books, deaths, friendships, wars—prevails here, too. As far back as I can remember, I have never been without it. I wonder where it comes from, and some days I think I know. I needed both to be taught to pay attention to Mystery and to experience it personally. Neither teaching nor experience alone would have sufficed for me to have a sense that Mystery has been present throughout my life.

I do not think experience and education are the same thing. Because of my experience in my family, I have thought, from the first time I read *Christian Nurture*, that Horace Bushnell was exactly right. There is—or at least, can be—a kind of "organic unity of the family" that is a bond by which "character, feelings, spirit, and principles must propagate themselves. . . ."[4] And this is true not only in the family but wherever there is what Moltmann calls "the fellowship which corresponds to the gospel,"[5] a community of friends rooted in the friendship of Jesus Christ.[6] To live in such fellowship and to experience its organic unity is to have one's life shaped in profound ways and to be caught up in Mystery through manners. All this happens without plan or purpose or conscious design. It happens in the experience of daily living.

In recent decades in the field of Christian education, this insight has received considerable emphasis through theories that concentrate on socialization and enculturation. These theories are on target insofar as they point out how profoundly our ways of seeing, valuing, believing, knowing, responding, and acting are shaped by the social forces of our communities. But they fail us if the manners are mistaken for Mystery. Beneath the level of norms, roles, institutional structures, rituals, stories, and symbols lies the level of our fundamental communal intentions toward one another and the world, which govern how we live in our roles and rituals and by means of which we apprehend the mystery of our existence.[7] Deeper still abide the everlasting arms of God.

I have been stuck by the power of an incident in the book of Ruth. When Ruth first encounters Boaz, he blesses her, saying, "The Lord recompense you for what you have done, and a full reward be given you by the Lord, the God of Israel, under whose wings you have come to take refuge" (2:12; RSV). It turns out, in chapter 3, that the wings of God take the form of the "wings" of Boaz, who spreads his skirt over her and redeems her (3:9). Eugene Peterson comments on this, saying, "Redemption is experienced in the story, because Boaz works through the legal details of an old Mosaic law."[8] Boaz minds his manners—embodies the spirit of those manners—in such a way that an ordinary act of responsibility becomes an experience of the redemptive activity of the Mystery at the heart of things.

All of this is experience: not just any experience but the kind of experience that arises in the context of what Christians call the fellowship of the Holy Spirit. We as educators are responsible for doing everything in our power to create opportunities in which such experiences may be had and in which the apprehensions of Mystery that come through such experiences may actually occur. But this responsibility is not ours alone. It belongs to the whole people of God, who create such contexts simply by their faithfulness.

As educators, we have an additional responsibility—namely, to teach. No one has stated it better than Martin Buber: "What we term education, conscious and willed, means a selection by man of the effective world: it means to give decisive effective power to a selection of the world which is concentrated and manifested in the educator. The relation in education is lifted out of the purposelessly streaming education by all things, and is marked off as purpose. In this way, through the educator, the world for the first time becomes the true subject of its effect."[9] How do we know that the wings of Boaz are the wings of God? How do we know that in the community of friends we actually experience the fellowship of the Holy Spirit? How do we know there is mystery revealed in the manners? Education is the work of bringing to consciousness the hidden dimensions embedded in and through our actions and relations and institutions, giving these dimensions names, and then helping each other take notice and live in their light.

Iris Murdoch pointed out that the "use of words by persons grouped round a common object is a central and vital human activity."[10] I suppose I find this activity so important because I have been fortunate to have teachers who have used words with such care that I have been able (in ways I never could have without them) to see beneath the manners into the mystery. Through this kind of gift, even rather ordinary lives such as mine can take on dimensions of depth, and a person's angle of vision can become such that "he begins to see before he gets to the surface and he continues to see after he has gone past it."[11] What Buber means by "a selection of the effective world" is not, I think, a selection of content to explore so much as an angle of vision by which all things are seen. An angle of vision does not come simply through experience. It comes through education, through teaching, through the use of words by people gathered around something they experience in common in order to interpret its meaning and discern it significance. I want this to happen to people. Otherwise, lives of purpose, value, direction, and meaning, lives less fearful and more free, are impossible. Educators are the people primarily responsible for helping this to happen.

Education in faith presupposes and depends on people's experience of the Mystery of God. Because this experience takes place in fellowship, Christian education also presupposes and depends on communities whose ways of being make the experience of this Mystery possible. But education is not the same as experience. In the context of religious community, education is our attempt to help one another understand our experience of this Mystery in its breadth and depth and in its implications for ourselves and for the world. One scholar has explained that *understanding* involves much more than "to know a good deal about" (though that is definitely included). It also includes intellectual and emotional appreciation for what one understands and experiences. Most of all, however, understanding means to be able to "see and grasp the inner character and hidden nature of things" [12] in that experience; one comes to insight into their reality and meaning. This requires of education in faith that it be at once an investigative process that guides people in the exploration of our experience of God; a critical process that liberates us from the patterns of thinking, feeling, valuing, and behaving that make it difficult for us to participate in this experience; and a caring process through which we graciously invite one another to enter freely and ever more deeply into this experience.

Education is, of course, itself a form of experience. (The distinction between education and experience should not be made too radically.) And because it is, the Mystery with which education in faith is concerned is not just its object but also its ground. Education has a transcendent dimension, which may arise as mystery through its own particular manners as we are in fellowship with one another in the Spirit. Thus, through investigation, criticism, interpretation, and care, education in faith may help people in a community of faith not only to see and grasp the inner character and hidden nature of the graceful Mystery that sustains their life together but also to experience it more profoundly. My hope for this book is that it will help its readers in that wondrous task.

Notes

1. Flannery O'Connor, *Mystery and Manners* (New York: Farrar, Straus & Giroux, 1961), 124.
2. Ibid.
3. Ibid., 153.
4. Horace Bushnell, *Christian Nurture* (New Haven, Conn.: Yale University Press, 1916), 76.
5. Jürgen Moltmann, *The Church in the Power of the Spirit* (New York: Harper & Row, 1977), 225.
6. See ibid., 114–21.
7. See Edward Farley, *Ecclesial Man: A Social Phenomenology of Faith and Reality* (Philadelphia: Fortress Press, 1975), esp. chap. 4, where Farley discusses the level he calls "the determinate social world."
8. Eugene H. Peterson, *Five Smooth Stones for Pastoral Work* (Atlanta: John Knox Press, 1980), 86.

9. Martin Buber, *Between Man and Man* (New York: Macmillan Publishing Co., 1965), 89. Throughout this book, I have not changed texts to make them gender inclusive, even where I am sure that the author or translator would have written differently today. Instead, I depend on the goodwill of the reader, who will take into account the historical context in which the older texts quoted here were written.

10. Iris Murdoch, *The Sovereignty of Good* (New York: Schocken Books, 1970), 32.

11. O'Connor, *Mystery and Manners*, 132.

12. Raymond Holley, *Religious Education and Religious Understanding* (London: Routledge & Kegan Paul, 1978), 75.

ACKNOWLEDGMENTS

Much of what appears in this book had its genesis in lectures I have given at a variety of theological schools. These include the Robert F. Jones Lectures at Austin Presbyterian Theological Seminary (1986); the Greenhoe Lecture at Louisville Presbyterian Theological Seminary (1986); the Bradner Lectures at the Protestant Episcopal Seminary of Virginia (1987); the Mary Charles Bryce Lecture at The Catholic University of America (1990); the Earl Lectures at Pacific School of Religion (1991); the Cranston-Irwin Lecture at Claremont School of Religion (1993); and the Petticrew Lecture at Christian Theological Seminary (1993). In addition, I received invitations to address the Presbyterian Missions Conference at Montreat Conference Center (1981), the Annual Meeting of the Indiana Academy of Religion (1989), and the Fortieth Biennial Meeting of the Association of Theological Schools in the United States and Canada (1996) and to teach at the Presbyterian Church (U.S.A.)'s Ghost Ranch Symposium on Faith and Families (1985). I thank my hosts at all these fine institutions for their warm hospitality and generous encouragement.

Articles and essays derived from these and other occasions have, over the years, been published in a variety of periodicals and books. They appear in this book as follows:

> The introduction is adapted from an essay, "Mystery and Manners: The Task of Religious Education" that appeared in *Religious Education* 79/1 (winter 1984): 61–66, and is used by permission.

> A portion of "Thinking Faith: A Theological Education for the American Churches," *Living Light* 27/1 (fall 1990): 7–16, is included in chapter 1.

> Chapter 4 includes portions of "Christian Education as a Means of Grace," *Princeton Seminary Bulletin* 13/2, n.s. (July 1992): 164–75.

A version of chapter 6 appeared as "The Formative Power of Congregations" in *Religious Education* 82/4 (fall 1987): 530–46, and is used by permission.

A version of chapter 7 appeared as "Family Promises: Faith and Families in the Context of the Church" in *Faith and Families,* ed. Lindell Sawyers (Philadelphia: Geneva Press, 1986).

A version of chapter 8 appeared as "Youth and the Language of Faith" in *Religious Education* 81/2 (spring 1986): 163–84, and is used by permission.

A version of chapter 9 was published as "Communities of Conviction and the Liberal Arts" in *Bulletin of the Council of Societies for the Study of Religion* 19/3 (September 1990): 61–66.

An expanded version of chapter 10 was published under the title *Love's Knowledge: Theological Education in the Future of the Church and Culture* (Pittsburgh: The Association of Theological Schools, 1996) as a special publication.

Chapter 11, "When the Bible Happens," originally appeared in *Alert* (August 1986): 9–12.

Chapter 12, "Learning to Be Sent," first appeared in *Presbyterian Survey* (September 1981): 44–45.

Chapter 13, "My Teacher, We Made Bread . . . ," first appeared in *Christian Century* (October 1, 1980): 901–2.

It was my privilege to serve as a member of a task force on Faith Development and the Reformed Tradition, commissioned by the Presbyterian Church (U.S.A.), and as writer of its report to the 201st General Assembly (1989). Titled *Growing in the Life of Christian Faith,* that report was subsequently published (with a study guide) by the denomination's Theology and Worship Unit in Louisville, Kentucky. Portions of chapters 2 and 3 in the present book first appeared in that report, and I am grateful for permission to use them here. I also express my appreciation for the conversation and collaboration of my fellow task force members, whose names appear on pages 1 and 2 of the report; to the Reverend George Telford, who provided staff assistance; and to the Reverend Edward Dixon Junkin, who ensured its wide distribution and use in the church.

I thank John August Swanson for permission to reproduce, on the cover of this book, his beautiful serigraph *The River*. In this, as in many of his other works, this extraordinary artist makes vivid connections between God's good news and elemental dimensions of ordinary life. It has been a pleasure for me to come to know Mr. Swanson, and I am grateful for his kindnesses to me.

Readers of this book's introduction will have noticed my gratitude for friendship. Two especially good friends made this book possible. Dorothy Bass, for almost ten years now my closest colleague in developing a "practices" way of thinking about education in faith, was the first to see in the occasional pieces I had written the possibility of a coherent book. She encouraged and guided me in putting it together. Tom Long, a constant friend since graduate school days and now my editor, did the hard work of turning manuscripts into chapters and ultimately moving these toward publication. I am deeply grateful for the confidence and generosity of these two wonderful people.

Other friends also helped. Geneva Press asked Don C. Richter, who knows my work well, to prepare the index. At an early stage, Frank Rogers reviewed much of what I had written and gave me sage advice on what was worth including in this book. Both Don and Frank are former students of mine whose current excellence as teachers and scholars I greatly admire.

This book was written with a deep sense of gratitude for pastors, teachers, friends, and family. They are too many to name, but I know those closest to me will recognize the ways in which they have shaped what I have written. My family's love and support have been constant. Through these words, I want my mother, Pauline; my sons, Peter and Andy, and now our daughter-in-law, Becky, to know yet again that I continue every day in thanks to God for them. I give thanks especially for my dear wife, Betsy, to whom this book is dedicated and with whom life together is a continuing joy.

Indianapolis, Indiana
All Saints Day, 1998

Hunger

Chapter 1

The Hunger for Daily Bread

There is in the Christian churches, and in the United States as a whole, a profound spiritual hunger for something. It is a hunger that I think may be met, at least in part, by a truly theological education in Christian practice.

Our country and its congregations are populated by a people who feel quite at sea. Careful listening to the conversations taking place in U.S. society about issues as diverse as work and family, sexuality, the public responsibilities of the media, and the shifting balances in international relationships reveals that thousands upon thousands of ordinary citizens recognize and are beginning to face the profound ambiguities intrinsic to contemporary political and moral life. We would like to be sure that what we are doing—as people, as citizens, as families, as a nation—is right and good, but deep down we are not at all sure that it is. Furthermore, most people do not know where to go to find resources adequate for dealing with our personal and cultural moral ambiguity. They are not satisfied with the supply of meanings our culture provides to deal with issues of right and wrong, pain, death, and violence.

People are beginning to ask questions about God again, and they yearn for coherent, thoughtful guidance as well as fresh access to the deep veins of wisdom that at least some of them suspect are still there to be mined from historic religious traditions. We know we live in dangerous times. And we know the dangers are not only "out there" but also "in here," within ourselves. We sense, even if only vaguely, that the forces with which we have to contend are not minor and manageable but "principalities and powers." The hunger each of us senses is a hunger to understand what that contending is about, what it consists of, and what it means for our lives.

I also sense a feeling on the part of many that the language, assumptions, and convictions of a radically secular culture no longer are rich enough to sustain the sort of life people feel in their bones it is in them to live. Still hoping that religious traditions have in them some wisdom worth mining, many of the most discerning members of our society are asking for help from those who are theologically conversant.

Each month a copy of the *Atlantic Monthly* comes across my desk. One issue was particularly striking. On the cover appeared a vague sketch, seemingly portraying God peering over desolate terrain, where a lone and lonely human figure was journeying. The drawing directed the reader to the title of the cover article: "Can We Be Good without God?"[1] I was frankly astonished by both the topic and the article. First, I wondered what a question like that was doing on the cover of the *Atlantic Monthly*. Its very prominence made me curious. Then, with some trepidation, I turned to the essay, not knowing how seriously the author would take this question. I half-feared that New Age spirituality was invading the *Atlantic's* covers, but there I found what turned out to be a lucid theological essay.

Glenn Tinder, a political scientist at the University of Massachusetts, articulated key and fundamental doctrines of Christian faith in a powerful and compelling way, while making their significance for our understanding of contemporary political culture perfectly plain. This, to my mind, is an almost crystalline example of what I hope for in theological writing— and a brilliant case of theological education taking place in the media.

But what was a finely honed theological essay doing in the *Atlantic*? How did it get there? Why were the editors of this very secular magazine publishing such material? My own response is that religious searching is going public, that a new taste for theology has sprung up among many, with a consequent yearning for theological education, not only in the church but also in the larger context of public life.

Tinder's article is not the only evidence of this yearning. Television is now exploring religious questions. PBS airs *Religion & Ethics NewsWeekly*, while popular dramas and even sitcoms have been giving sensitive treatments to religious questions and the ways in which people are struggling to ask and to answer them—especially those whose religious heritage has fallen by the wayside. The novelist Dan Wakefield says that "God— who long seemed absent if not 'dead' as a subject of concern in serious fiction, as in the culture at large—has returned as a force or a 'character' in the action" of many recent literary works.[2]

John Wheeler, president of the Center for the Vietnam Generation, a research and advocacy group, senses that "questions of faith and spirit have emerged . . . strongly at the close of this decade,"[3] especially among the cohort of the population we call the "baby boomers." Wheeler finds three causes. First, this is a generation that has faced and remembers death. Wheeler, who served as chairman of the committee overseeing construction of the Vietnam Memorial in Washington, says, "Memorials awaken questions of faith. Are things worth dying for? Is death the last word?" Second, young adulthood is a season of reevaluation for many, a time of asking what all the striving and acquiring really amount to and how what really does have value actually comes to us. Material security and self-concern, it turns out, do not save us from a sense of spiritual void, while the "deliverances of life lead us to the idea that God loves the world and acts within time and space." Finally, Wheeler maintains that science, though it gives us no final answers, drives us nonetheless to reminisce about Genesis.

All Wheeler's reflection takes place, interestingly, on the editorial page of the *New York Times*. Also in the *New York Times* in 1989 was a report on a monthly gathering of secular writers and editors for what one of the participants said was "the best conversation going on in New York City at this moment."[4] Among them were some of the nation's most dazzling literati—Cynthia Ozick, Max Apple, Philipe Lopate, and Lore Segal. And what were they discussing? They were discussing the Bible. A professor at the Jewish Theological Seminary (JTS), Burton Visotzky, recruited this group of believers and nonbelievers from backgrounds Jewish, Christian, and Hindu to meet in the back of the JTS cafeteria to read biblical texts and talk them through. He says, "My scholarly expertise is Rabbinic storytelling. I am a professor of midrash." The current way of studying the Bible in most settings, according to Professor Visotzky, virtually prevents people from engaging in interpretation. So, he decided, "Wouldn't it be nice to have a workshop where people actually did midrash? . . . I wanted people who would read the Bible as text—who know how to read between the lines." According to Cynthia Ozick, "What goes on in this room is more exciting to me than anything that ever happened. It's as if the text really matters." These conversations led to Bill Moyers's popular PBS series *Genesis*; and a subsequent PBS series, *Frontline's from Jesus to Christ: The First Christians*, which presents a historically informed and theologically sophisticated treatment of the development of early Christianity, has garnered significant attention and acclaim.

I do not know how widespread this taste for biblical and theological interpretation is, but I think the media have picked up on a reasonably extensive feeling in society that we are lacking something we desperately need. Among those who are turning to the churches and synagogues and to the scriptures of long-lasting religious traditions there is, in my view, a yearning for a firsthand encounter with the resources these traditions have accumulated, namely, texts and practices through which the grace and presence of God have been experienced.

For many people in U.S. society at the end of the twentieth century, this encounter may be the first in a long time, maybe the first in a lifetime. But it is a firsthand encounter that they want. They do not want their encounter with these texts and practices to come in summarized or diluted form. They do not want it second-, third-, fourth-, or fifthhand. They want it as directly as possible. They want to know it, handle it, interpret it, put it into play in their lives themselves. They want to feel it work in them—as a light to truth and as a way to be oriented to what is real and actual in the large universe and in their own daily lives. They yearn for what Edward Farley has described as "the wisdom proper to the life of a believer."[5] And this is what I mean when I say that part of what people may be hungering for is a *theological* education. They want to participate in those forms of learning, inquiry, and life together that make such an encounter possible. The hunger for them is not simply the result of a shift in taste; it is the consequence of a radical starvation.

George Lindbeck, who taught theology at Yale University for many years, provides a compelling analysis of why we may now be seeing a serious hunger for exposure to biblical texts. "Until recently," he says, "most people in traditionally Christian countries lived in the linguistic and imaginative world of the Bible." While this was "not the only world in which they dwelt"—the biblical world has always mixed with others— "the text above all texts has until recently been the Bible. Its stories, images, conceptual patterns, and turns of phrase permeated the culture from top to bottom."[6]

According to Lindbeck and many other commentators, this simply is no longer the case. Our society is no longer scripturally literate. The consequences of this are not simply that less of the Bible is quoted; not even just that people are less religious than they used to be. The most serious consequence is that fundamental questions are trivialized or become difficult even to pose. Why does the world exist? Why does it have its present order? Of what value are human beings, and how is that value secured? What is worth dying for? What is worth staying alive for? How should our lives be spent?

Lindbeck argues that "with the loss of knowledge of the Bible, public discourse is impoverished. We no longer have a language in which, for example, national goals . . . can be articulated. We try to deal with apocalyptic threats of atomic and ecological disaster in the thin and feeble idioms of utilitarianism or therapeutic warfare."[7]

The same is true for personal life. A deep, rich, complex, nuanced language of spirituality seems long forgotten as the church itself chases pop gnosticisms such as "codependency" and "twelve-step recovery" as proxy diction for telling the tale of redemption.[8] The language is skewed, and the images have gone flat. Similarly with what used to be called "devotional practices"; they have been widely abandoned. To most, they seem simply quaint. To some, they are regarded as harmful habits of conformation to oppressive religious socializing forces that squelch individual freedom and perhaps even the play of creative grace in our personal and social lives. But it is not only language and acts of interpretation that people require to live meaningfully and with integrity. They also require practices that regulate and shape their lives.

Margaret Miles, in a compelling book titled *Practicing Christianity*, argues that historical peoples have engaged in such practices as fasting, tithing, ordered worship, sabbath keeping, private prayer, devotional reading, meditation on death, and self-denying service to the sick and needy precisely as disciplines for rescuing their lives from dull conformity and spiritually unsatisfying existence. Well-formed, traditional devotional practices, she says, were used as means to "deconstruct the socialization and conditioning inscribed on the body [and mind and heart] by the 'world' [and] produce a new organizing center or 'self'."[9] Hardly mindless or thoughtless, engagement in disciplined piety made possible "the integration of thought and practice that defined the religious self."[10]

Devotional practices have historically been disciplined, patterned actions designed to create distinctive ways of seeing, understanding, and being. They were, Miles says, "specifications for producing simultaneously a consciousness, an experience, and an understanding"[11] that were at variance with the prevailing cultural ethos and message. At the same time, they were practices of a larger tradition and community. "Individual experiences [with them] . . . were preceded and confirmed by the interpretive rhetoric of a tradition and community; they were enclosed . . . in advance and in retrospect by the common language of the community."[12]

Such practices have been a mainstay throughout most of Christian history. But today, we are less schooled in them, and they are increasingly absent from our lives. Perhaps the calls we are hearing for "more spirituality" are, in large part, cries for help in developing anew disciplined *practices* of faith. Perhaps we should regard the burgeoning self-help books, pamphlets, articles, and courses we see all around us as contemporary substitutes for the manuals Miles studied when she looked at the popular and influential literature of devotional instruction produced in many cultures during nearly two thousand years of Christian history. The thousands of self-help groups that now flourish throughout our country are filling a vacuum created by the loss of practicing communities of devotion.

The question all this raises is not so much whether people are getting help for their needs—they are getting some kind of help, and they will, by hook or by crook—but whether the help they get in the practice of daily life is adequate to the depths and extremities that life presents. If, as Lindbeck says, we are left with only thin and feeble idioms as we try to deal with apocalyptic threats of ecological disaster and the atrocities of terrorism, are we not also left with synthetic and fragile practices and communities as we face death and dying and try to cope with the psychological and physical violence human beings perpetrate on one another?

A deep hunger, then, is not being met by the broadly available resources of our culture. Because of that, we will, I suspect, see increasing numbers of people turning again to the church in the decades ahead. But what will they find when they do? What kind of bread will the church have to feed the hungry?

I am disturbed by what seems to be a broad incapacity on the part of our churches to meet the hunger. I worry that our churches now find themselves generally ill-equipped and poorly poised to respond. The losses of meaning are not only the larger culture's losses. The church has, in large part, suffered such losses as well. I worry that as more and more people turn to the churches for renewed encounter with the texts and practices of Christian faith, they will discover too few who really know what these texts and practices are. Even more, I am afraid they will find there too many who are no longer sure that these texts and practices have any real power.

Edward Farley has argued that "in recent years, the theological community has entertained what might be called a nasty suspicion about itself."

> The rumor did not arise within that community but, once implanted, it had a certain self-fulfilling effect. Could it be that there are no realities at all behind the language of this historical faith? Could it be that the testimony, the storytelling, the liturgical expressions of [this] faith refer to entities that have only phenomenal status [that is, are only projections of our own consciousness or creations of our own cultural and economic systems]? Could it be that the mode of human existence which this historical religion calls faith involves no cognizing, no apprehendings at all? Are Christian theologians like stockbrokers who distribute stock certificates on a nonexistent corporation? In this situation, the "reality" of the corporation, its size, type, power, and promise, turns out to be simply the broker itself.[13]

In Farley's view, contemporary theology is plagued by insecurity on this most fundamental issue. It is not sure that it has or can have—or that anyone has or can have—knowledge of God. Since Immanuel Kant, Friedrich Nietzsche, and Ludwig Feuerbach, we have not been sure that theology is about anything beyond human subjectivity. That is the nasty suspicion.

At its deepest level, this suspicion means the loss of God to us. As Farley puts it, the question is: "Are there realities to which we can trace the normative language and the intellective acts of theology and the images resident in faith itself?"[14] More simply: Does our life together in the church, including our ways of talking, behaving, organizing ourselves, and relating to one another—much less our history, doctrine, and Scripture—refer to anything other than ourselves? Does this all point to God? Is it of God? Or is it all something that has no grounding beyond our own thinking and doing?

When the nasty suspicion takes hold, a kind of practical atheism infects church life, despite the fact that religious services continue to be conducted. We continue our rituals and manage the institutions, but we are not really sure that all the things we do in church and as church count for much. Does the practice of prayer have any point if we have no real confidence that our praying is anything more than a psychological defense mechanism or a corporate expression of opinion? What is the care of souls when we find ourselves entirely dependent on the latest techniques of modern therapy to guide us? For clergy and laity alike, "the residue [of the nasty suspicion in the church] is a thoroughly secularized religious institution which has traded religious for secular motifs masked in traditional language, rites, and polities."[15]

Somehow we do not seem to have a natural and deep conviction that through our practices and texts, the presence of God can be experienced and known. Somehow we are no longer sure that these are means of grace. And as long as this is true, our practices are nothing more than exercises in technique and management, unable to deal with the ultimate joys and tragedies of human existence, no matter how sophisticated, adroit, and well-grounded in social scientific theory these practices may be. Under these conditions, the hungers of our age are met with only coffee and doughnuts on Deck C.[16]

Can the church take on life, become vibrant, energetic, serious, alive? Can the practices of the church enable people to find something and receive something they could not otherwise have experienced, namely, the grace of God and the experience of new life? Are there certain conditions under which the people might sit forward in their seats, stand on the tip of their toes, put down their cups, and rush to see what's going on?

Toward the end of Luke's Gospel are two contrasting stories. First is the account of the visit to the tomb where the dead Jesus is expected to be. Grieving women, coming to tend the corpse, find it gone. In the midst of their astonishment they are asked a surprising question: "Why do you seek the living among the dead?" (24:5; RSV). The second story is of two disciples' lonely and discouraged walk down a path toward Emmaus. Their life with Jesus is over, and they have no hope. But a stranger surprises them, and when he "interpreted to them in all the scriptures the things concerning himself" and broke bread at table with them, "their eyes were opened and they recognized him," their "hearts burned within," and they ran to tell others (24:13–35; RSV)

Is the church a tomb or a path? If the church is a grave to which grieving people come to pay homage to a dead Christ, then God will burst its bounds and leave it empty. But if the church is a path, a place to walk and to practice the faith, we may be surprised along the way by the living God and recognize and know that Christ is present—to us, in our own lives.

Every week in church, and perhaps more often than that, we say the Lord's Prayer, praying that God might "give us this day our daily bread." We pray for a bread that will truly satisfy our hunger, a bread that feeds our everyday hungers. As Luther said in his *Small Catechism*, "Daily bread includes everything we need for this life, such as food and clothing, home and property, work and income, an orderly community, good government, favorable weather, peace and health."[17] We need these things, and they are good—gifts that God gives to us out of God's own grace and bounty.

But if we confine the meaning of "bread" to the mundane world of everyday need, then we will remain hungry. We must remember that Jesus told us not only "When you pray say . . . give us each day our daily bread" (Luke 11:2–3; RSV), but also "It is written, 'One does not live by bread alone, but by every word that comes from the mouth of God'" (Matt. 4:4; NRSV). Dorothee Soelle sums it up well in the title to her book *Death by Bread Alone*. It is not just that we do not live by bread alone; it is that we die by bread alone:

> Bread alone kills us. To live by bread alone is to die a slow and dreadful death in which all human relationships are mutilated and strangled. Of course, such a death by bread alone does not mean that we cease to exist. Our bodies still function. We still go about the chores and routines of life; we accomplish things; we produce and consume and excrete; we come, go, and speak. Yet we do not really live. . . . Death by bread alone means being alone and then wanting to be left alone; being friendless, yet distrusting and despising others; forgetting others and then being forgotten; living only for ourselves and then feeling unneeded; being unconcerned about others and wanting no one to be concerned about us; neither laughing nor being laughed at; neither crying nor being cried for by another. How horrible is this death by bread alone.[18]

Trying to live by bread alone leads us inevitably to succumb to the ancient temptation to attempt to turn stones into bread. How do we try to make bread from stones? By putting our nose to the grindstone, by doing our jobs, by running a company, by playing the stock market, or by making the right connections. We can turn everything from computer chips and laser beams to legal briefs and leveraged buyouts into daily bread. The bread that we feed on is the bread of business and busyness and boredom, a bread known both in and out of the church. This bread will not satisfy our deepest hunger.

We are hungry without fully knowing it, needy but unaware, in exile but unable to remember another home. We need to recognize our true hunger—hunger not for the things we can make, buy, and consume but for another kind of "daily bread," a daily bread we do not produce and cannot control all by ourselves.

There are places in the world where the church does seek this daily bread of the gospel, places where the church is vibrant and alive. Dick Junkin, a North American Presbyterian pastor and former professor who spent many years working in various places in Central America, once made the following observation:

> Somehow a Christian faith is being formed in Central America which is free, hopeful, patient, courageous, self-giving. And many of us North American Christians who rub up against that faith come away sensing how great the contrast is between what we have seen in some of those sisters and brothers and our own spiritual poverty. It is not that faith of that higher quality does not exist in the United States. Surely it does exist both here and there. But I and others like me testify that such a Central American Christian faith stands in great contrast with our own experience. Speaking very personally, the quality of our own discipleship and commitment is nowhere near that of theirs. And speaking very frankly, we haven't run across that kind of faith all too often in our life in the church here in the United States.[19]

Junkin wonders why this is the case. He tries out a variety of possibilities, including the fact that these people are poor, suffering, and persecuted in ways we are not. But he rejects these as explanations, for poverty, suffering, and persecution alone do not make people alive. By themselves, they kill and embitter; they produce passivity and hopelessness. Rather, in the face of suffering and hunger and oppression, a community takes form through common participation in a particular set of practices of interpretation, worship, and action. And in the midst of their participation in these practices, the community finds something and receives something they could not otherwise have experienced. They find and receive the presence of God and the experience of new life.

As the church lives true to its own practices—of prayer and studying the scripture, of worship and showing hospitality to the stranger, of feeding the hungry and feeding each other, of allowing our own hungers to be felt and fed—it participates in the work of a God who, ultimately, is the source for satisfying all hungers. The church becomes not the bread that kills but a taste of the bread of God that gives life, not a tomb but a pathway where the hunger deep in all of our souls is fed by the love of the living Christ. It is only in knowing our own hunger that we meet the One who, when we ask for bread, will not give us a stone.

Notes

1. Glenn Tinder, "Can We Be Good without God?" *Atlantic Monthly* 264/12, December 1989, 69–85.
2. Dan Wakefield, "And Now a Word from Our Creator," *New York Times Book Review,* February 12, 1989, 1.
3. John Wheeler, "Theme for the '90s: A Rebirth of Faith," *New York Times,* December 31, 1988, 23.
4. Eleanor Blau, "Writers and Editors Ponder the Bible," *New York Times,* March 6, 1989, C18.
5. Edward Farley, *The Fragility of Knowledge* (Philadelphia: Fortress Press, 1988), 88.
6. George A. Lindbeck, "The Church's Mission to a Post-Modern Culture," in *Postmodern Theology: Christian Faith in a Pluralist World,* ed. F. B. Burnham (New York: Harper & Row, 1989), 38.
7. Ibid., 47.
8. See Anne Wilson Schaef, "Is the Church an Addictive Organization?" *Christian Century* 107/1 (January 3–10, 1990): 18–21. For a sharp critique of this pattern of thinking, see Wendy Kaminer, "Chances Are You're Co-Dependent, Too," *New York Times Book Review,* February 11, 1990, 39–40.
9. Margaret Miles, *Practicing Christianity: Critical Perspectives for an Embodied Spirituality* (New York: Crossroad, 1988), 96.
10. Ibid., 90.
11. Ibid.
12. Ibid.
13. Edward Farley, *Ecclesial Man: A Social Phenomenology of Faith and Reality* (Philadelphia: Fortress Press, 1975), 6.
14. Ibid., xvi.
15. Ibid., 10.
16. This image is borrowed from Annie Dillard, *Teaching a Stone to Talk* (New York: Harper & Row, 1982), 40, where she asks, "Why do we people in churches seem like cheerful, brainless tourists on a packaged tour of the Absolute?"

17. Philip E. Pederson, *What Does This Mean? Luther's Catechisms Today* (Minneapolis: Augsburg Publishing House, 1979), 3–4.
18. Dorothee Soelle, *Death by Bread Alone*, trans. D. L. Scheidt (Philadelphia: Fortress Press, 1978), 3–4.
19. Dick Junkin, unpublished manuscript of the 1986 Greenhoe Lecture, given at Louisville Presbyterian Theological Seminary, September 29, 1986, 2.

Life

Chapter 2

The Faithful Life

People today, I have claimed, are hungry—hungry for the bread that truly satisfies, hungry for an authentic encounter with God and for a life shaped by that encounter. In essence, the hunger of our time is for a life-giving faith. But what is faith? The word *faith* refuses to be defined simply. Faith is a complex reality, and understandings of it differ. These differences in understanding often have striking, quite diverse, and very practical implications for our conceptions of spiritual growth and formation, as well as for patterns of church life and pastoral practice.

In describing what faith means, some start with general human phenomena such as believing, trusting, committing, and orienting life. Faith, in this view, is constituted by basic human activities, and accordingly, faith is a dimension of every human life, because belief, trust, and confidence in something seem inherent to being human. Some people place their faith in material goods or personal prestige; some in certain people, communities, or traditions; others in ideals or goals; still others in a transcendent Reality or Being. But everyone, from this perspective, has some form of faith.[1]

Others argue that faith can be understood rightly only by starting not with human activity but with God. In this way of thinking, faith involves being related to God in a particular way, indeed, being in right relationship to the true God. Ultimate relationship to anyone or anything other than God is considered to be idolatry, not faith. The notion of faith as a human activity is not denied, but this activity is set in the context of a relationship, and that relationship depends on the prior activity of God, who takes initiative in making the divine nature and presence known and accessible to human beings. Thus, faith is primarily a response to a gift, an activity of recognizing and accepting God's grace, which gives rise to a way of life—a way of believing, trusting, committing, and orienting all one's thoughts and actions.

The mainstream Christian tradition has always been aware that people must put their trust and belief in something to exist at all, and it recognizes and celebrates the religious need and sensibility that seems inherent to human being. Nonetheless, it has tended largely to reserve the term *faith* for trust and belief in the God known in Jesus Christ. Because of this, its way of understanding faith is couched in the recital of a story about this God. The story is the one told in the Bible. Christianity's classic creeds and confessions summarize this story in various ways, but these summaries always include the following basic parts: [2]

> The world and all its creatures (including human beings) have been created by God, and this creation is good.
>
> Within this good creation, human beings, out of their own freedom, have broken community with God and with one another, fracturing and distorting creation. We can do nothing to remedy this by our own power or through any other power in the world.
>
> We are not left on our own, however. God chose Israel for the sake of all, and now all are, in Christ, loved and, through Christ, saved, freed, forgiven, rescued, and redeemed by God, for no reason other than God's sheer gracious goodness.[3]
>
> That love and freeing rescue, active in the world today and in the future through God's Spirit, makes available to all humanity and to the whole creation a new kind of life in which we may now participate in part and ultimately in full.[4]

The place of faith in this story is at the point of our recognition and willing reception of the gracious love and saving liberation given by God in Christ.[5] As John Calvin put it: "We shall possess a right definition of faith if we call it a firm and certain knowledge of God's benevolence toward us, founded upon the truth of the freely given promise in Christ, both revealed to our minds and sealed upon our hearts through the Holy Spirit."[6] This is the basic, central meaning of *faith*, especially from the point of view of the Reformed tradition: acknowledging our need of God's love and freeing power; recognizing that this has been given to us and to all the world; and, in response, loving and proclaiming to the world the One who provides this tender mercy.

Faith gives rise to a new kind of life. The "life of faith" is the way of living that is organized by faith and that flows out of faith. In the life of faith, we come more and more to participate in the new reality God is opening to us. We live in it ever more fully and let it do its work in every aspect of our lives, as all our beliefs and understandings, feelings and emotions, values and meanings, commitments and actions become increasingly shaped by and conformed to it. Above all, the life of faith involves rejoicing in the love and grace of God, giving thanks to God secure in the knowledge that all God's promises are sure, and sharing that love and grace in the life of the world.

Faith and the life of faith are intimately related. Each includes and is dependent on the other. Thus, it is just as true to say that faith "flows out of" the life of faith as the other way around. Faith is possible only because the life of faith surrounds it and provides its context. This context is communal and historical. The life of faith is deeply personal, but it is not individual or isolated. Only because both faith and the life of faith are communal and historic realities can they belong to us as individuals. They come to us and are formed in us through our participation in the faith and life of faith of a community of faithful people. Let us explore more deeply these two key, reciprocal realities: "faith" and "the life of faith."

FAITH

Faith and belief. To many people, faith means belief. Faith is, indeed, closely related to belief, but the relations between the two are complex, and some ways of making the connections are unhelpful and even false. Belief sometimes mistakenly means mere opinion or unthinking assent. When faith is identified with belief in this way, faith becomes believing without knowing, a kind of shot in the dark. Faith does involves belief, but in a different sense. Faith includes particular beliefs about God, the world, and ourselves, beliefs that certain matters are, in fact, the case. Faith is conviction of truth, one so deep that, far from believing without knowing, faith always seeks knowledge. It is always willing to face the evidence, entertain doubt, and inquire as far as truth may lead it.

Faith and belief are also connected in another way. Faith involves more than believing *that* something is true; it also involves believing *in*, having confidence in, trusting. Trust and confidence in God and in God's promises have been classical Protestant emphases in describing faith. Belief that God exists means little unless one believes in God.

Another aspect of the relationship between faith and belief has to do with how central our believing is to who we are. Some of our beliefs are fairly peripheral to us; they can be given up without significantly affecting basic identity and life orientation. But some of our beliefs are central to our very selves. To change these beliefs would mean to change as persons. Such "core" believing is close to the heart of a person and thus tends to be nearly identified with faith.[7]

Talking about faith in terms of belief makes sense, then, where the word *belief* connotes the profound "believing in" and "believing that" which lie at the core of a person's or community's identity and character—at the heart of one's being. By itself, though, *belief* is not a strong enough word to convey the full experience of faith.

Faith and personal knowing. In Christian faith, God and the love, grace, mercy, and promises of God are not just believed; they are not even just believed in. Rather, they are *known*. As Calvin puts it, we should call it "a firm and certain knowledge . . . both revealed to our minds and sealed upon our hearts."

The "firm and certain knowledge" of faith is much deeper than merely knowing that certain statements are factually true. The pattern is more one of "address and response" than of "statement and agreement." The knowing involved in faith is like the knowing involved in *being addressed* by a trusted messenger with a life-important personal message (such as "Your execution has been pardoned" or "The one you love does, in fact, love you deeply as well"); *recognizing* that the message is meant especially for you; and *realizing* that you are now free and may live, that your deepest hopes have come true.[8] Thus, as the *Heidelberg Catechism* puts it:

> It is not only a certain knowledge by which I accept as true all that God has revealed to us in his Word, but also a wholehearted trust which the Holy Spirit creates in me through the gospel, that, not only to others, but to me also God has given the forgiveness of sins, everlasting righteousness and salvation, out of sheer grace solely for the sake of Christ's saving work.[9]

Because we have been addressed, received this kind of word, and accepted it, we *know* our very lives to be transformed. Now our lives are grounded anew, in the one who loves us and makes us free and able to love in response.

In such knowledge, there is assurance and comfort. The *Heidelberg Catechism* points to this dimension:

> Q. What is your only comfort, in life and in death?
> A. That I belong—body and soul, in life and in death—not to myself but to my faithful Savior, Jesus Christ, who . . . has completely freed me from the dominion of the devil . . . and makes me wholeheartedly willing and ready from now on to live for him.[10]

Faith involves accepting and receiving a liberating grace that truly frees us from every enemy to abundant life. Faith means freedom, the freedom at last to give up the anxious and impossible task of keeping oneself from falling. It means freedom to turn from oneself as the source of one's own life and hope, freedom to give up the struggle to control everything by one's own power. It means freedom to be at home in the presence of a loving God.

The *content* and the *source* of such good news are primary in the situation of faith and make possible the quality of its reception. The knowing that lies at the heart of faith gains its character from the urgency of the situation, the overpowering goodness of the good news, and the astonishing difference its reception makes in one's life. Faith is the deep, life-changing knowledge of something in particular: God's gracious freeing of us and God's abiding love for us and for the whole creation. To have faith is to know *this*.

If this way of speaking about faith leads to the conclusion that faith is still primarily a matter of knowing some *thing*, however, we have missed what is most fundamental about it. For faith is not only knowing the message; it is knowing the Messenger. Our response is not only to what is said but, above all, to the One who speaks. In the situation of faith, we encounter the *presence* of God in Jesus Christ in our lives. Ultimately, the "news" is the person; the good news *is* Jesus Christ. Thus, faith is a qualitatively different, extraordinary, and ultimately unique kind of knowing. It is knowing God, knowing God's own self, experiencing inwardly "God with us" as a present and personal reality. Fundamental to our knowing is the fact that we are known by the One we come to know. Christ's "true and efficacious presence" in the Holy Spirit is active in the inner heart and pervades the mind, and this is the ultimate condition of our knowing.

This kind of knowing is personal knowing—involving and affecting every dimension of our selves. Trust, loyalty, gratitude, love, adoration—even wonder, awe, and fear—all mark this relationship. Furthermore, the knowledge and the attitudes are not separate from one another. It is not because we know that we trust (or because we trust that we know). Rather, we know *in* trust, *in* love, *in* gratitude, *in* adoration. The attitudes and the knowing come together; they are parts of one another.

Faith and truth. The deeply personal nature of faith does not mean, however, that faith's knowing is merely subjective, much less irrational. The God who creates, sustains, forgives, and saves is a God who comes to us from beyond ourselves—indeed, from beyond human history and human experience. Therefore, though God is known in and through history and is experienced inwardly and personally, the knowledge of God and God's promises can never be reduced simply to internal individual experience or to a by-product of historical social processes.

Furthermore, this God is both the Truth who sets us free and the Source of all truth there is. Faith is oriented toward truth, and the knowledge of faith is the knowledge of Truth (John 8:31–38). From the Christian point of view, such truth, though not grounded in reason, is nonetheless understood to be credible to the discerning mind. Thus, intellectual inquiry into the meaning and intelligibility of God, of God's acts and promises, of everything in God's creation is an essential and constituent element of faith and the life of faith.

Christian faith, in its simplest, deepest form, is the knowledge of God in Jesus Christ through the Holy Spirit. It is profound acceptance of and utter reliance on the gospel, the good news, of Jesus Christ. Faith involves both the address of God and the response of humanity. The address is the originating impetus for faith. Without the gospel there can be no faith. Likewise, there can be no faith without human response. In faith, we answer—by recognizing and receiving God's gracious gift. Ps 85:10-11

THE LIFE OF FAITH

Faith issues in—even propels us into—a life of faith in which we come more and more to participate in the new life God has given us. In speaking of both "faith" and "the life of faith," we make a distinction and follow a pattern that is rather consistent in Christian theology, particularly in the Reformed tradition.[11] For example, Calvin says that:

the gospel is not a doctrine of the tongue but of life. It cannot be grasped by reason and memory only but is fully understood when it possesses the whole soul and penetrates to the inner recesses of the heart. . . . Our religion will be unprofitable, if it does not change our heart, pervade our manners, and transform us into new creatures.[12]

The *Westminster Confession* points out that faith, which is "receiving and resting on Christ and his righteousness," is "not alone in the person justified, but is ever accompanied with all other saving graces, and is no dead faith, but worketh by love."[13] A more contemporary American Presbyterian confession, the *Confession of 1967*, continues the same theme by saying that, as the gospel is proclaimed and believed, "the Spirit brings God's forgiveness to [human beings], moves them to respond in faith, repentance, and obedience, and initiates the new life in Christ."[14]

The Bible has many ways of speaking about this new life. It speaks of "newness of life" (Ps. 51:10; Ezek. 11:19; 18:31; 36:26; Rom. 6:4), of being "born from above" or "born anew" (John 3:3, 7; 1 Peter 1:3, 23), of "regeneration" (John 3:5; Titus 3:5), of "putting on the new nature" (Eph. 4:24; Col. 3:10), and of being "a new creation" (2 Cor. 5:17). Perhaps the fullest discussion of the life of faith, however, is that of the apostle Paul, who speaks of it in terms of "life in Christ" and "life according to the Spirit" (see esp. Rom. 8:1–39). Life in Christ and life according to the Spirit are, for Paul, two different ways of pointing to the same reality, namely, the life of Christian faith.

Life "in Christ" and "according to the Spirit." The life of Christian faith is life in such intimate relationship with Jesus Christ that, as Paul says, we may live "in Christ" and that Christ is "in you" (Rom. 8:10). Similarly, we are now free to live "according to the Spirit," so that "the Spirit of God dwells in you" (Rom. 8:9). This is contrasted by Paul with life "according to the flesh" (Rom. 8:5). The contrast is not one between life after death and our life on earth. Both life according to the Spirit and life according to the flesh are forms of present, daily, bodily, human living. But life according to the flesh is life aimed at and directed by things that have no ultimate, lasting value and power. "Life in Christ," "life according to the Spirit," is life-oriented, empowered, undergirded, and sustained by the Source of life itself.

Paul's phrases are not everyday terms, to be sure. But they describe realities of everyday life that are central to the meaning of the life of Christian faith. They point to those things in the life of Christian faith so basic that everything else is derived from them. To take one example, suppose a person lives in such a way that his or her life depends on and is fundamentally oriented toward succeeding in a career. When this is the case, failure in one's job would be a disaster. It would call into question one's very existence, all that one is and lives for. Fear that this disaster might take place compels one to protect against it, to do almost anything to make sure the failure never takes place. All one's energies, interests, understandings, feelings, and relationships become oriented toward career and toward keeping failure from happening. One's "world" is shaped by the career and its protection. Work becomes one's world. One becomes one's work: it is in you and you are in it. In Paul's terms, if this is going on in one's life, one is living in one's career "according to the flesh."[15]

Similarly, we can be related to our families, our leisure, even our religion "according to the flesh." In all these cases, these are good things to which we should be devoted—but only "according to the Spirit." "In Christ" we may love and care for them, as Christ does. But we cannot make any of them the very center of our lives, because none of them is God. Each of them ultimately passes away. Each is only a part of life, not the Source of life itself. When we center our lives on anything but God, we live "according to the flesh." And this, whether we know it or not, is living toward death.

In life "according to the Spirit"—life "in Christ"—our lives and everything that gives them value and meaning are not absolutely located in or dependent on what we human beings can do or create or protect. Rather, our lives are located "in Christ." God present to us in Jesus Christ becomes the source of our energy, the One on whom every aspect of our lives depends and to whom it is oriented. Life's meaning, value, and direction are all funded by and gathered together in Jesus Christ.

As this takes place, we actually experience our lives differently. Things change, individually and corporately—not all at once, but over time. We experience increasing freedom. Fresh ways of seeing and deeper insight into reality become available to us. New and different struggles emerge for us. We are given responsibilities that may not have been apparent to us, while we also receive new power to carry them out. And we are given new hope and perseverance.

We experience new life *together*, not in isolation. Life according to the Spirit is shared, corporate life. We are "in Christ" as members of "the body of Christ." Our intimacy with Christ takes place in community. So too, of course, with life according to the flesh. Whole nations and peoples live according to the flesh, not just individuals. Indeed, the ultimate overcoming of life according to the flesh is the fulfillment of the reign of God, the coming of the kingdom.

New freedom. Life in the Spirit begins with the profound assurance that we are loved—fully and unreservedly—by God. This love is the source and foundation of the new life we receive in faith. For many Christians, this proves to be a stumbling block difficult to overcome. Early childhood experiences or later trauma may leave some of us feeling that such love could not possibly include *me*. Others of us may never fully acknowledge our need for such love, secretly sure, perhaps, that it could never come anyway. In either case, the inability to receive the gift of love undermines the experience of faith and the life of faith, transforming God's gift into a burden or reducing it to irrelevance. But as we do receive this love, we receive new freedom as well.

The fundamental freedom of the life of Christian faith is freedom from all the powers that enslave, dominate, corrupt, and corrode. We become more *free from* being dominated by and inappropriately dependent on them. At the same time, we become more *free for* the things of this world that God has created and called good—free to love, respect, enjoy, and care for them, precisely because we are not controlled by them.

Dorothee Soelle has described the life of Christian faith as one of constantly "chiming in with the great 'Yes' to life." Faith is "choosing life" (cf. Deut. 30:19). This may not seem like much of a choice, given the alternative. But in the life of Christian faith, the choice for life is an emphatic and unconditional choice. As Soelle puts it:

We are inclined to affirm life under particular circumstances, under certain given conditions—when life is young, and beautiful and full of achievement. The "Yes" which is meant in the emphatic, biblical sense is a "Yes" without any conditions. It applies in sickness and dying as well. It applies above all to the people who have felt themselves to be denied and without dignity for so long that they have come to terms with the situation. But choosing life is the very capacity for not putting up with the matter-of-course destruction of life surrounding us, and the matter-of-course cynicism that is our constant companion.[16]

The new freedom of the life of faith is the freedom to choose life.

Fresh seeing. In life according to the flesh, our very world is shaped by what we are striving to defend and protect. We come to see everything through lenses distorted by such limited allegiances. In Christ, a whole new world in which to live is opened up to us. It is not just that we live new kinds of lives in the same old world. Rather, the very environment in which we live is both enlarged and transformed; the whole atmosphere is altered.

According to the Bible, the world made accessible to us by life in the Spirit is the real world. It is the world created and sustained by God, not a distorted, delusionary one born of fear and anxiety. This is why fresh seeing, discernment, and wisdom are regularly conceived in the Bible to be intrinsic to the life of faith. The life of Christian faith, life in Christ, involves being able to see what there is to be seen, to see beneath the surface of things, and even to see beyond what can be seen.[17]

In this sense, the life of faith is often contrasted with life lived in darkness or blindness. Our perception is veiled or distorted—by our own egocentric needs and desires as well as by familial and cultural structures and pressures. We see only what we want to see, out of fear and anxiety often refusing even to look at things to which we would rather not attend. In Christ, there arises the capacity to penetrate the haze, to face honestly what is there, both in the world and in ourselves. In the Gospel of John, for example, Jesus is regarded as the light of the world who makes sight possible. In him, John says, "you will know the truth, and the truth will make you free" (8:32).

Struggle with evil. The new seeing includes the ability to see evil more clearly, to recognize what the Bible calls "principalities and powers" for what they are. Recognizing the forces of evil and destruction that dominate life according to the flesh, we are faced in Christ with a continual struggle against them. Sometimes the struggle is with powers that work within us individually. Sometimes the struggle is with powers that work among us corporately and at large in the world. Usually we face both struggles at once.

In the life of faith, we may come to see our own selves more clearly, including our sin. Struggle with sin has been a central theme in Reformed theology from its earliest days. In Calvin's *Institutes* we read, for example, that the first of "the effects we feel" in the life of faith is repentance. "No one can embrace the grace of the gospel," Calvin says, "without betaking himself from the errors of his past life into the right way, and applying his whole effort to the practice of repentance."[18] But repentance meant more to Calvin than mere sorrow for our sin and the effort to avoid it in the future. It meant a lifelong struggle with sin that involved, at root, a fundamental turning from self to God. Repentance, he said, "is the true turning of our life to God."[19]

The struggle is not only with individual sin, however. Sin has a corporate dimension inseparable from its personal dimension. So the life of faith involves us individually and corporately in lifelong struggle against communal and political powers of sin and earth, deceit and alienation, injustice and oppression—in the church and in the larger world. It is not always clear in the midst of struggle that the powers of sin and death are not victorious. We must continually face up to the harsh realities of human existence and cannot avoid them. But as the apostle Paul has written:

We are afflicted in every way, but not crushed; perplexed, but not driven to despair; persecuted, but not forsaken; struck down, but not destroyed; always carrying in the body the death of Jesus, so that the life of Jesus may also be manifested in our bodies. (2 Cor. 4:8–10; RSV)

So the struggles, though often very difficult, are not humorless or devoid of joy. Just the opposite. For, to say it once again, the struggle is for life and is born of the life that is given us in and through the risen Jesus Christ. In the Spirit, we participate in Christ's living work in the world, which is at once a present foretaste and sure promise of the ultimate defeat of every power of death and destruction.

Consecrated service. Participation in Christ's living work is the heart of what is conveyed by the biblical word *sanctification.* Edward A. Dowey, Jr., put the matter this way in his *Commentary on the Confession of 1967:*

"Sanctified," in the Bible, means "set apart for a divine purpose," or commissioned to serve. What made the people of Israel holy (Latin, *sanctus,* the root of "sanctify") was not their moral condition but the fact that they were chosen and set apart for a special mission in the world. The same is true of the church and each of its members.[20]

Karl Barth made a similar point when he said that what supremely characterizes the life of Christian faith is the fact that in it we have been given a task, a vocation. For him, the life of Christian faith is "existence in the execution of this task."[21]

Obedience to Christ is a crucial dimension of the Christian life, but what that means can easily be distorted. Sometimes obedience is understood only in terms of adherence to moral rules regarded as expressions of God's will. There have been times in Reformed history when such understandings have inappropriately dominated the tradition. In such cases "the law" has been virtually identified with God (and sometimes a tyrannical God at that) and "moral righteousness" with faith.

But obedience is best understood as a response of gratitude and love to a gracious and loving God whose requirements are for the sake of creation. Furthermore, the God who calls us to obedience is the same One who has first freed us for obedience and who is able and ready to forgive our disobedience. God empowers obedience, encouraging and enabling us to live gratefully and responsively in relation to God's purposes and promises. In this way, obedience is true freedom.

We are often prone to identify "God's law" with our own law and God's purposes with our own desires, habits, and customs. Life in the Spirit, however, is life imbued with freedom from conventionality. To live in Christ is both to be and to do in new ways. There is a certain kind of predictability to those who live in the Spirit, if that predictability is seen from the point of view of consonance with the will and ways of God in the world. But because that will is not conformed to the will of the world, there is also an unpredictability to those who, following God's law and purpose, no longer necessarily think and behave in ways common to their culture and society or adhere to conventional and fixed patterns of response to people and situations. In the Spirit, God's will and God's instruction to us in the law are received as gracious gifts of guidance and direction, which point us toward the kind of new life that God intends for all people and the whole earth.

The life of Christian faith is obedient, above all, in love. The love of God for us and for all creation, made manifest in Jesus Christ by the Spirit, is the source and foundation of the new life we receive in faith, a life itself characterized by love. Love is the ultimate sign and manifestation of life in the Spirit, of new life in Christ. And the love that characterizes this life is one that moves out in all directions. It is not restricted. Obedience means freedom to share in God's love for all things, including one's own self, one's kin and neighbors, strangers and enemies, and the earth itself. Life in Christ is lived in love for God's whole creation. Obedience, therefore, takes the form of care for all the world. Its names include "healing" and "compassion" and "justice" and "mercy."

But our love is not only for creation. We love God. We love God as creatures who have been created and redeemed. We love God as God's own beloved. That means we worship God. So our obedience is not only in our political and personal care for the world but also in our worship of God.

Hope and perseverance. A life such as this demands perseverance. The life of faith involves faithfulness: holding firm, keeping faith, pressing on in confidence, courage, and hope. The life of faith must, therefore, be patterned, structured, kept in place and on course over the long haul through the development of disciplines and habits, both personal and corporate. The power of persevering faithfulness becomes especially evident when obstacles are faced and the struggles the life of faith involves bring suffering or persecution. The life of faith is no more immune to the devastations that evil can bring or to the powers of destruction and death than other kinds of life. Indeed, life in Christ may place us in harm's way more often and in more ways than life according to the flesh might. But, in the Spirit, we learn more and more to trust in God's power to do wonderful things, even in the midst of the bleakest of circumstances. The Bible recognizes this particular trust as an important element in the life of faith, and those who live in the Spirit are therefore not surprised when dead ends unexpectedly turn into fresh possibilities or when healing takes place—all by the power of God.[22] Moreover, as one contemporary creedal statement put it:

> In the life, death, and resurrection of Jesus
>   God kept his promises.
> All that we can ever hope for
>   was present in Christ.
> But the work of God in Christ is not over.
> God calls us to hope for more than we have yet seen.
> The hope God gives us is ultimate confidence
>   that supports us when lesser hopes fail us.
> In Christ God gives hope for a new heaven and earth,
>   certainty of victory over death,
>   assurance of mercy and judgment beyond death.
> This hope gives us courage for the present struggle.[23]

FAITH AND THE HUNGERS OF THE AGE

In chapter 1, we pointed out the widespread spiritual hunger that characterizes contemporary culture. This hunger for meaning, values, direction in life can lead people to Christian faith, if they know that in faith such hungers can be—and in fact are—met. But it is a mistake to *identify* Christian faith with a way of making sense out of life, with some way of finding meaning, direction, and value in it. Faith and the life of faith are indeed seen and experienced by Christians as filled with meaning, value, and life direction that is ultimately trustworthy and true. The God known in faith is the overflowing reservoir of all that is valuable and good, and to live "according to the Spirit," to live "in Christ," is to be placed in intimate contact with that God in every dimension of our lives. But "meaning" and "faith" are not the same. In fact, meaning, value, and direction in life can never be the main points of the life of faith. They are not faith's substance. Rather, they are its by-products, and altered by-products at that.

In the experience of faith and the life of faith, a transformation takes place. Meaning, value, and life direction all become relativized. They are no longer the prize we seek. In Christ, our very hungers become transformed, so that to live in Christ is the only food we crave. In Christ, we are free to give up all else—even meaning, value, direction, and our search for them. For they are not God. The surprise, however, is that in being free to give them up, we find them returned to us a hundredfold. Just as those who lose their lives for Christ's sake gain them back (Matt. 16:25), so also do those who, in Christ, let loose their strivings for meaning, value, and direction gain these back again, but indirectly, as a gift, and different in kind from that which they had expected, from that for which they had hoped. As H. Richard Niebuhr has written, God "requires of us the sacrifice of all we would conserve"—including meaning, value, and direction in life— "and grants us gifts we had not dreamed of."[24]

Notes

1. See, for example, James W. Fowler, *Stages of Faith* (San Francisco: Harper & Row, 1981). Fowler takes this approach in developing his theory of faith development.
2. This outline is patterned after Presbyterian Church in the U.S., *Declaration of Faith* (Atlanta: Presbyterian Publishing House, 1977). The opening chapter of this statement speaks of our relation to "the living

God" and introduces us to the story or narrative that follows. We are then told of God's creation and ruling of the world (chap. 2, 1–5), of how "the human race has rejected its Maker" (chap. 2, 6), of God's dealings with the people of Israel (chap. 3), of the coming of God in Christ and the deliverance brought in him (chap. 4), of the continuing activity of God in the world in the Spirit (chap. 5), of God's call to us to participate in what God is doing (chaps. 6–9), and of all toward which God's promises lead (chap. 10).

3. *Justified* is the technical word the Reformed tradition has most often used, and it has made clear that we are justified not by anything we have done but rather "by grace alone."

4. *Sanctification* is one traditional name given to this participation and to what happens in and to us through our participation.

5. See Office of the General Assembly, "The Westminster Confession of Faith," in *The Constitution of the Presbyterian Church (U.S.A.)*, part 1, *Book of Confessions* (New York: Office of the General Assembly, Presbyterian Church (U.S.A.) 1983), 6.079: "the principal acts of saving faith are accepting, receiving, and resting upon Christ alone."

6. John Calvin, *Institutes of the Christian Religion*, The Library of Christian Classics, Vol. XX ed. John T. McNeill, trans. Ford Lewis Battles (Philadelphia: The Westminster Press, 1960), 3.2.7.

7. See Sara Little, *To Set One's Heart* (Atlanta: John Knox Press, 1983), 14, for a discussion of "core beliefs." The whole of her first chapter is an excellent overview of the relationship between faith and belief.

8. See Walker Percy, *The Message in the Bottle* (New York: Farrar, Straus & Giroux, 1975), chap. 6, for a wonderfully illuminating essay on what it means to receive "news" and why receiving a certain kind of news is central to Christian faith.

9. Office of the General Assembly, "The Heidelberg Catechism," in *The Constitution of the Presbyterian Church (U.S.A.)*, part 1, *Book of Confessions*, 4.021.

10. Ibid., 4.001.

11. The distinction being made here is parallel and related to the distinction often made between justification and sanctification. That the two are so deeply intertwined as to be two parts of the same whole is conveyed by Calvin, who says that "this [justification, or the righteousness of Christ] you cannot attain without at the same time attaining to sanctification. . . . We may distinguish between them, but Christ contains

both inseparably in himself. . . . Thus we see how true it is that we are justified, not without works, yet not by works; since union with Christ, by which we are justified, contains sanctification as well as righteousness" (Calvin, *Institutes*, Book 3.16.1).

Likewise, "faith" and "the life of faith" are so deeply interconnected that they can never be separated from each other. Indeed, some feel that even to make a distinction between them is problematic. Nonetheless, for many purposes making such a distinction is useful, as long as making it does not lead to any kind of separation between them. We make the distinction here primarily to highlight the centrality of the deep and intimate knowledge of the gospel of Jesus Christ for the life of Christian faith, while not losing sight of the manifold and often intricately related dimensions of life lived in response to this gracious gift. We believe that by making this distinction we are helped to understand more clearly the nature and dynamics of growth and maturation in the whole Christian life.

It is important to point out, however, that the various dimensions of the life of Christian faith are not only related to and dependent on the dimension we have already discussed; they are also constitutive of it. That is, "a firm and certain knowledge of God's benevolence toward us . . . both revealed to our minds and sealed upon our hearts" involves the dimensions of discernment, freedom, struggle, obedience, perseverance, love, and hope that we are about to discuss. These cannot be central in our lives apart from the knowledge we call faith; but neither is the knowledge we call faith accessible to us apart from these other intrinsically related dimensions. And when we turn to the issue of growth in the life of faith, we will see that each dimension deepens precisely in the interplay among them all.

12. John Calvin, *Golden Booklet of the True Christian Life* (Grand Rapids: Baker Book House, 1952), 17.
13. Office of General Assembly, "Westminster Confession of Faith," 6.069.
14. Office of the General Assembly, "The Confession of 1967," in *The Constitution of the Presbyterian Church (U.S.A.)*, part 1, *Book of Confessions*, 9.21.
15. See Edward Farley, "The Work of the Spirit in Christian Education," *Religious Education* 60 (November–December 1965): 427–36, 479. Much of this interpretation of life "according to the Spirit" is indebted to Farley's presentation in this article.

16. Dorothee Soelle, *Choosing Life* (Philadelphia: Fortress Press, 1981), 7.

17. Cf. Heb. 11:3: "By faith we understand that the world was created by the word of God, so that what is seen was made out of things which do not appear" (RSV). See also Frederick Buechner's essay on this text, titled "Faith," in *A Room Called Remember* (San Francisco: Harper & Row, 1984), esp. 20–23.

18. Calvin, *Institutes*, 3.3.1.

19. Ibid., 3.3.5.

20. Edward A. Dowey, Jr., *A Commentary on the Confession of 1967 and an Introduction to "The Book of Confessions"* (Philadelphia: Westminster Press, 1968), 90.

21. Karl Barth, *Church Dogmatics*, vol. 4, part 3, second half, trans. G. W. Bromiley (Edinburgh: T. & T. Clark, 1962), 573–74.

22. See, for a few examples, Mark 5:22–43; 9:14–28; 11:22–25; Luke 18:35–42; and Heb. 2:1–5.

23. Presbyterian Church in the U.S., *Declaration of Faith*, chap. 10, 1–13.

24. H. Richard Niebuhr, *The Meaning of Revelation* (New York: Macmillan Publishing Co., 1960), 138.

Chapter 3

Growing in Faith

It is clear, both from experience and from the testimony of Scripture, that the kind of faith and life of faith we described in chapter 2 do not arise in a moment. The alterations and transformations that occur in faith and in the life of faith occur in time and over time. Though some dimensions of faith and the life of faith are born in the littlest child, others presuppose experience in the world and a meeting with the gospel. Besides, every dimension of faith may expand and deepen. The Bible speaks of both immaturity and maturity in faith, and we are called to grow up into the latter.[1] Furthermore, faith and the life of faith are dynamic, vital processes, not static conditions. For all these reasons, it is important to recognize and articulate what it means to grow in faith and in the life of faith and to ask how it happens. Calvin called the process "regeneration" and understood it to be long-term and dynamic:

> This restoration does not take place in one moment or one day or one year; but through continual and sometimes even slow advances God wipes out in his elect the corruptions of the flesh, cleanses them of guilt, consecrates them to himself as temples renewing all their minds to true purity that they may practice repentance throughout their lives and know that this warfare will end only in death.[2]

FAITH AND METAPHORS FOR GROWTH

The consistency of these insights with what we know about human growth and development in general is obvious. It is clear to almost everyone, and contemporary studies in developmental psychology underscore this, that not only our bodies but also our capacities to reason and use language, our emotions, our attitudes, our sense of self, and many other aspects of our lives undergo continual change in the dynamic processes of human life. Human life involves continual transformations and developments, and many of these, we now realize, occur according to some pattern and in an orderly and expected sequence. It is reasonable to wonder whether or not the same is true for faith and the life of faith. We know the life of faith involves change, transformation, growth, and maturation. Would it not be possible to chart out a consistent, general pattern by which this occurs?

Many attempts along these lines have been made over the centuries, though they have varied greatly in kind. Sometimes the pattern is that of an ordered series of works of the Spirit in a person (such as illumination, conversion, regeneration, justification, mystical union); sometimes people have talked about rungs on a spiritual ladder; the portrayal of growth and transformation as a journey on which crucial events take place is widespread (John Bunyan's *Pilgrim's Progress*, for instance); and in recent times, faith has been seen as something that moves through stages of human development or across eras in the normal human life cycle.[3]

One of two fundamental sets of metaphors is usually implicit in these various conceptions of growth in faith. Perhaps the most prevalent in contemporary thinking are the *organic* metaphors. To this way of thinking, growth is the expansion of an organic structure in size and complexity through a continuous series of transformations. Trees grow up from seedlings to maturity following a consistent pattern, the stages of which can be anticipated and systematically described. In much the same way, human bodies go through regular changes from infancy through childhood and adolescence to adulthood and old age. These changes and their sequence are more or less programmed in the organism from the beginning.

The second set of metaphors in our understanding of growth uses the imagery of a *journey.* Growth is seen as movement from some originating point to some destination. Here growth and transformation are not so much the development of an internal structure through an expected sequence as they are the results of events and interactions that take place between persons and their environments. The sources of transformation are thus both internal and external, and growth itself implies a certain degree of purpose on the part of the person who makes the journey.

Both sets of metaphors have been employed in the Christian tradition throughout its history and by contemporary thinkers who reflect on the nature of growth and transformation in faith, and both are helpful in capturing the dynamic, historical character of faith and the life of faith. But the tradition also contains warnings about too much dependence upon these metaphors.[4] Several fundamental themes in the tradition's understanding of faith and the life of faith keep it from adopting these metaphors without qualification and from using the language of growth and development without reservations to speak about faith:

> The tradition's emphasis on the priority of the activity of God as the source of faith and on the nature of faith as response to God in history makes it wary of organic metaphors which suggest that faith is a structure built into human beings that undergoes evolutionary or developmental transformation.
>
> In recognizing that our lives are ever endangered by powers and principalities and the threats of sin and death, the tradition has usually been hesitant to place too much emphasis on progress in the life of faith or to stake out any stages by which such progress might be marked.
>
> The tradition's emphasis on the freedom and particularity of new life in Christ has made it hesitant to define or describe maturity in faith and in the life of faith too exactly. There has been an effort to avoid a conformism and to recognize that the life of faith gains its concrete shape from the particular historical situation in which it is carried out.

Given these reservations, can we still speak appropriately of growth and transformation without obscuring, distorting, or oversimplifying faith and the life of faith?

FAITH AND HUMAN DEVELOPMENT

Faith and the life of faith certainly involve changes in the conditions and qualities of our lives, and these changes are heavily influenced by events and interactions that happen in various physical and cultural locations. The metaphor of life as a journey—and even as a "faith journey"—helpfully captures these characteristics of human existence in time. And indeed, certain aspects of human life (biological, psychological, and social) involve us in patterned developmental processes of growth and transformation. But faith and the life of faith should not be identified with the development of a structure or the itinerary of a journey. When they are, important dimensions of faith and the life of faith are obscured or distorted. Neither faith nor the life of faith is an organic structure intrinsic to human beings. Therefore, neither is the sort of reality that can grow in size or complexity through some patterned sequence over time. Nor are faith and the life of faith our movement from some point of departure to some place of arrival at the end of a journey.

Faith and the life of faith have power to transform and shape human development and life journeys. But this can be the case only if faith and the life of faith are recognized to be something more than and other than the outcome or sum total of development in the various natural human capacities (such as bodily motor operations, cognition, imagination, role taking, moral judgment, and various affective dimensions) or the result of a series of human events and interactions. Only then can it be clear that faith and the life of faith are never strictly determined by our developmental achievements or the accidents of history and, thus, never limited by any failure to reach some particular stage of development or to have some particular kind of event take place in one's life. The shape of one's faith and life of faith will certainly be influenced by one's developmental capacities and by the events that take place in one's life, but more significant, every aspect of one's human development and historical existence may be transformed by and employed in faith and in the life of faith.

This becomes especially important when we recall that no aspect of human development or of historical interaction is unambiguously good and life-giving. Rather, all of it is played out in the context of a contention between life "according to the flesh" and life "in the Spirit."[5] Human growth and development and human journeying lead us ultimately only to death and destruction if they take place according to the flesh. We live only to die, as the saying goes. But in Christ all things are transformed. From the point of view of Christian faith, this is the crucial point. The issue is not how much or how fast we grow but in what context. The ultimate context is known in faith to be the environment or communion of the Spirit, the creative and redemptive Spirit of God who makes all life-giving and life-sustaining growth possible.[6]

Coming to faith means coming to recognize that the context of all our growing and living is the world in which, over which, and through which the Spirit of God known in Jesus Christ reigns. We may fail to recognize this; or, recognizing it, we may refuse to accept it. We manufacture worlds of our own, of which we are the center and source, and we strive to control, guide, direct, and force our own growing and journeying within them. In these and many other ways, we often struggle against the fact that we live at all only because we live in an environment constituted by the graciousness of a loving God. But such recognition and acceptance are what define faith and originate, undergird, and mobilize growth in faith and in the life of faith.

GROWTH IN FAITH
AND IN THE LIFE OF FAITH

The life of faith is a living, moving, dynamic existence that takes place in the environment of the Spirit. This existence includes the experience of growth in the manifold aspects of our nature: our bodies, minds, feelings, judgments, social relationships, imaginations. In the Spirit we come to recognize this growth as God's gift. We come to see that "God has made us and not we ourselves," and this frees us to allow the Spirit to work in our growing, rather than to struggle against the Spirit by trying to control it through our own powers. This is part of what is involved in growth in the life of faith.

Growth in the life of faith also involves a lifelong, continuing process of encountering and entering into the inexhaustible richness of the mystery of God and of God's love, ever more deeply and profoundly. Just as the process of knowing a person is never finished or exhausted, so too the dynamic of uncovering the riches of God's grace and promises is unlimited. Thus we grow in the life of faith as we hear more and more of the good news of the living gospel, understand and appropriate more profoundly its unceasingly expanding meaning and significance, and dwell ever more fully on the presence of God with us.

We may also speak of growth in the life of faith in terms of extending our recognition of the consequences of God's grace into more and more aspects of our lives in the world. We grow in the life of faith as our seeing, our struggling, our obedience, our loving, our suffering, and our persevering—all the aspects of the life of faith discussed in chapter 2—are increasingly "quickened and strengthened."[7] Growth in the life of faith involves the penetration or infiltration of faith into ever-increasing dimensions of our existence.

Growth in the life of faith, then, has a number of dimensions. But what about growth in faith? Does faith grow? Do we grow in faith?

It is clear that we do not come to faith simply by growing. We do not

[handwritten annotations at top: "Faith: the smallest of all seeds becomes a mighty tree of refuge"]

grow into faith just by becoming more mature. But does faith grow? In a sense, it does. Faith—understood as the recognition and acceptance of God's enduring, saving presence—may grow in power, significance, richness, and depth as more and more dimensions of our individual and corporate lives are touched by and conformed to it. But in another sense, it is misleading to say that faith grows. If by "growth" we mean a patterned process of change in form, structure, or complexity, then faith does not grow.[8] Faith simply is what it is, and by being so, it provides the still point from which all other forms of life-giving growth and transformation may take place. *[handwritten: "or maybe the growth is through interaction w/ our will. see page 40 *"]*

[handwritten in right margin: "are you sure?"]

If faith—understood as the deep and personal knowledge of God's love—simply is what it is, the obvious next question is how we come to faith. How do we come to recognize and accept God's gracious presence in our lives? We may, in a sense, know it from the earliest days of our lives. The theologian James Loder has argued that when, at the age of three months, a child "seeks and learns to respond to the presence of a human face . . . and give a smile," what is established "is the child's sense of personhood and a universal prototype of the Divine Presence."[9] In other words, there is a sense in which infants may recognize the presence of God, though of course they cannot yet name it.

This recognition is short-lived, however, for, by six months, children already sense absence and disorientation, and in the brokenness of a world that lives according to the flesh, this gives rise to anxiety and the struggle to compose substitute "worlds" of our own.[10] Thus we need to be helped to make this recognition again. This happens as we come in contact with a people and a "culture" that has this recognition intrinsic to its way of life. The process by which we come to faith and grow in faith and in the life of faith is a process that involves a community. *[handwritten: "yes!"]*

THE COMMUNITY OF FAITH

Faith and the life of faith are communal before they are individual. A key New Testament text on growing in the life of faith is Ephesians 4:1–16, in which Paul speaks of Christian growth and maturity, saying that "we must grow up in every way into him who is the head, into Christ" (v. 15). The "growing up" that Paul has in mind is predominantly the growing up and maturing of the whole body of Christ (v. 12). Attaining "the unity of the faith and of the knowledge of the Son of God, [coming] to maturity, to the measure of the full stature of Christ" (v. 13) is something the people as a

[handwritten at bottom: "my motivation for class involvement"]

whole are called to. It is "we" together, as the body of Christ, who are to "grow up in every way into him who is the head" (v. 15), and it is only as "the whole body, joined and knit together by every ligament with which it is equipped, as each part is working properly," that the "body's" growth and upbuilding in love (v. 16) become possible.

The deep, almost physical knowledge of the love of God in Jesus Christ that constitutes faith is first of all and above all the whole community's knowledge. The presence of Jesus Christ is a presence in, to, and through the community of Jesus Christ. The new life in the Spirit, the new seeing, the vocation, the ministry, the suffering, and the perseverance are not simply the sum of individual new lives, visions, and vocations. Rather, all these are first and last the community's. The new life and all that comes with it are features of the community of Jesus Christ in every epoch, all around the globe, in every kind of cultural situation, including our own.

This does not by any means exclude the individual; just the opposite. The fact that faith and the life of faith are communal makes them possible for each of us. Faith is, indeed, profoundly personal, and the life of faith is given to each of us to live out in our own particular items and circumstances. God comes to each of us, God frees each of us, and God calls each of us in a personal way. The point is that faith and the life of faith come for each of us individually in the body, as parts of the body. And faith and the life of faith come in the body as a whole as each of us individually lives in faith and in the life of faith.

PARTICIPATION IN THE MEANS OF GRACE

The process of coming to faith and growing in the life of faith is fundamentally a process of participation. We come to recognize and live in the Spirit as we participate more and more broadly and deeply in communities that know God's love, acknowledge it, express it, and live their lives in the light of it. The Presbyterian *Confession of 1967* says that "the new life takes shape in a community in which [human beings] know that God loves and accepts them in spite of what they are."[11] In words that capture an older language, God uses the community of faith as "means of grace."

"New life in Christ" is made available to us in community, and such community carries on its life through certain "practices" that are constitutive of the shape of its life together in the world. These practices were called by Calvin "external means or aids by which God invites us into the society of Christ and holds us therein."[12] The *Larger Catechism* calls them "outward and ordinary means," or "ordinances."[13]

At times these "means of grace" have been mistakenly regarded primarily as means by which certain "benefits" were made available to individuals. And these benefits were understood to be available in and through the church, which alone "administered" the grace of God in Christ through certain ordinances that it controlled. This conception often led to distortions of the church's proper self-understanding and to destructive patterns of ministry and life in the world, and it still does so in some contexts today. But God's grace is not just for separate individuals or for Christians alone; it is also for the world. Nor is the church God's broker. Thus, contemporary wahoo developments in Reformed theology have led us to speak about these matters in other ways. To understand the place of the church and its practices in the economy of God's grace, it is helpful to consider, as Jürgen Moltmann does, "the participation of the church in the history of God."[14]

Just as faith and the life of faith are life in the communion of the Spirit, so a community "the whole being of [which] is marked by participation in the history of God's dealings with the world" becomes the concrete arena of our coming into faith and growing in the life of faith.[15] We participate in the life of the Spirit by participating in the life of such community, and this only because the community's own being and activity are constituted through participation in the life of the Spirit. Thus, insofar as the church is a community in the power of the Spirit, its whole life in the world becomes a means of grace for those who are its people and for all the world.

CHRISTIAN PRACTICES

The church, as community in the power of the Spirit, has over the course of its history learned to depend on the efficacy of certain central practices and disciplines in nurturing faith and growth in the life of faith.[16] The tradition itself bears witness to the fact that by participating in certain active forms of life together, an environment is created in which people may come to faith and grow in life in Christ.

At the same time, the tradition has avoided any sort of causal understanding of the relationship between these practices and faith. Participating in the disciplines of the church does not bring about or cause faith or growth in the life of faith. Rather, engagement in the church's practices puts us in a position where we may recognize and participate in the work of God's grace in the world.[17] This is precisely what we do when we "make diligent use of the means of grace." By active participation in practices that are central to the historical life of the community of faith, we place ourselves in the kind of situation in which we know God accomplishes the work of grace.

What are the practices and disciplines that Christians have found to nurture faith and growth in the life of faith? The *Larger Catechism* asks and responds to that question as follows:

> Q. . . . What are the outward means whereby Christ communicates to us the benefits of his mediation?
> A. The outward and ordinary means, whereby Christ communicates to his Church the benefits of his mediation, are all his ordinances, especially the Word, sacraments, and prayer.[18]

The catechism then goes on to discuss the ways in which these ordinances are to be carried out and instructs persons how to do so and with what intentions.[19]

Other official documents of the church likewise discuss such practices. *A Brief Statement of Belief* contains sections on "The Church and the Means of Grace" and "Christian Life and Work" that discuss various important practices.[20] *The Theological Declaration of Barmen* points out the significance in the Christian life of practices of criticism and resistance to powers that oppose Christ's work and calls us to the practice of "providing for justice and peace."[21] The various practices involved in the "ministry of reconciliation" are articulated in the *Confession of 1967*.[22] In addition, the *Book of Order* lists nine specific ways in which members are called to be involved in the ministry of Christ's church.[23]

Practices that appear consistently throughout the tradition and that are particularly significant for Christians today include:

1. worshiping God together—praising God, giving thanks for God's creative and redemptive work in the world, hearing God's word preached, and receiving the sacraments given to us in Christ;[24]
2. telling the Christian story to one another—reading and hearing the Scriptures and also the stories of the church's experience throughout its history;
3. interpreting together the Scriptures and the history of the church's experience, particularly in relation to their meaning for our own lives in the world;

4. praying—together and by ourselves, not only in formal services of worship but in all times and places;

5. confessing our sin to one another, and forgiving and becoming reconciled with one another;

6. tolerating one another's failures and encouraging one another in the work each must do and the vocation each must live;

7. carrying out specific faithful acts of service and witness together;

8. giving generously of one's means and receiving gratefully gifts others have to give;

9. suffering with and for one another and all whom Jesus showed us to be our neighbors;

10. providing hospitality and care, not only to one another but to strangers and even enemies;

11. listening and talking attentively to one another about our particular experiences in life;

12. struggling together to become conscious of and to understand the nature of the context in which we live;

13. criticizing and resisting all those powers and patterns (both within the church and in the world as a whole) that destroy human beings, corrode human community, and injure God's creation;

14. working together to maintain and create social structures and institutions that will sustain life in the world in ways that accord with God's will.[25]

These are the kinds of practices that the church's people engage in over and over again, because they are practices that constitute being the church, practices to which God calls us as Christians. They are, likewise, practices that place people in touch with God's redemptive activity, that put us where life in Christ may be made known, recognized, experienced, and participated in. They are means of grace, the human places in which and through which God's people come to faith and grow to maturity in the life of faith. From its own history and experience, the church knows that such practices enable the community and its people as individuals to continue their experience with God made present in Word, in sacrament, in prayer, and in the community's life in obedience to its vocation in the world.

I agree ☺

LIVING INTO THE PRACTICES

People come to faith and grow in faith and in the life of faith by participating in the practices of the Christian community. These are practices of
the whole church. Because and to the extent that the church is faithful in
its practice, it makes available to itself and to the world "external means"
by which the gift of God's Word and presence may come to persons and
take root in them. Those who participate in these practices are involving
themselves ever more deeply in processes by which faith may come, grow,
and mature.

People come to faith and grow in the life of faith in the context of these
practices as they themselves, participating in them actively, actually do
what these practices involve. We engage in them personally in particular
physical and material settings and in face-to-face interaction with other
people. It is not enough simply to know about them or think about them
or observe other people engaging in them. Each of us must actually pray,
read the Scriptures and interpret them, and provide hospitality to strangers.

We cannot start by doing all of them at once, of course, and in the beginning we will not be prepared for all that they involve. These practices
all involve multiple levels of complexity and broad ranges of participation.
It takes time and experience, for example, to extend one's reach beyond
simple attempts to say what a particular verse means toward more complex practices of interpretation in which many parts and themes of the
Bible are seen mutually to influence and resonate with one another and to
speak deeply to the most fundamental issues of our time. And over time,
we may come to participate in biblical interpretation in a wide variety of
settings and contexts, including not only worship and study but also devotional reading, moral decision making, and political action. We mature
in faith and in the life of faith as our participation in these practices involves increasingly broad, varied, and complex dimensions, and when the
activities we engage in become increasingly wide-ranging in their context
and impact. It is not only a matter of going into the practices in greater
depth; we are also enabled to take increasing initiative in beginning and
carrying them through.

We are not born with the abilities to carry out these practices, and they
do not come simply with age. We need to *learn* them. To learn them, we
need not only experience but guidance. We need at many points to be
taught. So we grow best in these practices when we participate in the ac-

tivities involved in them with others, especially with those who are skilled in them and are able to teach them to us. Then, as we are well taught, as our experience with them broadens and deepens, as our own engagement in them becomes more extensive, we grow more and more into the practices. Increasingly, we come to live into them until they live in us.

There are great advantages to learning and participating in these practices and disciplines from early childhood. They are not limited to adults. The faith of children is essential in the faith of the whole church. Indeed, adults can grow in the life of faith by participating with children in these practices, for the faith of children is a witness to us. Likewise, children grow in faith and in the life of faith as these practices become the fundamental habits of life around which their identity and character are formed. Furthermore, we are able to grow most fully in participation in the practices of faith when the people involved in them with us are, or are becoming, personally significant to us, and we to them. Bonds of affection and mutual support contribute greatly to growing into participation in every one of these practices. So the readiness of children to be open to such affection and trust makes possible deep participation with loving parents, teachers, and other caring adults.

No one practice is the key to faith and the life of faith. The life of faith involves participation in all of them. When any particular practice is isolated from the others, its power is limited. The power of each practice is enormously enhanced, however, when it is intimately related to the others and when each is experienced as a dimension of a whole. Telling the Christian story to one another and interpreting the Scriptures, for example, when done by people who are suffering for and with one another and who are talking about and listening attentively to one another's experiences in the world, have a power that they otherwise lack. Criticizing and resisting powers that destroy may themselves lead to the corrosion of human community if not done in a context where we also confess our own sinfulness and work to maintain and create sustaining, life-giving social institutions. In sum, we grow in any of these practices only as we come more and more to understand the significance and meaning of all of them and see how they are intimately connected with one another.

The practices and disciplines are means of grace, not tasks to accomplish or instructions to follow in order to grow in the life of faith. To do the latter would be to engage in the practices "according to the flesh" rather than "in the Spirit." Instead, these practices and disciplines are gifts to the community, by means of which God may use the community to establish and sustain all people in the new life given in the Spirit. We come to value and appreciate these practices and integrate them more fully into the structure of our own lives as we come increasingly to see this. Then we have reasons and motives of our own for engaging in them and take increasing personal responsibility for initiating, sustaining, and making them available to others. Then they become part of who we are.

Notes

1. See Eph. 4:13–16.
2. John Calvin, *Institutes of The Christian Religion,* The Library of Christian Classics, Vol. XX, ed. John T. McNeill, trans. Ford Lewis Battles (Philadelphia: The Westminster Press, 1960), 3.3.9.
3. See Karl Barth's sketch of various instances of this attempt within Protestantism, in *Church Dogmatics,* vol. 4, part 3, second half, trans. G. W. Bromiley (Edinburgh: T. & T. Clark, 1962), sec. 71.2 (see esp. 505–6); James W. Fowler, *Stages of Faith* (San Francisco: Harper & Row, 1981); Donald Capps, *Life-Cycle Theory and Pastoral Care* (Philadelphia: Fortress Press, 1983); and idem., *Deadly Sins and Saving Virtues* (Philadelphia: Fortress Press, 1983).
4. Barth is probably the Reformed theologian most emphatic in his warnings about the dangers inherent in trying to chart any kind of developmental sequence in faith and the life of faith. He says that "the essential interest in this matter has always been to outline the development of the natural man into a Christian, and the Christian into an increasingly perfect Christian, in a way which can be mastered and recounted." For him, "this whole attempt implies an attack on the substance of a genuine understanding of the process" (*Church Dogmatics,* vol. 4, part 3, second half, sec. 71.2, 506–7).
5. See, for example, James E. Loder, *The Transforming Moment: Understanding Convictional Experiences* (San Francisco: Harper & Row, 1981), chap. 6, where he discusses "the developmental history of negation" and argues for "the theological deficiency of normal development."
6. See Dwayne Huebner, "Christian Growth in Faith," *Religious Education* 81 (1986): 511–21. Huebner points out "the presence and necessity of God's grace for growth. Growth is mostly beyond our control and ken. To grow is one thing, to be conscious of that growth is another. If the mystery and grace are acknowledged, then faith can be connected with

growth. . . . The problem of faithlessness arises when we describe, depict, offer explanations, or think about growth. In such thinking activities, we usually fail to acknowledge the presence of God's gifts or God's grace."

7. A phrase borrowed from Office of the General Assembly, "The Westminster Confession of Faith," in *The Constitution of the Presbyterian Church (U.S.A.)*, part 1, *Book of Confessions* (New York, Office of the General Assembly, Presbyterian Church (U.S.A.), 1983), 6.067.

8. Thus, Huebner, "Christian Growth in Faith," esp. 517: "Faith is an awareness of God's presence . . . faith does not change form, structure, complexity . . . faith is openness to God, which is itself a gift of God. It does not grow."

9. See Loder, *Transforming Moment*, 166–67.

10. Ibid., 167ff. The same point is made by Huebner, "Christian Growth in Faith," 516: "In building our human world and our understanding, we, in effect, construct idols that detract us from memory, praise, and hope. This shows most clearly in the relationship between infant and parent/caregiver. The love and concern which made the infant a person is named human love and the Source of that love is forgotten. The intrusion of anger, disregard, selfishness in the relationship is brokenness or sin, unacknowledged as such. The clearings of faith, in which the presence of God is acknowledged and sought, are preempted by idols and the preoccupations which they produce. The infant, in growing with a cluttered adult and without the necessary clearings for remembering, thanking, and seeking God, constructs or takes on idols, not clearings of faith."

11. Office of the General Assembly, "The Confession of 1967," in *The Constitution of the Presbyterian Church U.S.A.*, part 1, *Book of Confessions*, 9.22. See Edward A. Dowey, Jr., *A Commentary on the Confession of 1967 and an Introduction to "The Book of Confessions"* (Philadelphia: Westminster Press, 1968), 86.

12. Calvin, *Institutes*, Book 4 (from the title, "The External Means . . .").

13. Office of the General Assembly, "The Larger Catechism," in *The Constitution of the Presbyterian Church (U.S.A.)*, part 1, *Book of Confessions*, 7.264.

14. Jürgen Moltmann, The *Church in the Power of the Spirit*, trans. M. Kohl (New York: Harper & Row, 1977), 64–65.

15. Ibid., 65.

16. A *practice* is an ongoing, shared activity of a community of people that partly defines and partly makes them who they are. A more complex and precise definition is proved and discussed by Alasdair MacIntyre in *After Virtue* (Notre Dame, Ind.: University of Notre Dame Press, 1981), 175. See also Robert Bellah, Richard Madsen, William M. Sullivan, Ann Swidler, and Stephen M. Tipton, *Habits of the Heart* (Berkeley: University of California Press, 1985), 335. The term *discipline* is virtually synonymous with practice, but we use both terms because several connotations of discipline are helpful in our context, particularly as we think of "spiritual disciplines" and "church discipline." Disciplines are practices and all practices are of necessity disciplined. In the Reformed tradition, "spiritual discipline" and "church discipline" (or order) have never been separate matters. Rather, they are reciprocal dimensions of one piety, a piety that is at once individual and corporate.

17. See Shirley C. Guthrie, Jr., *Christian Doctrine* (Atlanta: John Knox Press, 1968), 299–300: "In the first place, if new life is a gift of the Holy Spirit, we cannot give it to ourselves. We cannot simply decide to have faith, to live with hope and to love. Not only the New Testament but our own experience tells us this. . . . Secondly, there is nothing we can do to force the Spirit of God to come to us and give us faith, hope and love. We cannot manipulate him to work according to our schedule and desires. . . . He is free to work when, where and how he chooses. He takes the initiative and not we. But that does not mean that we can do anything we please or do nothing at all, excusing our lack of faith, our hopelessness or our unloving attitudes by complaining that the Spirit has not chosen to come to us. We have been told who he is, and where and how he is promised. Although we cannot control his coming and going, we can at least place ourselves in the kind of situation in which we know he accomplishes his work." (See also 307ff. and 323ff.)

18. Office of the General Assembly, "The Larger Catechism," 7.264.

19. Ibid., 7.265–7.306.

20. Office of the General Assembly, *Book of Confessions* (1988), xiv–xv.

21. Office of the General Assembly, "The Theological Declaration of Barmen," in *The Constitution of the Presbyterian Church (U.S.A.),* part 1, *Book of Confessions,* 8.22; see also 8.01–8.28.

22. Office of the General Assembly, "The Confession of 1967," esp. 9.31.

23. Office of the General Assembly, *The Constitution of the Presbyterian Church (U.S.A.),* part 2, *Book of Order* (Louisville, Ky.: Office of the General Assembly, Presbyterian Church (U.S.A.), 1988), G–5.0102.

24. Worship comes first on this list because it is the central and orienting practice of the Christian life. The Reformed tradition has always highlighted this point, because the worship of God is, in fact, the context and point of everything else Christians are and do.

25. This list is adapted from Craig Dykstra, "No Longer Strangers," *Princeton Seminary Bulletin* 6/3 (November 1985): 197. It was stimulated in the first place by a similar list in John Westerhoff, *Bringing Up Children in the Christian Faith* (Minneapolis: Winston Press, 1980), 36–52. This list should be compared with the somewhat different but nonetheless complementary list of Christian practices discussed in *Practicing Our Faith: A Way of Life for a Searching People,* ed. Dorothy Bass (San Francisco: Jossey-Bass, 1997).

<u>Practices</u> p.68

Chapter 4

The Power of Christian Practices

p. 42   p. 68

In chapter 3, I provided a list of practices constitutive of the kind of community life through which God's presence is palpably felt and known. The list included worshiping together, praying, reading and hearing the Scriptures and learning the history of the church, and interpreting all that to one another in the light of one's own and the community's experience. Also included were explicit acts of confession of sin and forgiveness and reconciliation, as well as mutual toleration and encouragement. Finally, I mentioned a number of activities that involved struggle and suffering, criticism and resistance.

Now I make explicit a claim that has been present, at least implicitly, in all that I have said: In the midst of engagement in these practices, a community comes to such an immediate experience of the grace and mercy and power of God that the "nasty suspicion" that permeates much of contemporary American church and intellectual life—the suspicion that theology is really about nothing more than human subjectivity—simply loses its power. I am aware that this is a very large claim, especially since the list of practices was a fairly simple one. I doubt if any of the items on that list surprised readers. To be sure, things such as worship and prayer are essential practices of the Christian life, but my hunch is that most readers probably consider the list, however accurate, to be somewhat mundane and obvious.

In this chapter, however, I think more about this seemingly obvious list of practices and, in the process, attempt to buttress my admittedly large claim. Certainly, the claim is not the kind that I think can be proven. It is more the kind of claim for which one can provide witness or testimony, and I hope to provide enough of that to see whether it stimulates testimony of a similar kind in you.

THE DEPTH OF THE PRACTICES

Each time I look at the list of practices, it occurs to me how ordinary most of them seem. Worshiping? But of course; we know all that! And we do it all the time. (And by the way, it rarely seems to have the effect I claim for it.) Telling the Christian story to one another? Yes, we do that. It seems obvious that Christians do that. We have Bible classes for all age groups, and we cover that stuff. We don't do too much church history (and maybe we ought to do more); but telling the Christian story? Yes, we do that.

Some other items on the list may be a little less obvious and ordinary. Suffering with and for one another and for all whom Jesus showed to be our neighbors, and criticizing and resisting powers and patterns that destroy human beings—those are rather difficult to do sometimes. For many of us, they are also perhaps the more controversial practices on the list, ones we might avoid if at all possible. But still, they do not really surprise us. Anyone who knows the Christian story at all knows that it relates a lot about compassion and resisting the powers and structures of the world. What is more, for all our reluctance and failings, we do, in fact, engage in such practices in various ways and at various times.

The first impression of the list of practices, then, is of its ordinariness. On second thought, however, we may begin to realize how rarely most of us really do many of the things on this list. We go to worship on Sundays; but when we worship, is each of us actually engaged in the practice of giving praise and thanks? Or are we just "singing the hymns" or "conducting the worship service"? How many of us actually engage in any regular way in the practice of interpreting something in scripture to someone else, in relation to its meaning for the community and for our own lives? Ministers do that a lot, I suppose, because they preach and teach. But even then, don't they sometimes find themselves just "giving a sermon" or "teaching a class," rather than engaging in an activity of interpretation as if our understanding of what's going on in our lives utterly depended on it? Beyond the minister, how many in the church are doing this? Are lay leaders of the church doing so as they struggle to make difficult decisions for the congregation? Are children given opportunities to do it, too? Where and how?

In sum, most of the practices on this simple list are, for most of us most of the time, relatively untried. This is true not only for lay people but also for pastors. Many pastors complain that their ministries are consumed by all sorts of activities that make real engagement in any of these practices almost impossible. Eugene Peterson, in his fine book on "the shape of pastoral integrity," *Working the Angles*, worries that

> the pastors of America have metamorphosed into a company of shopkeepers, and the shops they keep are churches. [We] are preoccupied with shopkeeper's concerns—how to keep the customers happy, how to lure customers away from competitors down the street, how to package the goods so that the customers will lay out more money. . . . Religious shopkeeping, to be sure, but shopkeeping all the same.[1]

For all of us, lay and clergy alike, if we feel our hungers for meaning and purpose are not being met, perhaps the fact that we have not engaged in the practices and disciplines of the life of faith has something to do with it.

Still further reflection on the practices on this list leads to another insight: how little we know of what is really involved in them. The more I think and read about them, the more I observe others engaged in them, the more I engage in them at some novice level myself, the more I realize what depths there are in each of these to plumb—and I recognize that I have hardly scratched the surface.

One of the most powerful guides I know to the practices of the Christian life is Dietrich Bonhoeffer's classic *Life Together*. Many of the practices I have mentioned, and more, are treated with power there. Take, for example, his comments on confession:

> "Confess your sins one to another" (Jas. 5.16). Those who remain alone with their evil are left utterly alone. It is possible that Christians may remain lonely in spite of daily worship together, prayer together, and all their community through service—that the final breakthrough to community does not occur precisely because they enjoy community with one another as pious believers, but not with one another as those lacking piety, as sinners. The pious community permits no one to be a sinner. Hence all have to conceal their sins from themselves and from the community. We are not allowed to be sinners. . . .
>
> In confession there takes place a breakthrough to community. Sin wants to be alone with people. It takes them away from the community. . . . Sin wants to remain unknown. It shuns the light. In the darkness of what is left unsaid, sin poisons the whole being of a person. This can happen even in the midst of a pious community. In

confession the light of the gospel breaks into the darkness and closed isolation of the heart. . . . It is a hard struggle until the sin crosses one's lips in confession. . . . Since the confession of sin is made in the presence of another Christian, the last stronghold of self-justification is abandoned. . . . Sin that has been spoken and confessed has lost all of its power. It has been revealed and judged as sin. It can no longer tear apart the community. Now the community bears the sin of the individual believer. . . . Now one is allowed to be a sinner and still enjoy the grace of God. He can confess his sins and in this very act find community for the first time.[2]

Here we see some of the depths of one of the simple practices we have listed, and they are all that deep.

In *Life Together*, so many practices are discussed in this kind of depth. Reading this book and remembering that it describes the practices engaged in by a small, underground seminary in the Nazi years in Germany, it begins to dawn on us how deeply these practices are related to one another. Indeed, the power of these practices does not fully emerge when any one of them is taken alone but comes only when they are in interrelation to one another. It is not just the reading and interpretation of Scripture that has power; it is the reading and interpretation of Scripture in the midst of providing care and hospitality to strangers while resisting powers that destroy.

These practices, when engaged in deep interrelation with one another, have the effect of turning the flow of power in a new direction. After a time, the primary point about the practices is no longer that they are something we do. Instead, they become arenas in which something is done to us, in us, and through us that we could not of ourselves do, that is beyond what we do.

This is not an easy point to make, but it is key. I know of no better way of making this point than with the example of the remarkable events that occurred in a small French town many years ago. One day in 1942, two khaki-colored buses pulled into Le Chambon, a little village in the mountains of southern France. They were the buses of the Vichy French police, and they had come to round up the Jews who were there. The police knew that Le Chambon had become a refuge for them, so they rousted everyone into the village square. The police captain stared straight into the face of the pastor of the Protestant church, André Trocmé, "warning him that if he did not give up the names of the Jews they had been sheltering in the village, he and his fellow pastor, as well as the families who had been caring for the Jews, would be arrested."[3]

The pastor refused, and the police, after a thorough and frightening search, could find only one Jew. They loaded him into an otherwise empty bus. Before they drove off, "a thirteen-year-old boy, the son of the pastor, pass[ed] a piece of his precious chocolate through the window to the prisoner, while twenty gendarmes who were guarding the lone prisoner watched." Then the rest of the villagers began "passing their little gifts through the window until there were gifts all around him—most of them food in those hungry days of the German occupation of France."[4]

This story is recounted in what I regard as a singularly important book for Christian educators, *Lest Innocent Blood Be Shed*, by Philip Haillie. It is, to quote Haillie's subtitle, "the story of the village of Le Chambon and how goodness happened there." A moving portrait of courage and character, of faith and cunning, of resistance and conviction, it is also a story of how the gospel can be taught when the church comes alive to face both the dangers that beset it and the concrete needs and hungers of the specific world in which they live. It is a story of youth groups and schoolchildren, of classroom teachers and adult Bible study groups. It is a story of how worship and preaching and studying and acting all come together to make a community into a people of God. It is a story of how a people read the Scriptures, lived their life with one another, and opened their doors to strangers as essential elements in their being the church in the world. But most of all it is the story of what happened to and in these people and in the world in the midst of what they themselves did.

THE PRACTICE OF READING
AND HEARING THE SCRIPTURES

One of the key elements of the church's experience at Le Chambon was its experience with Scripture. The community's life was full of hearing, reading, and interpreting the Bible, and doing so in the light of what they were experiencing in their town. The pastor, André Trocmé, established many intimate groups of young people, miners, women, and children who spent an enormous amount of time studying the Scriptures with his help. He visited home after home on daily sojourns and studied the Bible with the families there. They did all this as something much more than an extracurricular activity. They did it because they needed to, in order to know who they were to become and what they were to do in the world in which they found themselves. Through all this reading and study together, something happened to them. Through this reading in this context, they heard promises from God and, believing them, based their very lives on them. They also found out through the Scriptures what kind of world they really lived in, and this made it possible to tell lies from truth and to find courage to do what, had "their minds been conformed to this world," they could not have done. Finally, a way of life had been rendered to them, and they lived it.

The church has always claimed to know something, something we do not know except as it has been given to us. This is why some doctrine of revelation has always been central to Christian faith, and why revelation has usually been seen to have something to do with Scripture. The important thing to see about Scripture, for our purposes here at least, is that Scripture is not just a book we have and read, an object that *we do something to*, but an active force in the life of the church. It is something that *we have to do with*.

As David Kelsey has put it: "Part of what it means to call a text 'Christian scripture' is that it functions in certain ways or does certain things when used in certain ways in the common life of the church."[5] The Scriptures, he says, act on us in such a way as to solicit a response of some kind and have their authority by the fact that they do so.[6] When we ask about the Bible, then, we must not only ask, "What does the Bible say?" but also—and perhaps more importantly—"What is God using the Bible to do . . . to us and in us and for our lives?"[7] The Bible itself performs certain actions when told, heard, and remembered.

What is God using the Bible to do? The first thing the Bible does is render an agent, namely, God. This means that through the biblical texts we begin to see that behind and in everything that happens is an active Presence to whom it is all related and in whom it all holds together. The actions and characters that take place in the biblical narratives, for example, are not just isolated events and persons who appear and do what they do by chance. There is another agency, a will (if you will), that emerges through the action of the story. Thus this story is not just about a people who think that there is a God and that this God is doing something redemptive in history. Nor is God just one of the characters in the story. Rather, God is the agency who makes the story and who is revealed through the story. In other words, through the story God is revealed to its hearers as a present reality in the contemporary telling and hearing.[8]

The second thing the Bible does is render a promise. Ronald Thiemann has argued in his book *Revelation and Theology: The Gospel as Narrated Promise* that the God whose character and agency are rendered in the Scriptures is a God of promise and a God who can be depended on to keep promises. To be in relationship with God is to be related as one who has heard God's promises as promises to oneself, and as one who responds to those promises.

What is crucial to see here is that the Scriptures do not just tell us about a God who makes promises to some people. Promises are actively being made through the Bible—by God, to us. Thus the promising is not something we or others have made up or just tell about. It is an act not our own; it is an act of God toward us. As Thiemann puts it:

> The structure, content, and fulfillment of a promise depend solely on the initiative of the promiser. The promiser specifies the future act, expresses the intention to perform that act, undertakes the obligation implied in the promise, exhibits the necessary trust-worthy behavior, and alone can perform the action which will fulfill the promise. The hearer, on the other hand, though he or she would "prefer" that the promiser fulfill his obligation, cannot, if the act is to remain a promise, compel the promiser so to act.[9]

If we hear God's promises and accept them, something else happens to us. As Thiemann puts it, "the world of the Gospel narrative [is carried] into that of the reader."[10] Thus the Scriptures also render a world, the kind of world that is appropriate to the God who becomes present to us and makes promises to us through Scripture. What is meant here is not that we get to know something about the ancient Middle East or first-century Palestine or Rome (though we may), but that through this particular narrative, which is set in a variety of geographical and historical arenas, is portrayed what is really and ultimately going on in the creation as a whole.

"'World' in this sense," says Edward Farley, is the ultimate framework of the "origin and goal, the meaning and destiny of [humanity]."[11] As we hear, tell, think about, interpret, use, and appropriate this story, its world more and more becomes our world. Our thinking, believing, and behaving become shaped by it, so that we come to think, believe, and behave by means of it.† It is no longer a world outside of us, which we look at, but that world from which and by means of which we see at all. Furthermore, the world that is rendered is not a provincial world, the world of the church

† *Nicodemus. If you see it from the outside - you don't really see it*

apart from the world as a whole. Rather, it is understood to be the world itself, as it is; the world seen for itself rather than refracted through vision disfigured and distorted through deceit and alienation. Stanley Hauerwas suggests that if the world rendered through the story does not help us see the world as it is, then it should be given up. "But the claim of the Christian is that [this] language actually envisages the world as it is."[12]

Finally, the story acts on its hearers by rendering a way of living that makes sense in this world and in the light of the God who reigns in it. What I have in mind here is not so much that it presents ideals for how people should live or models of the perfect life. Rather, it marks out the kind of pilgrimage life is, the dangers it encounters, the limitations inherent in it, what sorts of things are necessary for sustaining it, the treasures that might be found there. It renders the adventure and gives clues both as to how ordinary human beings can get in on it and as to how it is they can miss it entirely.

In the reading, hearing, and interpretation of Scripture, then, the community comes to know a story; and by knowing the story it finds itself in a new world, on an adventure, and in relation to the Agent who makes the dependable promises that initiate and sustain it all. And this is what the people at Le Chambon actually found to be the truth of their experience.

Eventually, Pastor André Trocmé was arrested and carried off to prison camp. When he was taken, he too was given gifts. The first evening in the camp, he opened one of them, "a roll of toilet paper in order to share it with [the others]. On the outer sheets he found written in pencil verses of consolation from the Bible." They were put there by some of those whom he had taught, and it was those verses that reminded him, even in prison, "that he was still a part of Le Chambon."[13]

THE TRANSFORMATION OF ENEMIES AND STRANGERS

I just pointed out that one of the things the Bible does is render a way of living. That was clearly the case for the church at Le Chambon. But what is it that is so distinctive about the way in which a people live together in relation to a God who makes promises to them? The "peculiar" nature of such communal life resides in two profound movements that are made in relationships among people. The first is the movement from seeing and treating others most fundamentally as enemies to seeing and treating one another most fundamentally as fellow creatures. The second is the movement from seeing and treating others most fundamentally as strangers to seeing and treating one another most fundamentally as neighbors.[14]

Other people are often seen by us as a threat, sometimes even those who are near and dear to us. In many of our activities throughout our lives, we find ourselves striving to produce and control whatever it is we think can make life secure, be that material goods, personal prestige, or power over others. In such a context others may threaten us, in any number of ways. They may humiliate me, ignore me, try to control me, or take something that is important to me away from me. Others may have more status than I and thereby make me seem small in comparison. Of course, other people may in fact not be trying to threaten me at all. But that is not the point. I worry that they may bear threat to me, even without intending. And if I worry about that, I am, in fact, threatened by them. Therefore, my guard must be up. I must protect myself against any real or possible threat. The effects of this are isolation on the one hand and continuing calculation and evaluation on the other. Practically, the result is competitiveness, aggression, and self-protection, along with callousness, depersonalization, and forgetfulness.

The peculiarity of communal life under the promises of God is that these presuppositions toward one another undergo a modification. The other is not inevitably and necessarily presumed as enemy but is seen first and most fundamentally as fellow creature, limited and suffering like me but also, at least potentially, free to be with me rather than against me. This creates community. When another person is not presupposed fundamentally to be an enemy, some space is created by which it becomes possible for all of us, as fellow creatures, not only to refrain from hostility, ridicule, theft, even rape, torture, and murder but also to depend on one another for "help in surviving in the face of hunger, disease, and violence" and for the "subtle and enjoyable features of human interaction such as humor, play, sexuality, and cooperative pursuit of tasks."[15]

The second movement is from stranger to neighbor. This is an extension of the first, but an important one. The presupposition here is not just that *some* other people are fellow creatures and not enemies (others who are like me, for example; others whom I know and have come to trust; others who share my faith). It is that *all* others are potential participants in the life God is creating through God's redemptive work. As fellow creatures, therefore, no one is essentially a stranger; all are constituted by God as neighbors to one another.

Edward Farley argues that one of the fundamentally distinctive features of Christian ecclesial existence is "the transformed status of the stranger" it generates. Participation in the redemptive activity of God as communal delight in one another knows no provincial, ethnic, class, sex, or cultural boundaries. In fact, the redemptive activity of God often takes place right at the boundaries, on the margins that our ordinary social and cultural life creates. Indeed, Christianity began as a religion of the socially marginal and of those who were not so marginal but who, in Jesus Christ, were will-ing to make common cause with the marginal.[16]

Living in Christian community does not mean living only with others like us. It does not even mean living with an attitude of friendliness toward strangers. It involves actual hospitality to the stranger—face-to-face en-counter in which the stranger is given hospice, protection from danger and threat, and in which the stranger is welcomed into one's own home and life as if she or he could be nothing else but neighbor. "Who is my neigh-bor?" Jesus was asked. You'll remember the parable he told. A man fell among thieves. A Samaritan came and cared for him and took him to a place where he could find healing and rest (Luke 10:29–37). Who is my neighbor? Every stranger in need of hospitality.

In Le Chambon, we see both sides of this. The communal life in the parish was such that their lives were open to one another. Their doors were open, their kitchens places of communal conversation, and their fellow-ship with one another real. The communal life among them was not lim-ited to the members of the church or the neighbors in the town, however. The door was open to the stranger, literally. In the middle of the winter of 1940/41, Madame Trocmé was putting small pieces of wood into the kitchen stove to keep the house as warm as possible without wasting too much fuel in the midst of a swirling snowstorm. Startled, she heard a knock on the door. "There before her, only the front of her body protected from the cold, stood a woman shawled in pure snow. . . . Here was the first refugee from the Nazis to come to the presbytery door. . . . 'She said she was a German Jew, coming from northern France, that she was in danger, and that she had heard that in Le Chambon somebody could help her. Could she come into [the] house?' " At this point the answer that, accord-ing to Phillip Haillie, characterized who Madame Trocmé most essentially was and what the entire parish had become was spoken: "Naturally, come in, come in."[17] Their doors and their lives were open, to everyone as a mat-ter of course. None were strangers; all were neighbors.

But what about enemies? What about the Nazis and the Vichy police? Yes, even these were neighbors. They were resisted. They were not allowed to find the Jews hidden among them, to carry them away, or to kill them, if any cunning could stop them. But the people of the village would not themselves kill, not even these mortal enemies. As Trocmé's colleague Edouard Theis once took great pains to explain to Haillie, their resistance was their attempt "to prevent the Nazis and the Vichy from violating the commandment against killing. They were trying to protect the victims, but they were also trying to stop human beings who were hell-bent on becoming victimizers, hell-bent on doing evil. Trocmé and Theis believed that if they failed to protect those in Le Chambon, they, the ministers, would share the guilt of the evil ones who actually perpetrated the harmdoing."[18] Such is the radical nature of the practice of hospitality when combined with the practice of resistance.

HABITATIONS OF THE SPIRIT

I have been arguing that the practices of the life of faith have power to place us where we can receive a sense of the presence of God, especially when multiple practices are engaged in in relation to one another. This, I suspect, is especially true when among the practices are included some of the more difficult ones, those that involve resistance and risk and those that involve active reaching out to others in need. It is interesting how this was picked up by Phillip Haillie in his rendering of the story of Le Chambon. He writes as a moral philosopher who is not a Christian believer, one who wonders how this kind of moral courage and goodness is possible. Toward the end of his book, he is still trying to give an account of it, but he can't quite figure it out:

In physics the analysis of forces is useful. For instance, one may break down the various forces at work upon a door and upon the frame in which it is hung in order to hang the door well. But analysis is not all there is. There is another aspect to the full reality of this movement of the well-hung, opening door. There is the experience, so ordinary as to be unnoticed, of simply opening and closing the door.

If we would understand the goodness that happened in Le Chambon, we must see how easy it was for them to refuse to give up their consciences, to refuse to participate in hatred, betrayal, and murder, and to help the desperate adults and the terrified children who knocked on the doors in Le Chambon. . . . We fail to understand what happened in Le Chambon if we think that for them their actions were complex and difficult. . . . For certain people, helping the distressed is as natural and necessary as feeding themselves. The Trocmés, the Theises, and others in Le Chambon were such people.[19]

The ease with which they did things is the manifestation of the point this chapter has been trying to make. In the midst of their practice, the people of Le Chambon found that it was not really their practice. It was the practice of Another. It came with ease not primarily because they were strong and courageous but because their strength and courage were given to them.

Haillie can never quite explain these people. By the end, he senses he finally cannot, so he simply stands in awe of what he has witnessed. He senses that he has beheld a mystery and wishes simply to honor it, which he has done in a powerful and eloquent way in his book. But perhaps the people of Le Chambon know something that Haillie does not. In a series of offhand observations, which he does not seem to know what to make of, he tells us what Pastor Trocmé had to say. "He often talked," Haillie says, "about 'the power of the spirit,' which he described as being a surprising power, a force that no one can predict or control. He offered no systems or methods—this would be to violate the surprising force of the spirit. . . . [H]e himself embodied the surprising force he spoke about so often."[20]

This, in fact, is the experience of the church historically. The practices of Christian faith turn out in the end not primarily to be practices, efforts. They turn out to be places in the contours of our personal and communal lives where a habitation of the Spirit is able to occur. And it is this that is the source of their power and meaning.

Notes

1. Eugene Peterson, *Working the Angles* (Grand Rapids: Wm. B. Eerdmans Publishing Co., 1987), 1.
2. Dietrich Bonhoeffer, *Life Together*, in *Dietrich Bonhoeffer's Works*, vol. 5, ed. G. B. Kelly (Minneapolis: Fortress Press, 1996), 108–10.
3. Philip Haillie, *Lest Innocent Blood Be Shed: The Story of the Village of Le Chambon and How Goodness Happened There* (New York: Harper & Row, 1979), 3.
4. Ibid.
5. David H. Kelsey, *The Uses of Scripture in Recent Theology* (Philadelphia: Fortress Press, 1975), 90.

6. Ibid., 150.
7. Ibid., 213.
8. See ibid., 39–40, where Kelsey discusses this function of the Bible, drawing on the work of Karl Barth.
9. Ronald F. Thiemann, *Revelation and Theology: The Gospel as Narrated Promise* (Notre Dame, Ind.: University of Notre Dame Press, 1985), 110.
10. Ibid., 142.
11. Edward Farley, *Ecclesial Man: A Social Phenomenology of Faith and Reality* (Philadelphia: Fortress Press, 1975), 123.
12. Stanley Hauerwas, *Vision and Virtue* (Notre Dame, Ind.: Fides Publications, 1974), 46. See also Farley, *Ecclesial Man,* on "perceptivities," 191–93, 213–15.
13. Haillie, *Lest Innocent Blood Be Shed,* 33.
14. See Farley, *Ecclesial Man,* 169–74. I am indebted in what follows to Farley's whole account of the intersubjective dimensions of "redemptive existence," which can be found in *Ecclesial Man,* chap. 7.
15. Ibid., 161.
16. See Craig Dykstra, "Education, the Gospel and the Marginal," *Princeton Seminary Bulletin* 5/1, n.s. (1984): 13–20.
17. Haillie, *Lest Innocent Blood Be Shed,* 120.
18. Ibid., 283.
19. Ibid., 284.
20. Ibid., 170.

Chapter 5

Education in Christian Practices

In chapter 4, I described the practices of the Christian faith as habitations of the Spirit. They are not, finally, activities we do to make something spiritual happen in our lives. Nor are they duties we undertake to be obedient to God. Rather, they are patterns of communal action that create openings in our lives where the grace, mercy, and presence of God may be made known to us. They are places where the power of God is experienced. In the end, these are not ultimately our practices but forms of participation in the practice of God.

In chapter 3, I attempted to make the central point that people come to faith and grow in the life of faith by participating in the practices of the Christian life, practices such as those listed on pages 42–43. Whether children, youth, or adults, when people participate in these practices, they and the whole community discover a way of life that meets the world's deepest hungers.

With these ideas in place, we can now turn to the theme of education in Christian practices. This is not the first time we have talked about education; references to it have been scattered through every chapter so far, and the theme will appear again in later chapters. But here I discuss explicitly how the practices way of thinking about Christian faith and the life of faith may be helpful to all of us who have explicit responsibilities for the church's educational ministries.[1]

THE PROBLEM OF THE
TOO BIG AND THE TOO SMALL

A major problem that educators face is what I call the problem of the too big and the too small. The problem of the too big is that our purposes as Christian educators are rightly and necessarily large: They have to do, ultimately, with learning a whole way of life and of coming to knowledge of and trust in God. Those purposes are true, but they are too large, too grand, too big to guide us in direct and concrete ways. Purposes that large are impossible to get your mind around. They are too big to do.

The problem of the too small is the opposite one. In our actual work of educating, we do a little of this and a little of that and a little of something else. But too often these pieces do not seem to add up to much. We can't tell what larger wholes these smaller pieces are parts of. The connections get lost, and we lose any sense of the significance and import of particular educational activities and projects and events. That is the problem of the too small.

Part of the educational significance of the idea and social reality of Christian practices is that this concept provides a good answer to the problem of the too big and the too small. It breaks down a way of life into a set of constructive practices. At the same time, it draws together the shards and pieces of particular events, behaviors, actions, relationships, inquiries, and skills into large enough wholes to show how they might add up to a way of life.

In the present cultural context, Christian educators need to think about how to lead people beyond a reliance on "random acts of kindness" into shared patterns of life that are informed by the deepest insights of our traditions, and about how to lead people beyond privatized spiritualities into more thoughtful participation in God's activity in the world. In the Christian churches today, large numbers of members—and even many leaders—seem to be unaware of the rich insights and strong help the Christian tradition can bring to contemporary concerns. Thinking about our way of life as standing in dynamic continuity with our Christian heritage and with the worldwide church today opens fresh sources of insight into how the practices that pattern our days can shape our lives in ways that respond to the active presence of God for the life of the world.

The life of Christian faith is the practice of many practices. As individuals, we learn to participate in the whole large practice of Christian faith—this way of being in the world—through steadily and patiently learning and participating in each of the particular constituent practices. Thus it is on the particular practices that we as educators can most fruitfully focus if education in faith is our aim.

WHAT IS A PRACTICE?

In this book, I have consistently been using the word *practices*. Why? What am I trying to convey by that term? I suspect readers have noticed that this very familiar word is being used in a special way. What is at stake here?

As a matter of fact, my special use of that familiar word has a lot packed into it. A practice, according to the philosopher Alasdair MacIntyre, is

> any coherent and complex form of socially established cooperative human activity through which goods internal to that form of activity are realized in the course of trying to achieve those standards of excellence which are appropriate to, and partially definitive of, that form of activity, with the result that human powers to achieve excellence, and human conception of the ends and goods involved, are systematically extended.[2]

This is obviously a very complicated definition, and it is impossible to absorb what he is saying on first reading. But if we unpack it a bit, we can see what the important things being said here are.

It helps to use an example. Baseball is a practice, by MacIntyre's definition.[3] It is a specific example of a "coherent and complex form of socially established cooperative human activity." Let's look closely at each important concept in this first long phrase of the definition.

> Baseball is a *human* activity. Animals don't engage in practices. Only people do. This is because the kind of activity MacIntyre has in mind is not just random action and reaction but rather intelligible and purposeful action. Action of that kind is possible only because it draws from and makes use of language, concepts, images, and symbols in ways that only human beings can.
>
> Baseball is a human *activity*. It is something human beings *do*. While the activity is full of thought and purpose, it is still activity. There is no baseball if there aren't real people out on the field actually pitching and hitting, running bases, and catching fly balls.
>
> Baseball is something people do together; it is a *cooperative* human activity. Baseball cannot be played alone. It necessarily involves a group of people doing something in relation and response to one another.
>
> Baseball is *socially established*. People are able to do it together only because the practice has established rules and roles

that make the practice what it is. It has a character and consistency to it that makes it recognizable across time and place. Also, because it is socially established, it is possible for people to teach it to and learn it from each other. Finally, baseball is *coherent and complex*. It makes sense, but it is complicated enough that you have to work to learn the rules, the skills, the moves, and the nuances. For those who haven't learned at least some of the complexities, the game makes no sense; for them it has no form or meaning.

In the rest of his long, one-sentence definition, MacIntyre elaborates two dimensions of practices that make them deeply significant for human life. The first of these is that *moral goods* and *standards of excellence* are intrinsic to the practices themselves. Even baseball is morally significant, according to MacIntyre. It has standards of excellence built into it. There are real differences between poor pitching, good pitching, and brilliant pitching, and being able to recognize and to strive to live up to standards of this kind is part of what it means to be human. Also, profound human joys and deep satisfactions come simply from playing the game really well. These are the "goods" that are intrinsic to the practice of baseball. Great pitching and great hitting, and when all the pieces are put together at a high level of excellence, great baseball itself, are "goods" that make human life human.[4]

The second dimension of practices that makes them deeply significant for human life is that through participation in them, our *powers to achieve what is good are enhanced*. We become more capable of achieving excellence. Furthermore, our very *conceptions of what the good is are extended*. Our ideas about what human life is really all about, what its best purposes are, what we should strive for in life are all made larger and greater. And this is true not only for us as individuals but for us as communities and cultures as well. Human moral progress is made through participation in practices.

In sum, then, practices are those cooperative human activities through which we, as individuals and as communities, grow and develop in moral character and substance. They have built up over time and, through experience and testing, have developed patterns of reciprocal expectations among participants. They are ways of doing things together in which and through which human life is given direction, meaning, and significance, and through which our very capacities to do good things well are increased. And because they are shared, patterned, and ongoing, they can be taught. We can teach one another how to participate in them. We can pass them on from one generation to the next.

TEACHING AND LEARNING CHRISTIAN PRACTICES

Baseball, of course, is just a game. It is a great game, perhaps. It may even be the kind of game through which people can learn some of the "great lessons of life," as they say. But games are probably not the most significant of human practices. Others are much more important—and more spiritually and morally powerful.

Is the interpretation of Scripture a practice of that kind? Is prayer? Is confession of sin? How about forgiveness, or hospitality? I answer yes to each of these questions. Each of these is—in the context of Christian faith—a coherent and complex form of socially established cooperative human activity through which powerful internal goods are realized and through the pursuit of which our capacities as human beings to do and to be and to conceive of what God is calling us to become are systematically extended. Through participation in these specific practices—and others like them—the large, broad practice of Christian faith is made perpetually alive; at the same time, it is corrected and enlarged. Through the exercise of such practices, the "goods" that inhere in the life of Christian faith are realized in actual human existence. By learning them—and through long, slow, steady, patient participation in them—individuals and communities learn Christian faith, become Christian.

I do not know what a complete list of all the practices that constitute Christian faith would include. This, I think, is a matter for historical and theological investigation and for conversation and deliberation among Christians within and between their various smaller communities.[5] I am convinced, however, that the church needs to deliberate and be specific about which practices we think are essential to the life of faith, if the church's practice of faith and its educational ministries are to have any real vitality. We should become clear in each of our institutions and communities about which practices are crucial to us and why. We need also to get clear what moves, skills, understandings, and convictions are essential for engaging in these particular practices in the ways—and with the seriousness—that faith requires. We must examine (both historically and among our contemporaries) how people have learned and do learn the practices we find crucial and then shape our own educational efforts by what we discover.

In my view, an essential task of education in faith is to teach all the basic practices of the Christian faith. The fundamental aim of Christian education in all its forms, varieties, and settings should be that individuals—and indeed whole communities—learn these practices, be drawn into participation in them, learn to do them with increasingly deepened understanding and skill, learn to extend them more broadly and fully in their own lives and into their world, and learn to correct them, strengthen them, and improve them.

But how does one learn a practice? Let's go back to baseball for a moment. One learns baseball by playing baseball. You have to get in on particular games when they are being played. You also have to practice over and over again the particular skills and moves involved in doing it well. And besides that, you need to watch baseball being played. You have to watch attentively—and analytically—as the play of the game takes place. (If you ever doubt the analytical capacities of some ten-year-olds, just engage a young fan in a discussion about a particularly exciting game.) Learning baseball can be greatly aided by good coaching, by apprenticeship to those who have achieved some degree of excellence in the practice, and by reading, conversation, and argumentation about the practice of baseball in all its parts, complexity, and coherence. Indeed, to learn well the practice of baseball, it is essential to be involved in all these different kinds of activity, and in ways that steadily and carefully reinforce, correct, and supplement one another.

Learning baseball requires playing the game, making the moves, developing the skills, thinking it through, and practicing over and over again in order to do it well. Dance is similar. So is surgery. We have a lot to learn from all this for purposes of education in faith. The practice of Christian faith is a lot more physical than we usually recognize or let on. It is a body faith—an embodied faith—that involves gestures, moves, going certain places (where people are hungry and thirsty, for example; where suffering occurs), and doing certain things. As with every other practice, learning the practices of the life of Christian faith involves practice, repeated participation in the bodily actions that make up those practices.

At the same time that we need a renewal of emphasis on physical action in educating for faith, we must not lose sight of the fact that what is always at stake is *intelligible* action, action imbued with discernment and imagination, with understanding, purpose, and meaning. How is it that this intelligibility arises in the midst of learning a practice? The philosopher Iris Murdoch once wrote:

> Learning takes place when words are used, either aloud or privately, in the context of particular acts of attention. . . . Words said to particular individuals at particular times may occasion wisdom.[6]

This is precisely what coaches and mentors do—and work hard at doing well—when they are intentionally striving to help others learn to do something better. Often a coach will teach by demonstrating something, by making one of the essential moves and asking the learner to watch. Then words begin. Questions: What did you see happen at the start of my swing? Descriptions: What I'm doing here is planting my right foot and bringing my right arm close to my side to start the action of the swing properly. Explanations and reasons: What this does is begin to shift your weight and the momentum of the swing toward the target without letting your hands get ahead of the bat. Soon thereafter the coach will say, "Now you try it." And words flow some more. More questions, descriptions, explanations, and reasons, this time about the learner's own experience in action. Often similes and metaphors will be employed: "Imagine that you're swinging a chain with a heavy weight at the end of it. Try to hit the ball with that weight, not with the chain."

I won't go on, but you get the point. Intelligible action is full of imagery, concept, even theory—all made available and accessible through timely spoken and carefully chosen words that are shared back and forth among human beings. If the life of Christian faith is truly a practice of practices, shouldn't Christian education and theological teaching be more like good coaching? Isn't this how people learn actually to interpret Scripture themselves? Isn't this how people learn to pray and to confess and to forgive and to practice hospitality to strangers and enemies?

I would say so. And I would say so for the full range of Christian teaching. To learn these practices and learn in the context of them, we need others who are competent in these practices to help us: to be our models, mentors, teachers, and partners in practice. We need people who will include us in these practices as they themselves are engaged in them, and who will show us how to do what the practices require. We also need them to explain to us what these practices mean, what the reasons, understandings, insights, and values embedded in them are. And we need them to

lure us and press us beyond our current understandings of and compe-
tence in these practices, to the point where we together may extend and
deepen the practices themselves.

Children, youth, and adults best learn practices such as these when conditions such as the following pertain:

> when we ourselves are active in them, actually doing what
> these practices involve, engaging in them personally in
> particular physical and material settings and in face-to-
> face interaction with other people;
>
> when we participate in them jointly with others, especially
> with others who are skilled in them and are able to teach
> them to us;
>
> when the people involved in them with us are, or are be-
> coming, personally significant to us—and we to them;
>
> when we are involved in increasingly broader, more varied,
> and more complex dimensions of the practice, and when
> the activities we engage in become increasingly wide-
> ranging in their context and impact;
>
> when we come more and more to connect articulations of the
> significance and meaning of these practices (as well as the
> ways in which the various practices are connected and re-
> lated to one another) with our own activities in them and
> with the reasons we ourselves have for engaging in them;
> and
>
> when we come to take increasing personal responsibility for
> initiating, pursuing, and sustaining these practices and
> for including and guiding others in them.[7]

Participation in some of the practices of Christian life can and should occur naturally in the context of everyday life in a community constituted by
them. But communities, especially in such culturally and socially fragmented situations as our own, cannot depend entirely on the natural activities of everyday life for initiating people into these practices and guiding
them in them. Our situation requires planned and systematic education in
these practices. Such education must never be detached from participation
in the practices; it is not satisfactory simply to describe and analyze them
from afar. Nonetheless, education must order this participation in such a

way that all the practices are engaged in meaningfully and with under-standing at increasingly broader and more complex levels. And that pre-supposes systematic and comprehensive education in the history and wider reaches of the practices, as well as in the interpretation and criticism of the reasons and values embedded in the practices.

The need for planned and systematic education in Christian practices is complicated by the fact that we don't live in communities constituted only by Christian practices. Christian practices never exist in a vacuum. We both live and learn in multiple social contexts and institutions, each of which is constituted by a broader plurality of practices than those on which we have focused. Our wider intellectual, political, social, and occu-pational lives involve us all in a great variety of practices. And because these other contexts naturally infiltrate faith communities, this broad spec-trum of practices is internal to every part of Christian institutional and cul-tural life. We all live our lives at an intersection of many practices.

Education in Christian faith must concern itself with the mutual influ-ences that various practices have on one another, as well as with whatever complementarity or conflict may exist between the goods internal to Chris-tian practices and goods internal to others. Because we are all citizens, for example, we must inquire into the nature, effects, and implications of our simultaneous engagement in practices constitutive of Christian life and those central to public life in the broader culture. We need to inquire, for example, into the continuities and discontinuities between medical prac-tice in our society and practices of care for the ill and the dying that are now and have been in the past characteristic of the church. This applies also to a wide variety of other social practices.

THE PECULIARITY OF CHRISTIAN PRACTICES

These reflections on education in Christian practices lay out an agenda for those of us who bear responsibility for the church's educational min-istry. They suggest that the idea of "practices" provides a helpful way in which to organize the work of education, both conceptually and practi-cally. A focus on practices provides an educational aim and task that is at once concrete enough for us to accomplish and yet far-reaching enough to connect with faith's ultimate ends. This focus also encourages us to un-derstand that a good deal of the best teaching consists of a kind of coach-ing that helps those learning practices of faith how to be intelligent, purposeful, and active participants in them.

Having said all this, one issue remains for us to consider. *Christian* practices have a peculiarity about them, and this peculiarity must necessarily mark the character of Christian teaching and learning. For all the usefulness of the baseball analogy, the practice of faith is in one crucial respect *not* like the practice of baseball—or the practice of medicine or politics, for that matter. For all its similarities, the practice of Christian faith is fundamentally different from other practices. This is because the practice of faith is part of a distinctive story and is built on different assumptions from most other practices. A clue to the difference can be found in how odd it seems to talk of "excellence" or "outstanding achievement" with regard to the practice of faith.

The idea of excellence in the practice of faith seems at least a little inappropriate. It might not seem too strange to call a writer of a fine book on Matthew "one of the most accomplished interpreters of the New Testament in our time." But it would seem odd to say of Mother Teresa that she brought the practice of hospitality to strangers to a new level of excellence. Mother Teresa herself would have found such a comment off-putting. It seems to miss the point, in a seriously flawed way.

The very idea of achieving excellence or of attaining the highest standards possible in the practices of prayer or forgiveness or service seems, on the face of it, internally contradictory. Why? The reason is that excellence has to do with human achievement. But faith is not a human achievement; it is a gift.

The idea of excellence in a practice makes most sense when the point of a practice is the achievement of mastery. And the point of most human practices is just that—mastery over some set of forces that contend with one another, control over what threatens to run out of control, the creation of order in the face of chaos.[8] Have you ever wondered why major political figures and war heroes are the most celebrated figures in almost every society? It is usually because they have attained mastery in situations of great danger to the community. Almost by definition, a hero is a person who has mastered forces of chaos that threaten a community's peace and well-being. Excellence in the practice of politics means assuring, insofar as is humanly possible, that the powerful human forces that constantly threaten every human community, such as violence and greed, will not overwhelm or destroy it. The political task is to make sure that forces such as these are kept firmly under control and that the rights of the unprotected are justly defended. Mastery of political power is essential if the body politic is to endure in reasonable domestic and international tranquility.

Among those who make a society a good society are those who achieve excellence in the practice of politics in this sense.

Artists achieve a different sort of mastery, the ordering of words or colors or movements of the body to create new images out of the chaos of the materials at hand and to give rise to new understandings in the face of the threat of meaninglessness. Physicians seek mastery over illness and disease. Engineers must master powerful natural forces to fabricate machines that actually work or buildings that hold up. Athletes contend with the limitations of their own bodies and the competition of their opponents. They seek mastery, control in the context of the game. A home run to the upper deck against a ninety-eight-mile-an-hour fastball is the result of the mastery of forces of daunting proportions. Such mastery is a condition of excellence in baseball.

Our most important practices make sense only in the context of some overarching story that reveals to us fundamental convictions about what is ultimately real in and true of the universe in which we live. And most of the stories by which human beings live are *heroic* in character. They are stories about mastery over the forces of human evil and the threatening powers of nature. They are stories about how human beings (exemplified in their heroes) protect themselves against the undependability of the elements and the hostility or indifference of the gods. In such narratives, human mastery becomes ultimate virtue and the mark of excellence.

Christian practices are different. And that is because their story is different. While human achievement is valued in the Christian story, it has a different place and meaning. The human task is not fundamentally mastery. It is rather the right use of gifts graciously bestowed by a loving God for the sake of the good that God intends—*and ultimately assures.* In the Christian story, the fundamental fact is neither a violence that threatens to overwhelm us nor a chaos that threatens to undo us. No. This story's fundamental fact is that the everlasting arms of a gracious and loving God sustain the universe. So our basic task is not mastery and control. It is instead trust and grateful receptivity. Our exemplars are not heroes; they are saints. Our epitome is not excellence; our honor is in faithfulness.

Why does prayer show up high on a list of essential Christian practices? Because prayer *is* receptivity and responsiveness to the creative and redemptive grace of a triune God-for-us. Why would it seem odd to strive for the achievement of excellence in the practice of prayer? Because "achievement" connotes a kind of forceful striving that is inappropriate to the movement of body and spirit that prayer actually is. In the context of prayer, the abundance of God's grace relativizes all our excellences. Before God, our achievement is not the point; and it may be a hindrance.

The case is similar for hospitality to the stranger and to the enemy. Hospitality, like prayer, is receptivity and responsiveness. In the context of faith, there is always the hope—even the presumption—that grace is what one will meet in the encounter with the stranger. This can never be a naive assumption, for as a practice of Christian faith, hospitality is persistent in the face of threat and evil. It recognizes threat and evil for what they are and will manifest itself in behaviors that take fully into account the realities at hand. But it persists on the conviction that the peace of grace is more fundamental and primordial than violence or chaos. This modifies the character and ultimacy of whatever strategic elements of resistance and self-protection any particular moment or relation may require. This, I think, is precisely what the people of Le Chambon were up to in their protection of the Jews and their treatment of the Nazis.

The peculiar character of Christian practices operates also in the interpretation of Scripture. Excellence in interpretation, however much discipline and broad knowledge it requires, is never so much an achievement as it is a gift. This is not so much because interpretive insight does not often require great skill, training, and talent but because it comes in the midst of existence before God—which is formed, shaped, and given in the form of the whole broad practice of faith we have been trying to describe.

The relativization of achievement and mastery inserts itself into every Christian practice as a mode of behavior and attitude that always seems slightly puzzling in our society. The ethical compulsion to achieve excellence is paradoxically relaxed, because the ontological/religious compulsion to mastery and control is relativized by a peaceable Grace that is at the heart and ground of everything. And that makes an odd sort of difference.

The theologian Edward Farley wrote about this some years ago:

> We cannot avoid it, it seems. A certain "strangeness," a certain "peculiarity" marks everything which concerns in any way the Gospel of Jesus Christ. This means that everything in the church, including the church itself, is touched with this strangeness. Talking about the Gospel is strange. . . . Worshipping and praying have their peculiarities, and they are not exactly identical with these phenomena in all religions. Everything introduced into the church and its concerns is bathed in this strangeness.[9]

What is this strangeness? It is the strange freedom that comes when our deepest fear is relieved: our deep, deep fear that chaos and violence will overcome us unless we control it. That fear is relieved—that freedom comes—only in the strange gift of grace.

So what is the implication for Christian teaching and learning? The implication is that teaching and learning are not finally about mastery. Our task in learning is not to master the practices or the subject matter or ourselves. And our task in teaching is not to master our students. If, in striving for excellence, we find ourselves in pursuit of control over our own destinies as human beings, seeking to use education in faith as a means to secure ourselves before God, we will have missed the mark entirely. The practices of faith are not ultimately our own practices but rather habitations of the Spirit, in the midst of which we are invited to participate in the practices of God. So, too, education in faith is not ultimately an ethical or spiritual striving but rather participation in the educating work of God's Spirit among us and within us. In this way, education in faith is itself a means of grace.

Notes

1. I include here pastors and teachers in congregations, but I also have in mind those who have responsibilities for the programs and overall life of a congregation, including its governing board. In addition, I want to stress the role parents have in the education in faith of their children. Christians who are teachers in other institutions—primary and secondary schools, colleges and universities, theological seminaries—also have roles to play in the educational ministry of the church, though the ways in which they exercise their responsibilities may vary quite significantly, depending on the purposes and self-understandings of the institutions in which they teach. Finally, I believe leaders in a wide variety of institutions (from social service agencies to businesses) have educational roles to play, and I hope these reflections are useful to Christians in those contexts as well.

2. Alasdair MacIntyre, *After Virtue* (Notre Dame, Ind.: University of Notre Dame Press, 1981), 175.

3. Jeffrey Stout was the first to use this example; see his *Ethics after Babel* (Boston: Beacon Press, 1988), esp. 276 and 303. See also my other discussion of MacIntyre's definition of "practice" in Craig Dykstra, "Reconceiving Practice," in Barbara G. Wheeler and Edward Farley, eds.,

Shifting Boundaries: Contextual Approaches to the Structure of Theological Education (Louisville, Ky.: Westminster/John Knox Press, 1991), esp. 42–46.

4. *Intrinsic* goods are the goods inherent in the practice itself and that in large measure give it its character and value. There are other kinds of "goods" that may come as a result of a practice, however. Great pitching, for example, may lead to fame, fortune, and ownership of your own restaurant. These are what MacIntyre calls *extrinsic* goods. When too much attention is paid to extrinsic goods, they have a tendency to distort, diminish, and eventually corrupt the practice that generated them.

5. See Dorothy Bass, ed., *Practicing Our Faith: A Way of Life for a Searching People* (San Francisco: Jossey-Bass, 1997). This book is the result of a sustained ecumenical dialogue about the nature of Christian practices. The group that engaged in this endeavor arrived at a complementary but somewhat different list of practices from the one found in this book. I recommend Bass's book highly to anyone who wishes to pursue this way of thinking more deeply.

6. Iris Murdoch, *The Sovereignty of Good* (New York: Schocken Books, 1970), 32.

7. This list of conditions is influenced by Urie Bronfenbrenner, *The Ecology of Human Development* (Cambridge, Mass.: Harvard University Press, 1981); see esp. chaps. 3, 4, and 9.

8. See John Milbank, *Theology and Social Theory: Beyond Secular Reason* (Oxford: Basil Blackwell Publisher, 1990), particularly chaps. 11 and 12, where Milbank explores the "heroic" nature of MacIntyre's understanding of practice and then describes how the content of Christian faith gives rise to a substantively different meaning to virtue as well as to practice.

9. Edward Farley, "Does Christian Education Need the Holy Spirit? Part II," *Religious Education* 60 (November–December 1965): 432.

Places

Chapter 6

The Formative Power of the Congregation

I am by no means alone in arguing that the process of coming to faith and growing in faith takes place in the context of community and that God uses community as "a means of grace." Indeed, a near consensus prevails among religious educators that faith communities have formative power in the lives of people, nurturing faith and giving shape to the quality and character of their spirits.[1] Spirituality deepens in community, rather than in individualistic isolation. The beliefs, values, attitudes, stories, rituals, and moral practices of a faith community are the human forces most powerful in shaping a person's spiritual journey.

But religious educators worry about whether these communities are, in fact, powerful enough—and about whether the power they have is used for good, rather than for what is simply banal. So many strong socializing and enculturating forces are at work in people's lives that the formative power of faith communities, especially congregations, seems weak in comparison. Moreover, congregations are not always all that faithful. Too often, they seem more a reflection of the wider culture's values than an embodiment of the distinctive good news of the Christian gospel.

One obvious response to this situation is that if we could be more faithful as faith communities, we would indeed be less conventional and more influential. Closer knowledge of and adherence to this substantive tradition, rather than the kind of superficial civil religiosity that pervades most of our present corporate life, would generate more powerful faith. This is a good answer; but how do we get from here to there?

A prevalent answer to that question is one articulated by Thomas Groome: "Our religious education must promote a critical reflective activity in the midst of our socializing if our faith is truly to be our own and for the sake of the ongoing reform and faithfulness of the whole community."[2] This is a very good response, an indispensable one, in fact. But it begs still another question: Where does the capacity for critical reflection come from? Groome's answer to this is not entirely clear. He seems to suggest that critical reflection is possible for all people, given the appropriate developmental capacities, and that it emerges in dialogue with others when we think and talk together about our "present action" in relation to the tradition's "story" and "vision."

This is probably true, if we do, in fact, have the internal freedom to reflect critically on our present lives. But whether we are really free to do this is not evident. Reflecting critically on our present lives is a scary business. Much is at stake—namely, our present lives. To be free to reflect critically on our present lives, we must be willing to allow our lives to be changed, in a sense, to be given up. We ought not be too optimistic about people's freedom to do this. Anyone who has tried to get people in a congregation (much less to bring oneself) to reflect critically—really critically—on their lives probably will not be optimistic.

The way to a solution requires, perhaps, another look at the fabric of the life of faith communities, one that realistically examines its limits and what resources it may have for engendering the freedom we need to become what we are not. In an attempt to do something like this, I focus on the limits and power of the Christian congregation. What is said here may or may not have implications for other religious faiths and other forms of community life.

The exploration begins with and is structured by two basic claims: (1) a basic reality of congregational life is that we are often engaged in socially acceptable (indeed, socially celebrated) patterns of mutual self-destruction; and (2) in and through congregational life, these patterns are at the same time being redemptively modified, transformed. Congregations are profoundly caught up in powerful patterns of sin and alienation. This we must admit. But despite and even within the context of its embeddedness in these patterns, the congregation mediates redemptive power. Precisely in the midst of its sinfulness, rather than apart from it, the congregation has power to mediate the gospel in such a way that the "speaking" of it can restructure and transform human personal and social life.

To see how this may be so, let us begin with a story of an upper-middle-class church member, his family, and a few of his friends. It reveals, I believe, certain important dynamics going on in the daily lives of many people in our culture and in many of our churches.[3]

Carl Phillips walked back to his car after leaving Mary Matthews' house. His mind was reeling with the jarring awareness that he might have been able to prevent the death of Mary's husband and his friend, Tom Matthews. . . . As soon as he learned of Tom's suicide, Carl had gone immediately to the Matthews home.

As Carl drove slowly home he recalled his conversation with Mary. Carl thought he had known Tom Matthews pretty well but now was aware that he actually knew very little about him. Mary had confided that in the past few months Tom had had an increasing problem with alcohol, that he was frequently depressed, and was basically unable to accept being "phased out" of his executive position in a large New York firm six weeks ago. Carl repeated to himself what he had told Mary, "If I'd only known. . . . "

Carl Phillips was also being "phased out" of his managerial position in a New York advertising concern quite similar to Tom Matthews'. . . . At first Carl had fought for his job, appealing to personal friends higher up the executive "ladder." He had an impressive record . . . but [it soon became clear that] he would be one of six men to go. . . . Carl had not told his wife Marilyn that he was losing his job until three weeks ago. . . . Carl wondered again why he had waited so long to tell her. . . . "I guess it was . . . my male ego. I've been conditioned from childhood that the father is the head of the household and the provider of the family."

When Carl reached home he found Marilyn in the kitchen. . . . Carl told Marilyn what he had learned about Tom Matthews and put to her the nagging question in the back of his mind. "Marilyn, to what extent does my Christian responsibility demand that I share my own defeats with other people, especially if this kind of openness could give someone else the courage to share their burdens as well?"

Marilyn responded slowly but firmly. "If you're thinking about telling the world about being fired, that's nothing but masochism. You feel guilty about not having known about Tom Matthews. Maybe you could have helped him, but it's too late now. You would only be punishing yourself and your family by flaunting your failure. . . . Look, we live in a very status-conscious community and I don't want to have to deal with anyone else's pity."

Carl admitted that Marilyn hit some pretty raw nerves with that "status conscious" comment. . . . From the viewpoint of those "upstanding taxpaying citizens" in his economic bracket, "people on unemployment compensation are shiftless 'bums' waiting in line for a handout." Perhaps most problematic of all, could he really accept and face what he saw as personal failure to the extent that he could admit this to his friends?

But Carl also responded to what he saw as the "other side of the coin" as he argued with both himself and his wife. "Marilyn, Tom's suicide has painfully forced me to recognize the tremendous unspoken needs of people around us. I've talked before about the little 'pigeonholes' we put ourselves into and the crying need to break out of this pattern. We look to different kinds of programs in the church to do this for us, but we're not really willing to risk ourselves to get to know each other. I want to be honest with myself and with other people about where I am, but I don't know what that means for you or the boys or me."

PATTERNS OF MUTUAL SELF-DESTRUCTION

Tom Matthews, Carl Phillips, both their wives and families, their business colleagues, their local community, and probably the congregations of which they are members live under the power of a pattern of mutual self-destruction. This particular pattern is called, by social psychologists, the achievement-oriented lifestyle,[4] a style of life that has as its center the compulsion to succeed or achieve in whatever social world one lives in. A person whose style of life is structured by the achievement compulsion is one whose self-image depends on "making it" in one way or another. Who one is, one's identity, depends on earning the affection of others through the value of what one produces or does. This compulsion to achieve affects, almost to the point of determining, one's behavior, attitudes, values, and fundamental beliefs.

The achievement compulsion is socially mediated and socially expressed; it has its roots in early childhood (as Carl Phillips poignantly recognized) and is reinforced by many features of the American cultural system. People need and want nothing more than to be loved and found worthy—just for who they are. But in much American early childhood training, affection (the concrete sign of love) is not given unconditionally. It is used as a manipulative device. It is withheld until the child performs well, or at least it is bestowed with most intensity and enthusiasm when the child has done something that makes the parents proud. This pattern continues, and indeed is intensified, in school, where the ones who develop a sense of self-worth are those who produce. They get the rewards, the affection of their teachers, the acclamation of their classmates. And the more people succeed, the more they reap the benefits of the social system. Those who do not achieve, by contrast, struggle to find their place in the social matrix. Obvious evidence for this lies in our treatment of the mentally retarded, the "uneducated," the physically blemished, and the poor. Furthermore, this whole system of social priorities is sacralized by the language patterns, symbols, images, and rituals that define our culture. Thus, the achievement compulsion is a socially acceptable, indeed socially celebrated, pattern of social interaction. Who really argues with success—especially when that success is earned?

But it *is* a pattern of mutual self-destruction. The success-oriented society and culture gives birth to persons who do indeed produce and are purposeful. But they also tend to manipulate others for their own purposes and suffer from debilitating internal stress. Why? Because becoming a compulsive achiever costs something. One pays the price by repressing the natural and fundamental human need to be loved unconditionally. "The central tendency of achievement-orientation is repressive of a deep human cry for assurance of ascriptive (not achieved) worth. The outcome is aggression, tension, domineering control, and cruelty."[5] This repression is self-destructive and destructive of others. It is self-destructive not only because it produces ulcers and heart attacks (or sometimes, as in Tom Matthews's case, suicide) but more fundamentally because it locks the door to the one thing on which human life most fundamentally depends: unconditional love.

This pattern of socially acceptable mutual self-destruction pervades significant parts of the church. Achievement as a compulsion is fostered, accepted, and even celebrated in the church as much as anywhere. "Model churches" are successful, achieving churches. Persons who are honored in churches are persons who are purposeful, productive, and accomplished— persons who excel and succeed in and out of the church. Concrete evidence is the obvious sympathy we feel for Marilyn Phillips's response to her husband's thoughts about opening himself up to others in their congregation. We know that for him to do so would be very risky. Why? Because it would rupture the achievement-oriented norms, values, and expectations of the community. It would be, says Marilyn, "flaunting failure." It would create pain and conflict and might very likely lead to the rejection of the Phillipses by their friends.

Here we have, then, a painful reality of congregational life. In congregations and as congregations, we are engaged in socially acceptable patterns of mutual self-destruction. Furthermore, our participation in this pattern is institutionalized and passed on from generation to generation. It becomes a basic pattern of personality, within which individuals and communities are caught in all their feeling, thinking, imagining, and acting.

The compulsive and pervasive nature of patterns of mutual self-destruction is what limits our freedom in relation to them. Critical reflection on them is difficult to attain, partly because they operate largely at a prereflective level. As Edward Farley points out in another context, it is "too close to see because we 'see' by means of it, that is through a consciousness already modified by it."[6] Bringing such patterns to consciousness may elicit recognition. When the pattern is identified and articulated, people may say, "It's true. I hadn't thought about it before, but at the same time I knew it all along." But this does little to rob such patterns of their power. Consciousness of such a pattern in our own lives, of its contradictions and diabolical results, does not make us any less captive to it or free from it. Indeed, even our consciousness of the pattern may be co-opted by it. The achievement of critically reflective discernment may simply reinforce our dependence on our intellectual powers as our source of self-worth, make us compulsively critically reflective, and leave us unable to do anything more than strive further to be more critically acute than the next person. Critical reflection is not the primary source of freedom from a pattern of mutual self-destruction; it is, rather, a fruit of that freedom.

Furthermore, the mere presence of the story, vision, and language of the faith is no guarantee that powerful patterns of mutual self-destruction will be overcome. The patterns easily survive in congregational life, no matter how much that life may be filled with a talk about sin, crucifixion, the love of God, or the grace of the Lord Jesus Christ. Indeed, the achievement-oriented congregation learns to manipulate this language well. The compulsive achiever may simply strive all the harder to be articulate about sin, convincing in an analysis of the centrality of the crucifixion in contemporary theology, effective in proclamation, purposeful and disciplined in the work of the church—all in order to earn respect and love in the congregational context. "The achiever will take only 'appropriate' risks and probably therefore only 'successful' . . . risks, learn the 'winning' answers, interpret them to justify his style, and assume—perhaps not erroneously—that the church is celebrating his way of life."[7]

This achievement-compulsion pattern is a manifestation of one basic re-sponse to the human situation.[8] We are human beings in part just because we recognize our own nonnecessity.[9] That is, we recognize that we might not *be*. As we live anticipating death, we are also aware that we might just as easily never have come to be—if, say, our parents had never met or our particular conception had failed. We know that our existence, *the fact that we are*, is not necessary. But we also know that *who we are* is not necessary. Through different decisions and circumstances, we might have become very different from who we are now. And the future leaves open the as-surance that we will yet become different in significant ways.

The result of all this is a fundamental insecurity. Human life recognizes that it is surrounded by chaos. The creation stories in Genesis bear witness to this. (In the creation stories, God does not destroy chaos; God only pushes it back and separates the creation from it.) This recognition is ac-companied, however, by a correlative refusal. It is built into us as human beings, it seems, to refuse to allow chaos to be the ultimate fact and frame-work for human endeavor.[10] This refusal may take two basic forms, how-ever: what Edward Farley calls "self-securing," on the one hand, and faith, on the other.[11] Self-securing refers to our drivenness to refuse chaos by our own powers. Faith is the opposite of this. It is life lived in the trust and knowledge that God alone can refuse chaos, and in the confidence that God has done this and continues always to do so.

The human self is a very fragile thing. It is threatened on all sides. How is it to be established and secured? How can we know for sure that we are something, something good and valuable and worthy of being around, in spite of the fact of our physical and personal nonnecessity? We can know only if we are noticed. If no one notices that we are here, our lives, our very selves, are in jeopardy. It is in being noticed by others that children come to know they exist in the first place. If children are not noticed, if they do not feel their presence being felt by others, their being is not secured and the formation of a sense of self is impossible. The need to be established and sustained as a unique and valuable self can be met only by the devel-opment of a sense that one is profoundly and permanently noticed by an-other. To learn from one's parents when one is very young that one is accepted, valuable, and indispensable in the world is to learn that one *is*.

But note what happens when this certainty is not forthcoming or begins to break down. In this case, we begin to *make* people notice us. We begin to use people as mirrors in which to see ourselves reflected. We begin to manipulate others into responding to us, and on our own terms. This can have many different kinds of effects. It can make us so hungry for power that we begin to manipulate or even to destroy others in the process of trying to get it. It can virtually force us internally to engage in all kinds of unsavory or unethical behavior, all consciously or unconsciously designed to get us what we think we need in order to be somebody. I would say, in fact, that virtually every personal and social evil has its roots in our need to manipulate the world into paying attention to us.

And when our world does not respond—perhaps because it, too, is engaged in its own self-securing—our attempts to make it respond become continuously more desperate. This dynamic, I argue, is at the root of the achievement-compulsion lifestyle and every other self-destructive pattern of social existence. And when our desperate attempts to make the world take notice do not work, when achievement fails to bring love, we increasingly look for ways in which to anesthetize ourselves (through alcohol, prejudice, vainglory, or, in the extreme, suicide) against the knowledge that we are not being noticed in the way we want or need to be.

This dynamic operates in all of us to one degree or another. Another word for it is *sin*. Our sin is overcome, the dynamic is broken, only insofar as we are profoundly and permanently noticed in love. One of God's greatest blessings is the love and attention we receive from other people, especially love and attention that we somehow sense is not self-seeking. But because we are all sinners, none of us can be the source of permanent establishment and sustenance for another. We all grow up, and the existence that was secured for us in childhood by good parents always breaks down. We find out that our parents are not perfect, omnipotent, and eternal. They fail us, on the one hand, and they die, on the other. More disastrously, so does everyone else.

That is why our release from sin (and correlatively, from all of the patterns of mutual self-destruction in which we are embedded) depends on God and on faith in God. Unless there is this Reality that does, in fact, establish and sustain us, secure us in existence, notice us in love, permanently and utterly, and unless, through faith, somehow deep within our being we know that, we have no choice but to continue desperately to secure our own selves.

THE REDEMPTIVE POWER OF CONGREGATIONS

Now we are at the point where we may speak of the redemptive power of the congregation. Our second claim was that these mutually destructive patterns are being redemptively transformed, and that in this lies the power of the congregation to mediate the gospel. Since the patterns that destroy us lie at the prereflective level, and since the roots of these patterns lie in the desperate attempts at self-securing that characterize our historical existence, the redemptive power of the congregation must be a transformation of self-securing and must somehow be mediated at a prereflective level.

It is not enough for the congregation to speak religious phrases. Nor is it enough for it simply to try more ardently to become a community of mutual love. Because patterns of mutual self-destruction operate at a prereflective level, mere speech has no effect. And because the life of the congregation continues to be, to some degree and in a variety of ways, self-destructive, it cannot, under its own power, become a community of mutual love. Even to make the attempt is to continue the striving of self-securing.

It could seem, then, that the congregation has no redemptive power and there is nothing the congregation can do. But this is not the case. What the congregation can do is acknowledge its participation in patterns of mutual self-destruction (in theological language, this is called *confession*); recognize its incapacity to secure itself (this is called *repentance*); and accept, proclaim, and give thanks for the establishing and sustaining power that belongs to God alone. In sum, the congregation may worship. Worship is the core of congregational life and provides the paradigm for its peculiar form of life. In worship, the congregation *is* a congregation. Through worship, patterns of mutual self-destruction become redemptively transformed.

Worship, in this context, is not simply participation in a ritual (though the context and form of the ritual of Christian worship teach the congregation who they are). Worship is rather a style of life that may pervade the whole of a congregation's existence—even while it continues in sin. Look again carefully at the opening example. What Carl Phillips is yearning to do in sharing his defeats with other people is to worship. His yearning to be honest with himself and with others is a yearning to worship (to confess, to repent, and to proclaim and give thanks) in spirit and in truth. He is yearning to come before God as he is. And he knows that the only way to come before God as he is, is to come before God with others as they are. He also suspects that the others with whom he might come are yearning to worship in the same way. He suspects this because the testimonies and stories of the faith tradition of which he is a part (he speaks of his Christian responsibility) tell him that this is true.

Thus, right in the middle of the self-securing and mutually destructive form of social life of the status-conscious, achievement-oriented congregation of which Carl Phillips, like many of us, is a part is worship and the yearning to worship in spirit and in truth. And here lies the power of the congregation to mediate the gospel. For in a prereflective way, the worship that goes on from week to week, corrupted as it is, continues to break up self-securing, self-destructive patterns. This provides the fulcrum by which our life together may be and is being transformed for our redemption. It is worship, more than critical reflection, that is the context of our freedom. Insofar as (and as long as) the congregation worships, the congregation remains the church. And insofar as the congregation's whole life increasingly takes on the form of worship, to that extent the congregation increasingly more powerfully and influentially bears redemptive power.

Worship may seem an odd place to locate the source of the freedom that is required for the ongoing transformation of personal and corporate life. And, of course, it is not always so. Worship may degenerate into idolatry. Worship is what we once called "divine worship" only insofar as it is worship of God—the God whose nature and living presence the faith community's Story and Vision (to use Groome's terms) render. Furthermore, worship as communal style of life is worship only insofar as all its common expectations and processes of socialization (for both good and ill) are governed by and continually altered by apprehensions of and dealing with God. Unless this underlies all its practices, structures, and patterns of mutual human relationship (constructive or destructive), life in the community of faith is nothing more than participation in still another social group—no different in any essential way from participation in a profession, a club, or a social movement. In such cases, the ultimate reality becomes the community itself, with its beliefs, practices, values, and ways of seeing. Then idolatry reigns.

What makes a community *a worshiping* community is the fact that, as Farley points out, its "social structures and individual behaviors and attitudes are at best vehicles for whatever realities faith apprehends but are not the realities themselves."[12] Farley goes on to describe the way in which this conviction lies at the heart of Christian faith:

Historical study of the origin, development, events, personages, and "essence" of Christianity reveals a prevailing concensus that faith is directed to realities which are unreducible to the images, experience, or behaviors of this historical religion. Even if we grant the "doxo-logical" dimension in the language about God in this historical faith, the praise of God is not praise of praise. It is not intended as praise of a community engendered symbol or image. When an early church father or reformer criticized an opponent's Christology, a state of affairs was intended which pertained to Jesus himself, not simply the literary, psychological, or sociological features of the opponent or the tradition. There is no question that the historical faith in its very "essence" testifies to realities which transcend its own determinancy, representations, and theology.[13]

The loss of God as a known, believed, and present reality, transcendent to the community, is the loss of faith itself. Without God as the ultimate referent of all of a faith community's activities, distorted and corrupted as they may often be, faith simply reduces to the human construction of reality through social means. Socialization becomes nothing more than the incorporation of persons into a social group and its ways, and mutual human relationships lack any meaning that transcends personal and social immediacy. What, in faith, had been only means have become the end, or *telos*, itself.

In faith, however, patterns of mutual expectation and socialization are not ultimate. They are means by which the community as a whole and individuals in it come to know and live appropriately in response to God. Because the community and its ways are never ultimate, they are always open to change on the basis of deeper understandings of God and more authentic relationship to God. The community of faith is continually susceptible to judgment and renewal from its source and ground, because its source and ground is not itself.[14] This is why recognition of the need for confession of sin and repentance is more fundamental to the church's experience than any claims it might make for its own moral goodness.

When this is the case in the life of a congregation, the freedom that emerges is quite stunning. A marvelous example is reflected in a story Harvey Cox once told about a Sunday morning in his own little congregation in Cambridge, Massachusetts.[15] Cox begins his story by saying that one Sunday, "the minister of the small Baptist church I belong to did a very nice thing. During the pastoral prayer, along with remembering the sick and the shut-ins, he also asked the Lord to bestow a special blessing on our informer." The "informer," it turns out, was a person who had infiltrated the life of the congregation and was informing the FBI of its activities. Whimsically, Cox notes the congregants' surprise at the government's need for an undercover agent:

> There isn't anything very confidential about our church. The title of the sermons, such as "Begin the Faith Journey Today," are displayed on the bulletin board outside. The newsletter carries more information than most of our members want to know. The bulletins the ushers hand you on Sunday tell you whose birthdays and anniversaries are coming up and whose memory is invoked by the flowers on the communion table.
>
> What surprised us most was that the F.B.I. thought it would be hard to worm information out of us. Many people think our church's problem is just the opposite. Since we are Baptists and therefore maybe a little on the zealous side, we are more often accused of telling people too much. Indeed, some of our members feel that the last place they would tell somebody a secret would be at church—not because somebody might spill the beans but because in all probability people already know.

Cox goes on to tell the various kinds of things that go on in his rather active but not atypical congregation: Sunday school, morning worship, coffee hour, adult discussion groups, choir rehearsals, Bible studies, committee meetings, prayer circles, potluck suppers, and so on. Apparently, what had the government upset was that one of the church committees was helping a Salvadoran refugee whom the congregation had brought to Cambridge and whose children were still in El Salvador.

The presence of the informer had the congregation a bit worried, but not too much. It was something of a nuisance, and a few people had become wary of strangers. But Cox says:

> Still, in the meantime, I am glad our preacher asked the Lord to grant a special blessing to the informer. In fact, we all secretly hope our infiltrator does not get tired and quit. If he stays around long enough, he'll learn that when we say our church is a "sanctuary," we don't mean just for Salvadoran refugees. Churches are sanctuaries for homeless, lost and confused people of all kinds, including secret agents. They, too, are welcome to come and pray, listen to the Gospel reading and belt out "Beulah Land" with us. Who knows, they might even end up getting saved. It wouldn't be the first time.

In the context of a worshiping congregation, a remarkable freedom obtains. One senses it not so much in any acuteness of critical analysis (though one does not doubt that this can be done if it is needed); rather, the freedom comes through in the lightness of touch, the humor that proves that nothing, neither external threat nor internal order, is taken with ultimate seriousness—precisely because nothing is ultimate but the God whom they worship. It may not look much like freedom. But in praying for the sick and the shut-in; in all the open conversation at the coffee hours, the adult discussion groups, and the potluck suppers about things that matter in people's lives (and some things that don't); in the goings-on at the choir rehearsals, the Bible studies, the prayer circles, the committee meetings; and above all, in the high if somewhat comic drama of the worship service where God's presence is invoked, where the Word of God is read aloud, where the good news is preached, where God is praised in voices lifted up in song, where people come from east and west and north and south to sit at table with the risen Christ, and where, who knows, from time to time a few even end up getting saved—in all this there is considerable freedom.

There is freedom from compulsive self-securing. There is freedom from the patterned, prereflective forces that generate mutual self-destruction. The worshiping people are never utterly or perfectly free, of course. The self-securing is redemptively modified, not eliminated. The mutual self-destruction is ameliorated in some ways, though never completely. Still, there is a point of leverage and some movement—maybe even enough to enable the people to open their arms to strangers, both Salvadoran refugees and FBI informers.

Notes

1. If there is such a consensus, John Westerhoff has undoubtedly had considerable influence in bringing it about.
2. Thomas Groome, *Christian Religious Education* (San Francisco: Harper & Row, 1980), 108.
3. The story is a case reported in Robert Evans, Alice Evans, Louis Weeks, Carolyn Weeks, *Casebook for Christian Living* (Atlanta: John Knox Press, 1977), 66–68. The case is a write-up of an actual incident, though the names are fictional.
4. I am depending, in my discussion of this lifestyle pattern, on James E. Loder, "The Fashioning of Power: A Christian Perspective on the Life-

Style Phenomenon," in A. J. McKelway and E. David Willis, eds., *The Context of Contemporary Theology* (Atlanta: John Knox Press 1974), 187–205. Loder uses the phrase, "socially acceptable patterns of self-destruction," which I modify here; see 187.

5. Ibid., 191.

6. Edward Farley, *Ecclesial Man: A Social Phenomenology of Faith and Reality* (Philadelphia: Fortress Press, 1975), 141.

7. Loder, "Fashioning of Power," 192.

8. See Farley, *Ecclesial Man*, chap. 6, for a phenomenological description of this situation.

9. Ibid., 132–33.

10. Ibid., 133.

11. Ibid., 143.

12. Ibid., 15.

13. Ibid., 15–16.

14. The criticisms of socialization theory in religious education, including Groome's, have been made largely on the grounds that socialization necessarily implies domestication and the preservation of the status quo. This seems to me to involve too simplistic a reading of socialization theory. I believe there is more dialectic built into both C. Ellis Nelson's and John Westerhoff's positions than is usually recognized, though neither is, to my mind, adequately clear or forceful about this. In any case, a more fundamental problem than any perceived lack of dialectic between the faith community and the larger world or between the community and its members is the problem of what Farley calls "reality loss" (the loss of a believable sense of the reality of God as a foundation for the community's life). Advances can be made over both "socialization" and "critical dialectical hermeneutical" theory only by confronting this issue directly. This is a project yet to be undertaken.

15. The story appeared in an editorial. "The Spy in the Pew," *New York Times*, Monday, March 3, 1986, A15. The following quotations are taken from that source.

Chapter 7

Family Promises

What is essential to being family, and what are the connections between the family and Christian faith? Families are people who make promises to each other. When we see what those promises are, we see what a family is. I am not saying that first there is a family, and then those who are that family start making promises. What I mean, rather, is that family is constituted by promises. "Family" is a peculiar set of promises. It is the promises that make the family, before it is the family that makes promises.

A fairly common sense definition of *family* runs as follows: "family" is that group of persons with whom we are linked as parents or children or siblings or spouses or kin, by birth, by adoption, or by marriage. This definition suggests that every person is part of a family—unless, of course, one has no kin at all. It does not by any means limit family to a married couple and their children. Never-married and formerly married people are part of families, whether they have children or not. Married couples without children are in family. People who live alone are almost always still in families. Family does not mean "people living together under one roof." If people have parents, sisters, brothers, children, uncles, aunts, nieces, nephews, or cousins, and so forth, they are in family. *Family* is a very inclusive category when the tracings of kinship are brought to our attention and our imaginations are not limited by stereotypes.

This definition, however, standing by itself, does not tell us much about what family means. The crucial phrase in the definition is "we are linked." But what is the nature of this linkage? Is it simply biological or sociological? Or is something deeper implicit in all of this? Here is where the notion of promise-making comes in. It helps us see what is at the heart of being linked.

Marriage is not the only way to become family. If we start with marriage, however, we find a fairly clear way to open up the promise-making nature of all kinds of family constellations. How do people get married? How does a person become a husband or a wife? It is by making a promise, by saying "I promise . . . " or "I take thee . . . " or "I will . . . " or "I do. . . . " That is it. An act of promising constitutes the marriage. This, in and of itself, creates a family. To be a spouse, to be a wife or a husband in relation to someone else, means nothing else but to have made some particular promises.

What are people doing when they make promises like this? In an act of promise-making, people are saying something about their intentions for the future, committing themselves to a particular way of moving through the present into the future. And what is it that people are promising in the act of marrying? The most fundamental promise is henceforth to see the other as spouse, as wife to me or husband to me. This means a number of things. It means mutual acceptance of responsibility for each other's welfare. It means commitment to work out together, as husband and wife, the financial, personal, cultural, and social problems that arise in life. It means to see each other and both together as the human matrix of whatever children may come from their sexual relationship and to take mutual responsibility for them. To see another as spouse means seeing the other in terms of a future that involves mutual responsibility in sexuality, in sustenance, and in dealing with realities and forces that impinge on the lives of each of us.[1] All this is involved in regarding each other as a spouse. A family comes into being when two persons become spouse to each other (and are seen as spouse to each other by others) through a public act of promise-making.

Can we think of other relationships in family in the same way? Do we become parents, daughters and sons, brothers and sisters, grandparents, aunts, uncles, and cousins through making promises? The matter is not nearly so clear, since there seems to be no explicit act of promise-making involved and the connections seem largely biological. Still, a strong case can be made that all of the various relationships that make us kin or family are constituted ultimately in promising.[2]

Ordinarily, we tend to think that the paradigmatic case of the establishment of the parent-child relationship is the one in which the child is biologically born from the union of the parents. But if promising is really at the heart of being family, then the process of adoption may offer a better example. When people adopt children, they do something similar to what is done in marrying. They say, in a sense, "I promise," in answer to the question "Will you take this child to be your son or daughter?" In saying, "I promise" (or "We promise"), people are promising henceforth to see this child, regard this child, as son or daughter to them. Again, to regard a child as one's son or daughter involves implicit (if not explicit) intentions to live out the future in a particular way, a way that includes commitment to and responsibility for the child's welfare, identity, and future. And it means that it is *as* father or *as* mother that the person shall carry out these commitments and responsibilities to the child as son or as daughter.

When a person adopts a child, this promise-making is fairly explicit. Adopting parents have to make certain promises publicly and explicitly to adoption agencies (and have their fitness for making those promises checked up on and tested out) before they are allowed to adopt. The promise-making involved when children issue out of our own bodies is not as obvious. But it is no less the case. We make promises, I think, whenever we engage in sexual intercourse—whether we know it or not. An act of promise-making is occasioned by this sexual act. Ronald Green, in an essay on the ethics of abortion called "Abortion and Promise-Keeping," argues as follows:

> The mere fact that coitus, when followed by conception, initiated a series of events that normally culminates in a set of legitimate expectations on the part of another human being (the future child) places the individual who has helped initiate that act . . . under particular obligations to fulfill those expectations.
>
> Precisely because these expectations have an objective basis, we contend that any [person] capable of understanding the implications of coitus must eventually realize the promise-making nature of [his or] her sexual acts. Thus, we are not so much saying that a promise is implicitly made as that a promise is implicit to this act.[3]

Sexual intercourse is, in and of itself, implicitly promissory. Just by having intercourse, we make promises to any potential offspring of that action.[4] If a child is conceived, he or she becomes son or daughter to us (whether we like it or not) precisely through the promises implicit in our act. The promissory nature of family that arises from children biologically born to us is no different from the promissory nature of family constituted through adoption. Here, too, we "promise" henceforth to be father or mother to sons or daughters.

What about from the other side? Do children make promises to be sons and daughters? Or to be brothers and sisters? Such an idea seems odd, at least. Children have mothers, fathers, sisters, and brothers through no choice of their own. From the point of view of the offspring, no volition is involved. None of us chooses even to be born, much less to be born into the particular family we are given. How can any promising be involved in being a son or daughter, a brother, or sister?

Here the promises are implicit and arise out of receiving and responding to the promises made to us by our parents. In being parents to children, parents engage their children in an ever-developing web of mutuality. This mutuality is founded initially, to be sure, on the promises of the parents. But in responding to those promises, children implicitly make promises back. To be seen as daughter or as son by one's father or mother evokes the response on the child's part of seeing oneself as son or daughter and, reciprocally, the parent or parents as mother or father. The reciprocal seeing has implicit in it a reciprocal promising. This is experienced quite powerfully at a rather early age. But it is only later that these promises may become explicitly conscious to the child; and even later still, perhaps, that they may be intentionally owned.[5] Nevertheless, at the point where the child's promises become conscious and owned, promises are not newly being made. Rather, the promises are existing, already-lived promises becoming articulated and affirmed (or perhaps, rejected).

This same kind of process goes on in making us brothers and sisters in families. Parents see all their children as their sons or daughters. As children see their parents seeing them and the other children in the family as all being their children (in short, as brothers and sisters), each child comes to see herself or himself that way too. That is, each child comes to see himself or herself as incorporated with the other children in the family into that particular set of promises that constitutes the family. The same kind of analysis can be made in relation to more distant kin, though in such cases (especially in cultures such as our own) the promises quickly become much more restricted and the opportunities for seeing other kin at all—much less seeing them *as* kin—diminish rapidly.

All families, then—not just Christian families or families in the church—are constituted most fundamentally by promises. Families are people who make a particular set of promises to one another. One thing that must be said at this point is that it is promise-*making*, not promise-keeping, that constitutes the family. As a matter of fact, the promises that constitute the family are very ofdifficult promises to keep, and we all continually fail at doing so. We fail for all sorts of reasons. We may fail because certain cultural, social, and economic forces quite beyond our control make it extremely difficult, if not impossible, for us to fulfill our promises to promote one another's welfare, to work out problems and difficulties mutually, to attend to one another as husband, wife, father, mother, daughter, son, sister, brother. War, poverty, racism, sexism, societal violence, pornography, and dislocation are all powerful forces that make our promise-keeping difficult to fulfill and sometimes impossible. Or we may fail because of our human limitations. Often the promises involved in being family are too many and too overwhelming for us to fulfill, just because there are limits to our energy and to our capacity to know and see and be in the ways that the fulfillment of our promises would require. Or again, our failure may be due to our own sinfulness: our deceiving, insincerity, manipulation, idolization, ridiculing, and self-centeredness.

It is not the failure to *keep* promises, in and of itself, that destroys family. Such failure happens in every family and can be expected. Family can remain family in the midst of unfulfilled promises. What destroys family is the collapse of promise-*making*. It is when the very making of promises is no longer believed in that families die. The failure to keep promises and the collapse of promise-making are, of course, related. The continual failure to fulfill promises acts as a corrosive to the promise-making. But when this happens, it is the promise-making itself that becomes null and void. Then the constituting ground of family is dissolved. In divorce, for example, a certain set of promises is no longer being made. The promise-making that constitutes two persons as husband and wife comes to an end. That is what makes them no longer husband and wife.

CHRISTIAN FAITH AND FAMILY PROMISES

Many of the promises that are involved in the constitution of family are somewhat hidden and implicit. It is not obvious what promises we are making when we marry or have children or just find ourselves to be kin to someone. Because of this, it is very easy to marry or have children without knowing what we are doing—without knowing exactly what promises we are making and even, perhaps, without even knowing that we are making promises at all. This is all the more true as our culture becomes more secularized. In fact, one thing secularization may mean is the removal of the context and grounds for the visibility, significance, and meaning of promise-making.

Promises can be very slippery. So often in our lives we cannot tell whether we have been promised something or not. Suppose someone tells me, "I will be there." Has that person made a promise? It is an open question. It depends on whether that person was just stating a hope or a wish or a reasonable expectation—or making a promise. We cannot always tell just from the words themselves, which are continually open to further questioning by all parties involved, unless the words have been said in some context that secures them as a promise.

Richard Fenn, in a fascinating book, *Liturgies and Trials*, suggests that liturgies are contexts that secure promises. He says that secure promises

> are rare in human conversation. When they occur, they are given and received with signs and symbols that something out of the ordinary is occurring. I am thinking specifically of wedding ceremonies in which extraordinary care is taken that all the conditions are fulfilled that make full-blown promises possible for mere humans. Announcements of intention to marry and a final pronouncement begin and conclude a process in which both persons promise that only death will part them. There can be no mistake about the seriousness of this promise, and its seriousness is guaranteed by those who watch with "the eyes of God" as rings are exchanged, hands clasped and solemn steps taken. Even those who know of conditions that would prevent a full-blown promise from taking place are told to speak (now) or keep silent forever. The liturgical language of religion is therefore the last human defense against the slipperiness, ambiguity, and uncertainty of all human acts of speech; and even these liturgical guarantees are widely known to fail.[6]

Fenn is suggesting that a secular culture, a culture without liturgies that make promises secure by the promises of God, is a culture that allows our promise acts to be continually open to question and thus continually unstable. A radically secular culture is one in which no adequate context and grounds are provided for the visibility, significance, and meaning of promise-making.

What happens to marriage, childbearing, and child rearing; relationships between brothers and sisters; responsibilities of children to their parents—in short, to family—in a culture that fails to make implicit promises visible, significant, meaningful, and secure? What happens is that the promissory foundations that constitute family are undercut. In a radically secular context, divorce is not seen as grievous failure in the sacred matter of promise-making, thus requiring confession, repentance, forgiveness, and the grace that is needed to continue to keep making promises. It is simply the (perhaps sad and even painful) ending of one phase of two person's lives and the beginning of another. What it requires is only readjustment.[7] Similarly, parents and children, brothers and sisters, come to be seen (and to see themselves) to be moving through stages of relationship in which everything may change from one stage of life to another, with nothing tying one stage to the next or each person to the other except a partly common past. The human task in such a situation is simply to cope and adjust. We can make no demands on one another or call one another to account. We cannot even cry out, "But you promised!"

At this point we can see some of the significance of the Christian faith for family. Two points are crucial. First, in the context of Christian faith, the promises that are constitutive of family are made conscious, public, and binding. Second, in the same context, these promises are linked with other, similarly serious and binding, but wider promises. The linkage of the family promises with these other promises deepens the significance of the family promises and to some extent transforms them, at the same time providing support and empowerment for the fulfillment of the family promises.

One of the important ways in which the Christian faith makes conscious, public, and binding the promises that are central to the family is through its liturgies. Among the most obvious of the liturgies that deal with family is the marriage service. Let us take two Presbyterian liturgies as an example. In the 1946 edition of *The Book of Common Worship,* used for many years in Presbyterian churches, there is an "Order for the Solemnization of Marriage."[8] The idea of "solemnization" suggests that something very serious is going on and that it should be recognized as such, that what is going on has dignity and form to it that need to be respected, and even that there is something sacred about what is taking place, to which we are to respond with a sense of awe and humility.

In the service itself, all of this is made quite clear. The minister tells us that "we are assembled here in the presence of God" and that what is happening is "instituted of God, regulated by His commandments, blessed by our Lord Jesus Christ, and to be held in honor among all." Once this context is set, it is made very clear that promises are about to be given and received; and what those promises are is articulated: "By His apostles, [our

Savior] has instructed those who enter into this relation to cherish a mutual esteem and love; to bear with each other's infirmities and weaknesses; to comfort each other in sickness, trouble, and sorrow; in honesty and industry to provide for each other, and for their household, in temporal things; to pray for and encourage each other in the things which pertain to God; and to live together as the heirs of the grace of life." Then follows the question to all present as to whether any impediment to the making of these promises is known. And then, as if to reinforce the seriousness of the matter, the persons to be married are charged to examine themselves: "I charge you both, before the great God, the Searcher of all hearts, that if either of you know any reason why ye may not lawfully be joined together in marriage, ye do now confess it. For be ye well assured that if any persons are joined together otherwise than as God's Word allows, their union is not blessed by Him."

After a prayer for God's blessing but before vows are taken, the minister asks both of those to be married the same question. The question is framed in such a way that the nature of the promises to be made is clearly stated. It asks, in essence, whether these persons know what they are doing and are ready to do it. And the minister expects and must get an answer before going on: "N., wilt thou have this Woman (Man) to be thy wife (husband), and wilt thou pledge thy troth to her (him) in all love and honor, in all duty and service, in all faith and tenderness, to live with her (him), and cherish her (him), according to the ordinance of God, in the holy bond of marriage?" Each must answer: "I will."

Only then is it possible actually to make the promise. The nature of the promise has been articulated already, so in the vow the statement goes directly to the heart of the matter: "I, N., take thee, N.; to be my wedded wife (husband); and I do promise and covenant; before God and these witnesses; to be thy loving and faithful husband (wife)." But it is not left to chance that the promise-makers know how significant and binding this promise is. So the conditions are set out. This promise holds under all conditions: "In plenty and in want; In joy and in sorrow; In sickness and in health; As long as we both shall live."

I have taken us through this marriage service in order to show the kinds of promises that the whole church (not just the Presbyterian church) has thought basic to the constitution of family and to illustrate the clarity with which they are articulated and the firmness with which they are made secure. One sees nothing like this in a secular ceremony. Interestingly, in some of the more contemporary Christian worshipbooks, produced to make our worship more in tune with modern culture, one can see some compromises with the tradition's efforts to be clear and firm about the nature of the vows being taken. For example, in the 1970 Presbyterian service book, *The Worshipbook*, the liturgy is called not a solemnization but simply "The Marriage Service"; and the nature of the promises and the seriousness of making them are not nearly so clearly spelled out.[9] The vows are these: "_____ , I promise with God's help to be your faithful husband (wife), to love and serve you as Christ commands, as long as we both shall live." This vow still points to the heart of the matter and makes it binding. But little else in the liturgy articulates exactly what this promise means and involves or assures the seriousness of the parties making the promises. Questions arise about the nature and seriousness of the promises constitutive of the family through what is not said.

There is something quite good about the marriage service in *The Worshipbook*, however, that is not made nearly so evident in the liturgy in *The Book of Common Worship*. It is the way in which it helps put the marriage promises in the context of a set of larger promises. As an "order for the public worship of God," it places marriage not only in the context of prayer but also in the context of confession of sin and the declaration of God's mercy, the reading and hearing of lessons from the Old and New Testaments, and the interpretation of God's Word through preaching. Used rightly, this liturgy makes clear the second dimension of the relationship between family promises and Christian faith, namely, that marriage in the context of Christian faith places promises that are constitutive of family in inseparable relation to wider promises.

Marriage is not the only promissory act of Christian faith, nor the only one celebrated in liturgy. Christian faith is imbued with a promissory structure as a whole. This promissory structure is made especially clear and is enacted anew for each new Christian in the Sacrament of Holy Baptism.

The Sacrament of Holy Baptism, as observed in the most recent official liturgy of the Presbyterian Church (U.S.A.), begins with a series of Scriptural quotations, all announcing the promises of God, and then states:

Obeying the word of our Lord Jesus, and confident of his promises, we baptize those whom God has called.[10]

In response to these promises of God, corresponding human promises are made. For example, an adult candidate for baptism is asked to promise to turn away from the path of sin and toward new life in Christ. In the case of the baptism of a younger child, the child's parents are asked, "Relying on God's grace, do you promise to live the Christian faith, and to teach that faith to your child?" The whole congregation is asked to promise to guide and nurture those baptized "by word and deed, with love and prayer, encouraging them to know and follow Christ and to be faithful members of his church" and to confess its faith by reciting the Apostles' Creed.[11]

What these rubrics make prominent are (1) the promissory nature of the whole set of relationships (including God, the individual, and the wider Christian community) involved in the Christian life; (2) the vocational character of the Christian life as discipleship; and (3) the church as the context for the living out of that vocation.

So it is not just the family that is founded on promises. The Christian faith as a whole is. Promise making runs straight through the Judeo-Christian tradition from beginning to end. Israel came into existence on the basis of God's covenants with (God's promises to) Israel. And Christians are understood as the people of the new covenant, the people of God's new promises, made known in the life, death, and resurrection of Jesus Christ. Christian faith is belief in and trust of those promises and the God who makes them, and it is our response to those promises with corresponding promises of our own, to God and to each other.

What God promises is, most simply put, our redemption and the redemption of the world. The apostle Paul describes the whole world as "groaning in travail" (Rom. 8:22; RSV). We live in a world shot through with patterns and powers of destruction, and we participate in them ourselves. Afraid of one another, we fight with one another or flee one another's presence. Afraid of ourselves, we deceive ourselves and make ourselves out to be both more and less than we actually are. Afraid of death, we try to secure ourselves—either with the use of force or, more subtly, through competitiveness, callousness, forgetfulness, selfishness, self-protectiveness, deceitfulness, depersonalization, manipulation, and ridicule. Afraid of God, we summon our powers against God or try to ignore God. And we seem to have no power of our own to keep ourselves from living in this way—in our families, in our work life, with our friends and colleagues, and, all the more, with our enemies. As much as we would do and be otherwise, we cannot. Sooner or later, in one way or another, sometimes not even knowing that this is what we are doing, we cry out. We want to be saved from this way of living. We want, because we need, redemption.

And behold, this is what God has promised. This is what God gives. Another way has opened up and is possible. We are given the gift of salvation and are called to participate in the redemptive and transforming way of life that God makes possible for us. We are promised new life. The response of faith is the response that believes and accepts God's promises and in turn promises simply to participate in that new way of life. This is the Christian vocation, the vocation of discipleship. The most basic promise made in the baptismal liturgies is the promise to be a disciple: "Do you intend (your child) to be [Christ's] disciple, to obey his word and show his love?" To be a disciple means nothing other than to be one who follows Jesus into the new life—the new way of life—that God promises and makes possible through him.

The connection between the family promises and the baptismal promises is that the promises we make as family are a distinctive set of promises through which we live out, in part, our promise to be disciples. As Christians, we are to be family in the mode of discipleship. We are to be family in the context of following Jesus Christ into new life. That is what we promise when we follow the path of being baptized and being family in the church.

The way in which this connection in some ways intensifies and transforms the family promises may not be obvious. The Christian vocation of discipleship means that we live our lives in a peculiar way. It is a way characterized by confession of sin and repentance to God, together with confession to and repentance in relation to one another; by the recognition of God's grace and forgiveness and reconciliation with one another; by prayers of thanksgiving and praise and intercession to God, which involve giving thanks and praise for one another under all circumstances as well as intercession for one another; and by being servants of God in the world, which includes serving one another in the family and serving the world together as family. All these disciplines of the Christian life are very difficult. And in some ways, they make family life more difficult. They place responsibilities on us as families and as individuals in our families that, outside the context of Christian faith, we would not see or take on. They make us more vulnerable and require us to take risks, face conflicts, and endure sufferings—both within our families and as families—that we would otherwise ignore, flee, or never encounter. They also, however, bear the fruit and bring the joy of the Christian life and allow the family to participate in that.

Even when, because of our finitude, our sin, or some tragedy, our family promise making fails or comes to some end, our discipleship promises do not. When we divorce, for example, and we no longer make family promises to the one who had been our spouse, our discipleship promises to God in relation to our former husband or wife do not cease. We may not be called and committed any longer to marriage, but we are still called to a life of confession, repentance, forgiveness, reconciliation, prayer, and service with and in relation to that person. This holds not only when there are still children to be cared for but even when there are not. We may no longer love a person as husband or wife, but we are still to love each other as children of God and face each other in these terms.

The baptismal promises, as responding promises to the promises of God, open up one further dimension. In the baptismal liturgy, it is made clear that we are not only receiving God's promises and making our own in response. We are also being incorporated into the family of the church. We promise to be faithful members of a particular congregation and to seek the fellowship of the church wherever we may be. We also receive the promise of the people of the church to tell us the good news of the gospel, to help us know all that Christ commands, and to strengthen our family ties with the household of God. Our family promises are thus sustained and supported by being incorporated into the family promises of the household of God.

One implication of seeing the connection between faith and family in these terms is that the particular sociological shape of one's own family now has no primacy. Whether one is married or has never been married or was formerly married; whether one has no children or two children or ten children; whether one has no sisters or brothers or ten, twenty-five cousins or none—this is not terribly significant. What is significant is the nature of our personal discipleship in the context of whatever kind of family we happen to be a part of, as well as the nature of the discipleship of that family as a whole. Our discipleship can be exercised faithfully in any of a multitude of family constellations, and families of very diverse arrangements can themselves be faithful. What becomes normative is not the kind of family situation we are a part of but the way in which our baptismal promises are carried out in relation to whatever family situation we are in.

The second implication is that family promising is no longer merely private. Family promising is no longer something that is just between two or a few persons (the kinship family alone). When family promises are incorporated into our discipleship promises and the family itself is incorporated into the family of the household of God, our family promises and activities become the concern of the whole church. This means the end of any attitude that suggests, "What I and my family do is our business and nobody else's." As Christians together, even though we are not kin, the character and quality of my family promise-making is your business too, just as these matters in your life are my business. We have a responsibility now for one another's family promises—the making and breaking of them, the fulfilling and the nonfulfilling of them. It is a responsibility that requires of us not only mutual concern, care, and support but also mutual instruction and even discipline in these matters. We have now both the freedom and the responsibility to be involved in one another's family life. This, of course, is not sanction for aggressive nosiness or a neurotic preoccupation with one another's situations and problems, and even less for vindictive judging of others. It is, instead, a call for the gracious and appropriate mutual pastoral care of one another—both individually and corporately—in families and as families. The idea that we have such freedom and responsibility is quite different from the common secular assumptions.

CHURCH AND FAMILY

What does this understanding of faith and family mean for the family in relation to the church and the church in relation to the family? It means, in the first place, that we must stop thinking of church and family as two completely separate entities. We do this so often and so easily, usually without really intending to. We speak, for example, of the church's ministry to families, as if the church were a body of people who were not in one way or another participants in families (or even as if the church were an institution without people at all). Or we speak of what families can do in and for the church, as if the church were not made up of people in families.

Rather than seeing families as one thing and the church as another, we must learn to see Christian people as participants simultaneously in the promise-making that constitutes church and in the promise-making that constitutes other covenantal relationships—including the family relationships we have as daughters or sons, sisters or brothers.

The commitment made in partnership is never one in which we can be sure we will be faithful. All relationships entered into by Christians are lived in the threefold tension of the "already, not yet" of the eschaton. We are already partners even before we know one another, because God has reached out to us in Jesus Christ and has reconciled us, making us partners of one another and God. But we are always in the process of becoming partners. And this is very difficult. It involves partnerships where commitments are broken, and persons betrayed, as well as the few relationships where there are signs that partnership might be a possibility. And at the same time we live in the hope that we will become partner, when the provisional signs of koinonia in this life are realized fully in God's promised future. We are all partners, yet we experience not only growth but decline as we search out ways of living now, as if our relationships were those of full partnership.[12]

All our partnerships are weak and remain at least partially unfulfilled—in our families no less than elsewhere. But in their weakness, they are sustained by the promises of God. Further, the partnership of the family may be nurtured, developed, and sustained partly through the promissory relationships with others—within the congregations or in friendship, work, educational, political, or other settings—that individuals in families may have, either on their own or together with spouses, sons, daughters, brothers, or sisters. Our hope, as Christians, is that all our partnerships may ultimately be so interwoven and mutually enlivening that each contributes to the other toward the common aim and task of participation in the redemptive activity of God. This is why the church historically has recommended, for instance, marriage between persons who are both Christian. It can make this all somewhat less difficult. But the church does not prohibit marriage outside the faith, because it recognizes that in such marriage, too, redemptive partnerships can be formed. Our task, in all circumstances of family life, is for all of us to live our family promises as part of our own baptismal promises, participating there, too, as fully as we can in the redemptive activity of God for the sake of the whole world.

When church and family are both understood as partnerships based on the promises of God and on our own corresponding promises, we can see that the roles of church in relation to family are no different from what they are in relation to any other partnership, relationship, or activity. The roles of the church are liturgical, missionary, and educational. The church is people in partnership in the worship of God. In liturgy, God is praised, given thanks, confessed to, heard from, and responded to through our own promise-making and going out to fulfill our promises. In marriage liturgies, we, in partnership with the whole church, make promises in the context of the worship of God. In baptismal liturgies, we—including not only parents or a parent but also aunts and uncles, grandparents and friends, the various members of the particular congregation as sponsors, and, in some traditions, godparents—in partnership with the whole church, make promises for ourselves (and for our children) in the context of the worship of God. In going out to fulfill these promises, we engage in the mission of the church. In partnership with the whole church, we—in congregations, in families, and in local, national, and global arenas of work, education, and politics—go out to carry on the caring, sustaining, and reforming activity that is crucial to participation in the redemptive activity of God. And for the sake of both worship and mission, we educate. We do the work of training and educating ourselves in order that we become able to see, understand, and participate ever more deeply, widely, and powerfully in our worship and mission.

Notes

1. See Edward Farley, *Ecclesial Man: A Social Phenomenology of Faith and Reality* (Philadelphia: Fortress Press, 1975), 95–98, for the discussion of the meaning and nature of marriage on which I am drawing.
2. By defining family in terms of promise-making and by arguing that promise-making is constitutive of all families and family relationships, we do not limit family to the traditional family structure of married parents with children. For example, some families did not begin with marriage, but this does not mean they are not families, since promise-making also occurs there.
3. Ronald M. Green, "Abortion and Promise-Keeping," *Christianity and Crisis* 27 (1967): 110.
4. The whole set of issues concerning whether or not family is constituted promissorily in cases of rape or even when voluntary intercourse involves no intentions toward childbearing is very complicated and cannot be satisfactorily addressed in the scope of this chapter.
5. Interestingly, the *Heidelberg Catechism*, by using the structure of commandment and obedience, confirms the idea of the promise-making of children, at least in relation to their parents, when it says:

> Q. . . . What does God require in the fifth commandment?
> A. That I show honor, love, and faithfulness to my father and mother and to all who are set in authority over me; that I submit myself with respectful obedience to all their careful instruction

and discipline; and that I also bear patiently their failures, since it is God's will to govern by their hand.

[See Office of the General Assembly, "The Heidelberg Catechism," in *The Constitution of the Presbyterian Church (U.S.A.)*, part 1, *Book of Confessions* (New York: Office of the General Assembly, Presbyterian Church (U.S.A.), 1983), 4. 104.]

6. Richard K. Fenn, *Liturgies and Trials: The Secularization of Religious Language* (New York: Pilgrim Press, 1982), xiii.
7. For a complementary view of the relationship between secularization and the undercutting of promise-making, see Robert N. Bellah, Richard Madsen, William M. Sullivan, Ann Swidler, and Stephen M. Tipton *Habits of the Heart: Individualism and Commitment in American Life* (Berkeley: University of California Press, 1985), esp. chaps. 3–5.
8. *The Book of Common Worship* (Philadelphia: Board of Christian Education of the Presbyterian Church in the U.S.A., 1946), 183–88. Subsequent quotations are taken from these pages.
9. *The Worshipbook* (Philadelphia: Westminster Press, 1970), 65–68.
10. *The Book of Common Worship* (Louisville, Ky.: Westminster/John Knox Press, 1993), 404.
11. Ibid., 406
12. Letty M. Russell, *The Future of Partnership* (Philadelphia: Westminster Press, 1979), 545–55.

Chapter 8

Youth and the Language of Faith

In a short story by Flannery O'Connor, two fourteen-year-old girls have taken to calling each other "Temple One" and "Temple Two." Each time they do, they convulse in laughter, "getting so red and hot," as O'Connor describes them, "that they were positively ugly." The source of all this hilarity is a lecture they had recently received at their convent school from the oldest nun, Sister Perpetua, on what to do if a young man should "behave in an ungentlemanly manner with them in the back of an automobile." They were to say: "Stop sir! I am a Temple of the Holy Ghost—and that," according to Sister Perpetua, "would put an end to it."

All this is explained by the two girls, amid renewed torrents of giggling, to a woman to whose home they have been invited for the weekend. On hearing the explanation, the woman, without laughing, responds:

'I think you girls are pretty silly. After all, that's what you are—Temples of the Holy Ghost.'

The two of them looked up at her, politely concealing their giggles, but with astonished faces as if they were beginning to realize that she was made of the same stuff as Sister Perpetua.

The entire episode takes place in the presence of the host's twelve-year-old daughter, who takes it all in, thinking that this is in fact a wonderful idea, one that these girls are just too stupid to grasp: "I am a Temple of the Holy Ghost, she said to herself, and was pleased with the phrase. It made her feel as if somebody had given her a present."[1]

O'Connor's story has to do with religious language, faith, and youth. In the story, an image from the Bible (taken out of context and put to a different purpose, to be sure) is given by a teacher to a group of young girls. The teacher captures that image in the phrase "You are a Temple of the Holy

Ghost," and its use, as it is passed on to others (including a twelve-year-old) through conversation, evokes a variety of images in various minds and a variety of uses in speech in various people and contexts. The images in use result in convulsive laughter in some; in others, a sense that truth has been spoken, even if those who speak it do not realize it; and in still others, a sense of wonder and giftedness that provokes—in relation to other events, as the story goes on to show—a new way of seeing and being.

This story raises questions about why and how and to what effect people use religious language. It raises questions about the place of religious language in everyday discourse and its effects on our ways of understanding ourselves, our experience, and reality as a whole. And for those who are concerned with the lives and faith of adolescents, it raises questions especially about religious language in the mouths and minds of youth. Is it something to celebrate or something to fear, when adolescents make jokes using biblical images? Can the images that religious metaphors and concepts may convey really evoke a sense of wonder and giftedness that leads to a kind of human deepening, even in children as young as twelve? Under what conditions? Is there anything especially powerful and truthful about biblical images and images from a faith tradition that, when gathered into language and used in our speech, forms us particularly well as persons? If so, is it important and good for youth to be exposed to religious language? Are there better ways than others for this to happen? What can we expect of youth in their own use of religious language? Are there different kinds of uses of religious language? If so, how can adolescents be helped to use it well?

RELIGIOUS LANGUAGE AND FAITH

Religious language and faith are on rather intimate terms with each other, though the relationship is complex. But what is the connection? George Lindbeck argues that

> a religion can be viewed as a kind of cultural and/or linguistic framework or medium that shapes the entirety of life and thought. It functions somewhat like a Kantian a priori, although in this case the a priori is a set of skills that could be different. It is not primarily an array of beliefs about the true and the good (though it may involve these), or a symbolism expressive of basic attitudes, feelings, or sentiments (though these will be generated). Rather, it is similar to an

idiom that makes possible the description of realities, the formulation of beliefs, and the experiencing of attitudes, feelings, and sentiments. Like a culture or language, it is a communal phenomenon that shapes the subjectivities of individuals rather than being primarily a manifestation of those subjectivities. It comprises a vocabulary of discursive and nondiscursive symbols together with a distinctive logic or grammar in terms of which this vocabulary can be meaningfully deployed. Lastly, just as a language . . . is correlated with a form of life, and just as a culture has both cognitive and behavioral dimensions, so it is also in the case of a religious tradition. Its doctrines, cosmic stories or myths, and ethical directives are integrally related to the rituals it practices, the sentiments or experiences it evokes, the actions it recommends, and the institutional forms it develops.[2]

Lindbeck's claim is that the connection between religious language and religious faith is so intimate that we can think of religious faith itself as a kind of linguistic structure. But this is a complicated thesis, and it will help to point out and discuss several key elements involved in it.

The first thing to point out is that religious faiths are distinct ways of life. Distinctly different ways to live are available to us as human beings, and different faiths may most fundamentally be understood as different ways of life. Whether or not this is apparent today, the early church certainly thought of Christianity as primarily an alternative way of life. The ancient Didache starts out by saying: "Two Ways there are, one of Life and one of Death, and there is a great difference between the two ways." It then goes on to describe both in rather concrete terms.[3] A look at the catechetical lectures of Cyril of Jerusalem shows the emphasis in his third-century church on putting off an old way of life and taking on and being incorporated into a new one.[4] The particular way of life that Christian faith is has been described somewhat differently in different historical eras and contexts, but the ancient idea has never really been lost. And difficult to articulate and explain as it may now be, faith understood as a way of life always seems to involve the fashioning of distinctive emotions; of distinctive habits, practices, and virtues; of distinctive purposes, desires, passions, and commitments; and of distinctive beliefs and ways of thinking.[5]

Christian faith is, of course, not the only example of this. The same is true of other religious faiths. To say that religious faiths are ways of life is not to say that there is only one. Rather, it is to say the opposite. Nor does it necessarily imply that one is better or more adequate than all others—though some faiths may well claim that. Even then, however, the claim that each is distinctive does not entail that these ways of life have nothing in common or nothing to learn from one another. Nor does it imply that every way of life is necessarily religious. There are ways of life that are not. And it may be possible, as well, to live lives that are so chaotic, so lacking in direction and sense, that they can hardly be called a *way* of life at all. We may be able to go on from year to year without living with the coherence and integrity that is implied in the word *way*. The point here is not to make judgments about how people live, to evaluate the various possibilities, or even to discuss how similar to or different from one another various ways of life may be. It is simply to claim that religious faiths are, in a fundamental sense, ways of life, each of which is distinct in some significant manner from alternatives.

Another important point is that a religious faith is always communal and involves a distinctive way of living *together*. Religious faith has to do with the way in which we live our life, and all of us always live our lives in relation to others. Living a way of life means involvement with others in reciprocal relationships that have some pattern and consistency. Living in a way of life with others means that we can come to expect certain things of others who share that way with us, and they of us—some common ways of doing things, some common understandings, some common hopes and desires, some common obligations and responsibilities, and involvement in some corporate activities that are done together.

More is involved, however, than just common life. The communal character of religious faith also affects who we, as individual persons, become. We do not become involved in and take on communal religious life without changing. We cannot live it without becoming, in some ways, different people ourselves. People tend to take on as features of their own identities the values, beliefs, patterns of activity, and ways of seeing of their primary social groups. The norms and roles of our religious community's life together are incorporated into our own selves through processes of imitation and identification. This insight is widely accepted and commonly articulated in religious education literature under the rubric of *socialization* or *enculturation*.

Common expectations of one another and the socialization of persons into community are crucial dimensions of religious faith. But there is a dimension even more significant that both underlies and gives vitality and dynamism to these other features of religious community. That has to do with how these features correlate (and do not correlate) with the ultimate reality toward which the community moves and to which it most fundamentally attends. Faith is religious faith only insofar as it apprehends and has to do with God. And a religious community is religious only insofar as all its common expectations and processes of socialization are governed by and continually altered by apprehensions of and dealings with God. This is what gives religious faith as a way of life its real distinctiveness: the God it knows and strives to respond faithfully to.

In light of all we have said about faith being a distinctive communal form of life based in a relationship with a reality that transcends it, it is apparent that religious language is absolutely indispensable. Religious faith as a way of life is borne, necessarily, by language, and each distinct way of life necessarily has a language of its own.

The first reason that religious language is indispensable has to do with the common, mutual expectations that people living a particular way of life have of one another. People signal to one another through language what they are doing and why. To carry out their ordinary, everyday, face-to-face relationships, the members of any community must speak to one another. In a religious community, the people's way of speaking will, in most instances, be no different from the wider culture's common discourse. But occasionally their speech will contain images that, in perhaps very subtle ways, will reveal how their ordinary relationships are embedded in the faith community's distinctive way of life.

An example of this can be found in the transcript of the 1960s trial of the war protesters known as the "Catonsville Nine." At one point the defense attorney asks Daniel Berrigan, one of those on trial, what his intention was in burning the draft files. He responds: "I did not want the children or the grandchildren of the jury or of the judge to be burned with napalm." The judge questions this response. He cannot understand what this means as a literal statement and therefore cannot understand it at all. He does not see that, by answering in this way, Berrigan is signaling a fundamental biblical image that suggests that all children are the children of God and, hence, are related to each of us as our own children. Since the judge does not catch this, however, he queries Berrigan suspiciously: "You say your intention was to save these children, of the jury, of myself, when you burned the records? That is what I heard you say. I ask if you mean that." Berrigan responds: "I mean that. Of course I mean that or I would not say it. The great sinfulness of the modern way is that it renders concrete things abstract. I do not want to talk about Americans in general."[6] Here Berrigan's religious language becomes more explicit. He does not say, "The great mistake . . . "; he says, "The great sinfulness. . . ." There is a huge difference, because the word *sinfulness* places both Berrigan's own actions and the actions of those he protests against before God and in relation to God's will. Those who understand Berrigan's religious language will understand who he is and what he thinks he is doing. Those who do not, will not. Later, Berrigan confirms the centrality of his religious faith to all this when he responds to a question from the defense attorney.

> DEFENSE: Was your action at Catonsville a way of carrying out your religious beliefs?
> BERRIGAN: Of course it was. May I say if my religious belief is not accepted as a substantial part of my action, then the action is eviscerated of all meaning and I should be committed for insanity.[7]

The Berrigan case is perhaps a dramatic example, since it takes place in a famous trial; but the same sorts of references to religious faith as the context and medium for ordinary relations come in more mundane speech. Jews and Christians often give their children biblical names, quite consciously to remind the children, the community, and themselves who they are and what way they are living. Even what seems like purely "secular" speech may be religious language functioning in this way. "I promise" may well mean in some contexts "I covenant" and thereby be related to the whole convenantal structure of a faith tradition and its understanding of and relation to God. And certainly, when Sister Perpetua tells the girls, "You are a Temple of the Holy Ghost," however quaint that may seem, she is signaling to the girls an understanding of who they are that relates them in a complex way to an entire way of life, one that she hopes will be foundational to and presupposed in every ordinary activity they engage in—including those in the backseat of an automobile.

The second reason why a religious language is indispensable to religious faith and community is that such language makes possible historical continuity. It is a factor in the perpetuation of the faith and community over time and across generations. Here we find perhaps the most obvious and visible uses of religious language. It is the religious language we use in liturgy, preaching, education, and explicit religious ethical discourse to retell the stories and ethical mandates of the tradition; to carry out our worship, sacraments, and ordinances; and to measure our decisions as a community against traditional norms. It ranges from Bible stories told in church schools and at seder meals to confessions of faith, hymns, prayers, and benedictions in morning worship.

But this use of language raises the possibility of a great temptation. The community may fall into self-idolatry. When the religious community uses its language simply for self-perpetuation, then God has been captured as the god of the religious cultus and is no longer the God of all of life. And this, in turn, makes the valid use of religious language in everyday life impossible. Insofar as religious language reflects not a pervasive way of life but only the language of an institution or a particular social group within a person's life-world, there arises an impermeable wall between religious language as "church talk" and religious language as a foundation for ordinary discourse. This is the "ghettoization" and ultimate death of religious language. When the life of a religious community has little to do with life as a whole but is only turned in on itself, its language will surely be of little use outside its own provincial boundaries. When, in contrast, the life of a religious community forms a way of living in a people's whole life, then its language—though used within the community and for its own perpetuation—is also useful for the perpetuation of that way of life in the world as a whole.

All this points to the third and most significant purpose of religious language: to help us to see, understand, and participate rightly in reality as a whole. As George Lindbeck puts it: "To become a Christian involves learning the story of Israel and Jesus well enough to interpret and experience oneself and one's world in its terms."[8] Religious faith is a way of living that intends to be in touch with what is true and real. But it implies that to see, understand, and live rightly require living in a particular way. This means that religious language is not just language about "religious things" (i.e., the religious community, its institutions, and traditions) but about the whole of reality made evident and available through the community's faith.

It is important to emphasize that religious language involves not just *what* is said but also *how* things are said. Indeed, "God-talk" can be irreligious, and discourse that contains no obvious reference to "religious" subjects can be religious language of a most important kind. Hubertus Halbfas is extremely helpful on this point when he says:

To talk about God you do not have to use theological terms. The word "God" itself is often unnecessary, and (as so often used) awakens the suspicion that what is being talked about is really a very, very long way away. . . . It is not the "what" that gives human language (religious) "content," but its "how." Some people just speak about children, their house and garden, supper and bed, and yet their discourse is full of faith and hope, thanks and prayer. Others, of course, talk in a highly learned, theological manner, using the kind of concepts that would make you think they were on intimate terms with the Holy Trinity. But what does that kind of talk produce? Emptiness, helplessness, and often anger. . . . The "content" of religious discourse is "God," but it is not this word, together with the vocabulary of Church doctrine, that communicates God, but only the life-revealing language of other human beings.[9]

This does not mean that specifically religious terms such as *God* are to be forbidden. Not by any means. Their use is, in many contexts, crucial. But whenever they are used, they must be used in a way that is faithful to the form of life in which they find their essential home.

ADOLESCENT HUNGER FOR THE WHOLE

What does this view of religious language have to do with youth? The issue is a matter not of getting young people to talk "church talk" but of helping them find a way to speak and images to speak with that make religious language, as it was for the twelve-year-old in O'Connor's story, a gift.

Adolescents invest significant energies in striving to interpret themselves and their world in coherent, meaningful, workable, and personally satisfying ways. We do not have to promote this; it goes on quite naturally. They are involved in a search for a way of life, and the process is at once social and linguistic. If Erik Erikson is right that a central dynamic of adolescence is the development of a sense of identity, the significance of language—and hence, potentially, of religious language—in the lives of youth becomes apparent. Erikson describes the process through which this takes place in the following way:

Identity formation employs a process of simultaneous reflection and observation, a process taking place on all levels of mental functioning, by which the individual judges himself in the light of what he perceives to be the way in which others judge him in comparison to themselves and to a typology significant to them; while he judges their way of judging him in the light of how he perceives himself in comparison to them and to types that have become relevant to him.[10]

This process is a "hermeneutical endeavor." Our responses to others are responses to interpreted actions. This is not unique to adolescents; but what arises at adolescence is at least the beginning of a sense of personal responsibility for interpretation. The identity crisis is a crisis of interpretation.

Moreover, adolescence is a time of disorientation and conflict for some young people in our culture, partly because so many diverse patterns of interpretation are available. There are many competing subcultures, each offering a more or less different pattern of interpretation. Thus adolescents, according to Erikson, hunger for some larger whole, for a broad, full-orbed pattern of interpretation of the world and of the significance and meaning of the events, circumstances, and interactions that take place in that world. That is the only way in which they can come to interpret coherently, find a place for themselves in a meaningful world, and establish a sense of personal self in that world that is significant and workable.

We come to have a world and find a place for ourselves in it by learning the language, symbols, stories, metaphors, images, rituals, and modes of speech of the community of interpretation that gives us our world. If we do not know the language of a community, we can neither see the world as that community sees it nor become a part of that community ourselves. But when a community's language becomes the language we use, we ourselves become members of that community and increasingly come to see the world and structure our own lives through the lenses of that language.

A major task for adolescents is to find, among the available alternatives, a way of life that they can make their own. The search for such a way is made partly through experimentation. And the test by which adolescents finally make enduring choices is whether or not one (or more) of the patterns helps them make sense of themselves and the world. Of course, enduring choices often are not made during adolescence but only later. Still, the questions appear: Does this way of life help me understand the experiences I am having? Does it put me into relationships that are satisfying to me as a person? Does it help me see things the way they are, or does it lead me down blind alleys that are personally destructive? Does it enable me to make use of my talents and gifts? Does it place me in a context that promises to support and sustain me over the long haul? Does it make possible for me experiences that seem worth having?

This may convey a greater sense of freedom to choose and a greater degree of conscious evaluation than is actually the case for adolescents, especially younger ones. For many, the experimentation may better be described as a form of play. When the girls in O'Connor's story arrived for their visit from the convent school,

> they came in the brown convent uniforms they had to wear at Mount St. Scholastica but as soon as they opened their suitcases, they took off the uniforms and put on red skirts and loud blouses. They put on lipstick and their Sunday shoes and walked around in the high heels all over the house, always passing the long mirror in the hall slowly to get a look at their legs.[11]

The giggling about being Temple One and Temple Two is all part of this play and testing. They are finding out who they are and in what form of life they belong. And they know there are alternatives to be tried out. Indeed, play with religious language may very well be an important part of the process for those who have been exposed to it in some significant way.

ADOLESCENTS AND RELIGIOUS COMMUNITY

As important as religious language is in religious faith and, at least potentially, in the lives of adolescents, we really know very little about adolescents' actual use of it, especially in everyday discourse. To know, for example, that "eighty-six percent of all young adolescents in this study are quite sure or sure that God exists, and 87 percent affirm the central axiom of the Christian tradition—that Jesus dies and was resurrected"[12] does not tell us much. It tells us only that the young adolescents surveyed have, somewhere in their experience, encountered the claims that God exists and that Jesus died and was resurrected and that they, for some reason or another, agree with the statements.

Discerning something as subtle and elusive as an adolescent's everyday use of religious language requires observation and participation in conversation with youth by persons who are both sensitive to religious language and to young people's struggles to live in reality meaningfully. Those most likely to discern its presence or absence will probably be discerning parents, teachers, pastors, and friends who themselves use religious language authentically and participate in the form of life from which it comes. Only rarely will a social scientist conducting a formal study be able to see this.

Some studies, however, do provide clues about the meaningfulness of religious traditions, practices, concepts, and imagery to adolescents. Years ago, Merton Strommen found that when asked, "Over all, how important is religion in your life?" 80 percent of mothers and 67 percent of fathers of the church youth who were studied "affirmed that 'it is the most' or at least 'one of the most important influences in my life.'"[13] A majority of the youth (between 60 percent and 46 percent; it varied with age and sex, decreasing from the fifth to the ninth grade) responded likewise.[14] But as Strommen pointed out, there is an enigma:

> Though religion is identified as important by both parents and adolescents, it is almost a taboo subject in the home. When asked, "How often does your family sit down together and talk about God, the Bible . . . or other religious things?" 42 percent of the young adolescents say this never happens; 32 percent say this topic is discussed once or twice a month; 13 percent say it is discussed once a week. And this, it must be noted, is the finding from a survey of largely church connected families, of whom 97 percent are members of a church.[15]

Strommen's question does not get at the more nuanced understanding of religious language. Nevertheless, the responses probably suggest that few adolescents include much religious "content" (in Halbfas's sense or any other) of any quality in their daily discourse. Many of Strommen's respondents (both parents and youth) expressed a desire and a sense that such discussions would be a good thing. But it may be safe to assume that the reason such conversations do not take place is that they so often seem artificial, abstracted from life, and a matter more of duty than anything else.

RELIGIOUS LANGUAGE AS POETRY

If a religious community cares at all about helping young people establish a sense of identity that is coherent, meaningful, workable, and satisfying, then it must help young people to learn its language and see how it affects the life experiences they have. Unless a religious community's language of faith is actually used with adolescents and taught to them, and unless they can be helped to find a way to make it their own more or less natural language for describing and understanding their life experiences, there is no way young people can participate more fully in the community of faith, and no way they can establish a sense of identity that provides the resources for the way of life available through it.

Why, then, do we so often fail to teach young people this language and use it with them? I suggest two possible alternatives. The first is that we ourselves, as parents, friends, teachers, and pastors of youth, do not really know and use the language of faith in any meaningful way. The second is that far too much of the language that we think of as religious language is either so abstract and lifeless or so authoritarian and moralistic in character that it either is simply useless in daily discourse or is something rightly to be avoided.

It is not enough to bewail biblical illiteracy and theological amnesia. There must be reasons for our lack of knowledge and facility with the language of faith that go beyond sheer laziness or lack of will. Could it be that we do not know our faith's language because we simply do not live the form of life out of which such language grows? Perhaps our form of life is, in reality, so fully governed by another language that religious language is simply quaint and irrelevant. If this is the case, we can do nothing to offer meaningful religious language to young people. No new curriculum, no new educational techniques, no new ways of forming groups will remedy the situation. What will be required is a kind of conversion on our parts, one that requires a good deal more than language.

This is the darkest view. A more hopeful view, and one I have been claiming is more true to our situation, is that we do, in fact, hunger for this language. Often enough we also find it immensely useful when we hear it and use it ourselves. But we are unsure about it because we too often have confused it with its counterfeits. Halbfas, in a blazing critique of the curriculum materials and books usually used in the churches and in schools, says that

> most of our religion books . . . are deficient. They still offer concepts and formulas, and try to fix the universal principles of being, of morality, of belief, in a system and in laws, and thus to arrest the never-ending multiplicity of historical phenomena. They offer "doctrine," that is, abstract insight which cuts out all the multitudinous paths and circuitous particularities of human experience, and provides the child with ultimate goals that cannot possibly affect him because they are deprived of the versatility, hazard, and truth of debate and encounter.[16]

The same could be said, I venture, for a great many of the sermons, lectures, and discussions that people hear and participate in.

Religious language is, at its heart, the language of poetry and story. This, perhaps, is why singing in a church choir is for many young people their most important and profoundly affecting introduction to religious language. When the music is good, the poetry remains alive and touches the heart. Furthermore, it is religious language that they can utter without embarrassment, in a kind of indirect communication of their own faith. When, however, the only religious language we hear and read lacks these qualities, it is no wonder that we find it useless and even embarrassing.

Religious language can be perverted into "theologizing" and "moralizing." This ultimately bores us. But it is also perverted when it is turned into a tool for creating artificial boundaries between and antagonisms toward people who are in some way "different from us." When religious images and terms are used to stir racial hatred and create outcasts, sensitive people become wary of almost any use of religious language, and rightly so. Religious groups often have and still do use language involving religious references in order to circumscribe a world in which "God" is identified with the ideology of a limited and hostile social group that compels unthinking obedience. In such cases, good and evil are so sharply defined and so sharply separated that a "we/they" mentality is developed, in which one's own position is fortressed and those in alternative positions are made into enemies. Our society is full of such groups, and so is the church's history. It is not just a secular, tolerant society that rejects and fears such groups and the language they use. Religious communities do and should as well. Nevertheless, if this is what a religious language does and means for a person, and no meaningful alternative comes into view, obviously religious language will be of no interest.

THE CARE AND EDUCATION OF YOUTH

The care and education of youth (as well as the well-being of our society) demands, then, the recovery of a lively, vital, usable religious language. This is not simply a task for youth leaders, teachers, and ministers with youth. It is a task for the whole religious community. But those in the religious community who have most to do with youth are in a position to work on this problem. The way will not be found by academic theologians. It will be found by theologians in practice, who, in regular and real conversation with youth, find ways of using religious language to help them interpret their lives and live them more fully.

This is a very difficult task. It involves the recovery of language that is clear enough to be comprehended by young people, rich enough to be meaningful, concrete enough to relate to the world as it is, and critical enough to keep open the dynamics of inquiry and continuing conversation. Moreover, it involves providing help in—teaching of, even—the art of interpretation.

Groups that use religious language rigidly and in an authoritarian manner have a seeming advantage. They are able to use "religious" language concretely and clearly (in one sense) because they are satisfied with literalistic and univocal religious understandings. The task of nonauthoritarian religious communities is to find ways to use religious language that are at once concrete and clear but not literalistic. It must be a language like that of poets and artists, using the concrete to open up dimensions of transcendence, depth, and mystery. The "classic" texts of religious traditions are usually texts that themselves have these qualities,[17] but for far too long we have kept our young people from reading and interpreting them, often because we have failed to study them and use them ourselves. If we are to recover the constructive power of religious language, we will have to make these texts available to our young people in new and compelling ways. If we do, we will find there not only concreteness and clarity but also inexhaustible richness and critical dynamism.

The appropriation of a language does not happen just from hearing it. It happens through understanding it and speaking it. This usually requires some teaching—not necessarily formal but certainly quite intentional. More is involved, however, than just introducing young people to the texts, words, concepts, metaphors, and images, important as this is. New vocabulary and new grammar need to be used by young people themselves, employed by them in such a way that the new language increasingly involves them in a faith's way of living. The way of living deepens the understanding of the language, while a deepening understanding of the language enables new levels of participation in the way of living. Language and action cannot be separated. Thus an exploration of religious language must take place in the context of experiences in the way of life to which it is appropriate, and always venturing out into new experiences of it.

This all takes time and effort. If new language is to be learned, it cannot come all at once or just at random. It must be thought about, talked about, spoken, written, acted on with real thoroughness—and all in relation to a young person's own experience in life. Clearly here, everything depends on having someone to talk with. Young people cannot make religious language their own unless the religious community as a whole uses religious language as its own, and unless particular adults who love and care for particular young people engage in conversation with them.

Under conditions such as these, young people can be given the gift of the language of faith. It may then feel to them as if they have been given a present.

Notes

1. See Flannery O'Connor, "A Temple of the Holy Ghost," in *The Complete Stories* (New York: Farrar, Straus & Giroux, 1979), 236–48. This part of the story and these quotations are found on 236–38.
2. George Lindbeck, *The Nature of Doctrine* (Philadelphia: Westminster Press, 1984), 33.
3. *The Didache*, vol. 6 of Ancient Christian Writers, trans. J. A. Kleist (Westminster, Md.: Newman Press, 1948), 15.
4. William Teller, ed., *Cyril of Jerusalem and Nemesis of Emesa*, Library of Christian Classics, vol. 4 (Philadelphia: Westminster Press, 1955), esp. 64–68.
5. See Paul L. Holmer, *Making Christian Sense* (Philadelphia: Westminster Press, 1984). See also Edward Farley, *Ecclesial Man: A Social Phenomenology of Faith and Reality* (Philadelphia: Fortress Press, 1975), especially chap. 6, for a phenomenological description of Christian faith as a distinctive way of life, which Farley calls "redemptive existence," that I find both illuminating and persuasive.
6. All the quotations in this paragraph are from Daniel Berrigan, *The Trial of the Catonsville Nine* (1970), quoted in Richard K. Fenn, *Liturgies and Trials: The Secularization of Religious Language* (New York: Pilgrim 1982), 187.
7. Ibid.
8. Lindbeck, *Nature of Doctrine*, 34.
9. Hubertus Halbfas, *Theory of Catechetics: Language and Experience in Religious Education* (New York: Herder & Herder, 1971), 136–37. Note, for example, the responses of Daniel Berrigan quoted above (pp. 117–18). In the first response, no explicit "religious" vocabulary was used at all. But the way in which Berrigan used ordinary terms both caused confusion in the judge (who knew, implicitly, that something out of the ordinary was being said here but could not understand it) and communicates religiously to those who know the form of life Berrigan is speaking from.

10. Erik Erikson, *Identity: Youth and Crisis* (New York: W. W. Norton & Co., 1968), 22–23.

11. O'Connor, "Temple of the Holy Ghost," 236.

12. *Young Adolescents and Their Parents: Summary of Findings* (Minneapolis: Search Institute, 1984), 20.

13. Merton P. Strommen and A. Irene-Strommen, *Five Cries of Parents* (San Francisco: Harper & Row, 1985), 131.

14. See ibid., 133.

15. Ibid., 133–34.

16. Halbfas, *Theory of Catechetics*, 151.

17. See David Tracy, *The Analogical Imagination* (New York: Crossroad, 1981), for a helpful discussion of the nature of a religious "classic."

Chapter 9

Communities of Conviction in Religion and Higher Education

Contemporary interest in moral and character formation in the context of higher education waxes and wanes. Currently, it seems to be on the rise again. Higher education in the United States has been shaped by a historical commitment to moral education, arising largely from the intense moral seriousness of the religious traditions that played a major role in developing American higher education in the first place. That historical commitment may still be strong in many quarters, but the field of play has changed significantly. Robert Morrill, in his fine book, *Teaching Values in College*, pointed out in the early 1980s that

> the autonomy and professionalization of the disciplines, the increasing hegemony and prestige of value-free scientific methodology as a model for all inquiry, and the secularization and pluralism of both our society and the university have established a new educational context. This is a strange and foreign world for moral education. In the academic community, there is little confidence about what can be known in the moral realm, and even less about why, how, and to whom it should be taught.[1]

This is still an accurate portrait; it shows the terrain to be treacherous. These are mighty forces to be dealing with, and any reemerging commitment to moral formation must deal with them.

Nonetheless, interest in moral formation in the context of higher education is growing. What might be responsible for this resurgence? Perhaps it has something to do with the disarray of contemporary liberal arts education—and an accompanying sense of having lost something precious. I am referring to disciplines (especially in the humanities and social sciences) that seem more interested in their own logic and methods than with the realities they are ostensibly designed to explore. I am referring to a series of calls for relevance—personal, social, and occupational—to which liberal education has seemed to some incapable of responding. I am referring to an overall sense of fragmentation in thought and work, of a narrowing of interests, and of removal from intimate "contact with the dilemmas of human experience and [silence] about critical questions of personal and social choice."[2] Those who work and study in the world of higher education feel this disarray, whether they articulate it or not. Many of them are searching for a way to integrate the scattered bits and pieces and find some perspective on the whole. Perhaps moral formation could provide such a path.

Our society and the world in general also are experiencing disarray. Ours is an era of critical issues and tough choices, some of them ultimate in nature. We sense that our inherited values and present character provide us neither the vision nor the courage to deal with them. The result is moral uncertainty and confusion, both standing in the shadow of a temptation to hopelessness. Our survival as a people, we sense, depends on an ethical revitalization—and as a people, we still expect our colleges and universities to play a crucial role.

Whatever the reasons, a renewed interest in moral education is being experienced even while the terrain is difficult to negotiate.

RELIGIOUS COMMUNITIES AND HIGHER EDUCATION

In chapter 1, I noted an *Atlantic Monthly* article by University of Massachusetts political scientist Glenn Tinder that asks, "Can We Be Good without God?"[3] Tinder gives an unabashedly Christian theological reading of our sociopolitical situation. He develops the political implications of such concepts and doctrines as Christian love, the love of God for persons, providence, fallenness and sin, Christology, and Christian love, arguing that together these make profound descriptive sense of our contemporary situation, accounting for our ideologies and ambiguities at the same time that they show us a way forward at once radical and hesitant, realistic and hopeful.

The very appearance of the article in a secular publication such as the *Atlantic Monthly* is of interest. Equally fascinating is the kind of offensive taken here on the secular foundations of modern liberal political thought. The notion that politics is secular activity, that it is best described and thought of on the basis of the secular assumptions of the Enlightenment, and that we can live best as a people only by adopting a secular mentality upheld by secular institutions are assumptions brought under intense scrutiny. As Tinder puts it:

> Politics is properly spiritual. The spirituality of politics was affirmed by Plato at the very beginnings of Western political philosophy and was a common-place of medieval political thought. Only in modern times has it come to be taken for granted that politics is entirely secular. The inevitable result is the demoralization of politics. Politics loses its moral structure and purpose, and turns into an affair of group interest and personal ambition. . . . Politics ceases to be understood as a preeminently human activity and is left to those who find it profitable, pleasurable, or in some other way useful to themselves. Political action thus comes to be carried out purely for the sake of power and privilege.[4]

The question can be asked whether this description of the demoralization of politics is not also apt regarding higher education—which is, of course, among any society's central political institutions. Is higher education demoralized in much the same way as is the larger political context? Is higher education losing "its moral structure and purpose," turning into "an affair of group interest and personal ambition"?

Some commentators argue that indeed this is the case. Among the most vocal on this point is Christian ethicist Stanley Hauerwas, who wrote the essay "How Christian Universities Contribute to the Corruption of Youth." In Hauerwas's view, colleges and universities, even religious ones (and among them, especially so-called Christian ones), contribute to the corruption of youth in several ways. The most significant is that "the university underwrites the assumption that morality is created through individual choice rather than by the shaping of our thorough disciplined discovery of the good."[5] We live in a consumerist culture, and it is therefore no surprise to an ethicist like Hauerwas that the main body of contemporary ethics focuses on the choices individuals make among a panoply of possibilities. Decisionist ethics is the philosophical complement of consumerist market economics, and both are reinforced by a system of higher education that sees its task as to

> convince those who come to it that any of their needs can be met. The university or college must appear to be a gigantic cafeteria. The student comes as a diner filled up by pushing a tray along the line, taking

a salad of math or computer science, potatoes of philosophy . . . a little corn of literature, and finally some meat of the major in business, physics, or history . . . to supply nourishment for their career.[6]

The very language of "values" in higher education, Hauerwas hints, betrays such an assumption.[7] *Value* is a term of economic pedigree. It is the purchase price, the cost, the exchangeability of something. To teach values is to teach something's relative worth on the market.

But is moral life really best conceived through this imagery and the assumptions borne by it? Is morality most fundamentally about making choices? Or is there some alternative way to conceive it? In *Vision and Character*, I tried to make the case that we should understand moral education as having to do with the formation of character, which means most fundamentally to become persons who see deeply into the reality of things and who love that reality—over time and across circumstances.[8]

Such seeing and loving involve the long, hard, patient formation of our desires; struggle with our fears; learning ways of thinking and speaking that disclose what is true and good; participation in traditioned practices— many of which place the self at risk and even in danger—and the shaping and testing of fundamental convictions, all of which take place through profound involvement in some particular community.

Iris Murdoch once wrote that

> there are people whose fundamental moral belief is that we all live in the same empirical and rationally comprehensible world and that morality is the adoption of universal and openly defensible rules of conduct. There are other people whose fundamental belief is that we live in a world whose mystery transcends us and that morality is the exploration of that mystery insofar as it concerns each individual.[9]

I count myself among the latter. Murdoch also said that

> we are not isolated free choosers, monarchs of all we survey, but benighted creatures sunk in a reality whose nature we are constantly and overwhelmingly tempted to deform by fantasy. Our current picture of freedom encourages a dream-like facility; whereas what we require is a renewed sense of the difficulty and complexity of the moral life and the opacity of persons.[10]

In the light of such portraits of the human creature and the human condition, values are thin reeds. What moral formation requires is something much more profound than options—and patterns of thought more capable than critical inquiry alone of fructifying the landscape of the moral imagination. Here, I think, is one important place where we can ask about the significance of religion in the moral life. Religious communities, precisely because they bear within them a long, deep, rich, historical tradition attentive to ultimacy, have the capacity to provide the denser resources required for the formation of character and vision. They are what I describe in the title of this chapter as "communities of conviction."

By "communities of conviction" I mean peoples who are intersubjectively related to one another across time and space by a body of convictions, language patterns, and practices that they hold in common. Such communities must last over time, long enough to have and to be historical dramas. As one becomes a member of such a community, that drama is adopted as one's own. The story of the founding of the community becomes a part of one's own story. Great events that most clearly illuminate the character of the community become events in one's own history. Further, the drama does not belong solely to the past. Current members of the community recognize that they have parts to play in the continuing drama and so form their own lives as to continue its development.

Such communities also carry conviction—fundamental convictions about the nature of reality in its broadest scope. Members of such communities share those convictions. They may argue about how the convictions should be formulated and expressed. Individuals may struggle for years with the meaning of these convictions and their roots in reality, often undergoing periods of profound doubt and intensive criticism. Many may even feel they have rejected these convictions, only to find out later that at some deep level they were being shaped by them all the while. Whether or not one's views clearly conform to such convictions at any particular moment, a person finally leaves such a community only when his or her quest for meaning and truth is no longer framed in their terms.

A community's convictions are borne through languages and practices the community shares. Particularly important here are the key images, metaphors, and symbolic actions that give a community's language and ritual life its particular distinctiveness. In addition are patterns of corporate action—and institutional structures that support and shape them. Communities of conviction are more than linguistic systems. They are patterned processes of social interaction. They act on individuals, and they call forth action from them.

All these elements of communities of conviction have profound effects on their members. They shape what persons believe and how they think. They influence what persons do and how they do it. They shape their members' sense of self and identity. They modify people's very desires and help pattern the feelings they have. They influence what persons pay attention to, what they notice when they do, and what they make of what they see. In sum, communities of conviction are fundamental formative influences on persons' character and vision.

Religious communities of long-standing tradition have the capacity to be communities of conviction. And for many people, they in fact are. Religious communities can and very often do function in all these ways, and they do so with a degree of ultimacy that makes it possible for them to "permeate the total life-world," as Edward Farley once put it—not necessarily in the sense, by the way, of "a world-devouring fanaticism" but in a way that gives unity to every level and dimension of human existence as well as to the mystery beyond its horizons.[11] In this way, they form the contours of human lives and also give them foundation, freeing selves from debilitating anxiety and neurotic fear and providing a context for human access to actuality and truth.

THE UNIVERSITY: A COMMUNITY OF CONVICTION?

Reflections such as these obviously carry complicated presuppositions and demand careful argument. But suppose we accept for the moment several of the claims I have made or implied thus far. Suppose we accept: (1) that we live in a culture—which includes a politics and a general pattern of higher education—that is increasingly demoralized, partly, at least, as a result of the rationalistic, secular assumptions on which pervasive beliefs, structures, and practices in our society are based; (2) that moral formation may involve some significant degree of participation in the ways of thinking and in the practices of some living "community of conviction," in the context of which alternative ways of being and seeing are formed; (3) that such communities actually exist and in some flawed but still potent ways do form people in ways that give us some freedom from neurotic fears and egocentric compulsions to control and distort, and that they thus can help us develop the capacity to love reality itself; and (4) that such communities are likely to be religious in nature. All of this is debatable, of course; but suppose for the moment we accept it. What, then, might we say about moral formation in higher education, about moral formation and the liberal arts?

Much depends on what one understands the relationship of such communities of conviction to institutions of higher education to be. Hauerwas, for one, would regard all secular institutions of higher education to be intrinsically antagonistic to such communities. Even Christian higher education is, in his view, largely corrupting, since secular assumptions govern the structure of the curriculum, contemporary methods of inquiry, and virtually every other important dimension of the educational environment and process. For Hauerwas:

> The university is the place where we should train those with the wisdom to help us all know what is best about us. Such training comes by the discipline of confronting texts and figures of the past and present to continue the discussions of our forebears. For the university is the way a community insists that its forebears have not lived (or died) in vain.[12]

But if a school were to understand itself this way, the content of its very discourse would be different from that which prevails in the larger culture. It would involve challenging "reigning intellectual paradigms in the study of religion and in other disciplines." It would mean "that what is taught as history or psychology or sociology at such schools might be different."[13] In Hauerwas's view, such work has hardly begun.

Hauerwas may be overly pessimistic, however. Perhaps the relationships between religious communities of conviction and contemporary higher education are not nearly so antagonistic as he portrays. In his eloquent 1987 Ryerson Lecture at the University of Chicago, Wayne Booth opened up another possibility. Booth recognizes many of the dis-integrating features of university life that Hauerwas points to. He describes, for example, the enormous difficulty faculty have in simply understanding one another's work. He tells of asking a number of his colleagues, "Could you, given a week's warning, read an article or book in a given field and then enter into a serious dialogue with the author, at a level of understanding that the author would take as roughly comparable to his or her own?"[14] The response, according to Booth, was that all confessed for the most part they could not— not only across disciplines but even within their own departments. In the university, according to Booth, where dealing with the front lines of each other's knowledge, the faculty members barely speak the same language.

But, says Booth, such specialist languages are only one kind of rhetoric prominent on the university landscape. Despite the fact that, in one sense,

nobody knows what the other is saying profoundly enough to test particular scholarly judgments with great accuracy, scholars still know how to
test one another's judgments relatively fairly. They do this through another rhetoric. Specialist languages are rhetoric of suspicion and critical inquiry, dependent on refined jargons relatively inaccessible to any not
intimately involved in the particular inquiry. But much of the rest of the
life of the university—hiring and promoting faculty, admitting students,
giving prizes, conducting daily business—depends on other rhetorics,
which have other grounds. As Booth puts it:

> We depend upon appraising the testimony and authority and general
> ethos of other people as they appraise the testimony and authority of
> still others, who in turn depend on others . . . and no one can say
> where these circles of mutual trust end, except, of course, when soci-
> eties and universities destroy themselves by losing the arts of deter-
> mining when trust is justified. . . . As Polanyi puts it, we are all
> inherently "convivial," . . . [we] live . . . even as specialists, in "fidu-
> ciary" structures that we have not constructed and could never con-
> struct on our own.[15]

This description of the university includes key elements of what I have
called a "community of conviction." Might it be that even secular universities are not so thoroughly fragmented as they might seem? Might critics of
the university such as Hauerwas be focusing too much on surface features of
university life and thus missing the more latent but nonetheless still powerful constellation of common practices that sustain the university as a community of conviction itself? And might not these latent features have the
power to form participants in the university in ways that are morally quite
good, ways that other communities of conviction might celebrate? Could it
be the case that many colleges and universities are forming both students
and faculty through such practices in ways that are sometimes more satisfying and powerful than those that religious communities of conviction have
been able to accomplish? Such possibilities should, I think, be entertained.

DESCRIBING THE REALITY
OF HIGHER EDUCATION

Religious communities are not nearly so successful in the formation of
vision and character as many of us might hope. Nor, I think, are universities intrinsically so corrupting as they are sometimes accused of being. The

two kinds of communities of conviction might, in fact, share more in common than first seems evident. Among the convictions central to some religious communities is that all fall short of the glory of God and are deeply in need of forgiveness and grace. At the same time, the spiritual foundation of intellectual inquiry may not ultimately be hubris, but humility in the face of realities that do not finally submit to our fantasies and manipulations. These are complementary convictions, and that fact suggests a way in which religious communities and colleges and universities, even secular ones, might fruitfully understand and relate to one another—namely, by searching out as many complementarities as possible and by working to redeem one another where sins are being committed.

The end of that last sentence is, I know, a religious recommendation. It is the kind of thing a Christian might say about what both religious communities and colleges and universities might, even ought to, do. And the fact that it is a religious recommendation points to one of the ways in which I think religious communities ought to live in complementarity to higher education. They ought to use their own language to describe the reality of higher education they see before them. Through such description, religious communities can be of service to colleges and universities and help them be better formers of character and vision.

Such description is open for debate, of course—not only between religious communities and higher education communities but also among religious speakers (many of whom are, of course, in colleges and universities). Stanley Hauerwas, for example, employs religious language as a tool of criticism. Not all would agree that his descriptions are full enough or nuanced enough. And he might be flat wrong at a number of points. Nonetheless, his way of describing what is going on in the university and college provokes inquiry and insight wherever it is not simply dismissed.

Parker Palmer, to take another example, also brings religious language to bear on higher education.[16] Russell Edgerton, president of the American Association of Higher Education, says about Palmer's contribution that "he's on to something people have felt but have not been able to articulate."[17] Are there realities that religious language is somehow especially well equipped to articulate? If so, there is wisdom in employing it to say what otherwise might not be said at all.

For academic communities to be able to take advantage of such possibilities, they must recognize and validate other sources of insight and wisdom than those that now predominate in the university. That such sources are *worthy of study* often seems easier to recognize in the university than that they might be *valuable to employ.* Is prayer a way of knowing that a university can possibly consider?

Perhaps the hesitation about other ways of knowing comes from the high valuation placed on criticism and analysis in academic culture. One often gets the sense that academicians regard themselves as the inventors and sole proprietors of critical analysis. But they should not forget that religious communities, too, have powerful internal critical capacities. What else is prophecy, for example? And who is more often the object of that criticism than the religious community itself? Critical inquiry was not invented with the Enlightenment. Nor, for that matter, were tolerance and openness. Every major religious tradition has found ways to deal with pluralism, and often with great staying power. Powerful intellectual and practical resources—not always employed, to be sure—are available in these traditions for sustaining hospitality to the stranger and even love of the enemy.

At the same time, no pathology is so potent as religious pathology, and no fantasies so distorting and disfiguring as those that covet and claim for themselves the benediction of God. Pathological religion always fears unencumbered search for truth. In relation to such pathologies, colleges and universities have often played crucial, critical, and healing roles. The arts and sciences of our colleges and universities have not perfected searching for truth, but they do provide remarkably fertile contexts for such endeavor.

FORMING CHARACTER AND VISION

In an essay that has been a part of my own mental equipment since the day I first read it, Simone Weil sets down her "Reflections on the Right Use of School Studies with a View to the Love of God." She says that if two conditions are met, "there is no doubt that school studies are quite as good as a road to sanctity as any other."[18] The two conditions are these: first, "when we set out to do a piece of work, it is necessary to wish to do it correctly."[19] "Students must therefore work without any wish to gain good marks, to pass examinations, to win school successes."[20] "The second condition is to take great pains to examine squarely and to contemplate attentively and slowly each school task in which we have failed, seeing how unpleasing and second rate it is, without seeking any excuse or overlooking any mistake . . . trying to get down to the origin of each fault."[21] If we can do these things, says Weil, we have become people capable of paying attention, which itself is the substance of prayer, which in turn is the substance of love.

Now, it is obvious that not every college or university student accomplishes such attention. And no one is able to keep it up continually. But I believe that it may happen more often in college and university studies than anywhere else in our society. For some people, that is the only place it happens—the only place it is taught and encouraged.

Hauerwas once wrote that the church does not *have* a social ethic but rather *is* a social ethic.[22] Maybe he was right. But if so, it is equally and in the same sense true of colleges and universities. Colleges and universities form students morally most thoroughly and most powerfully through the fundamental patterns of inquiry, learning, and teaching that they practice. To the extent that they succeed in guiding students into attention to what is real, they succeed in the formation of both character and vision.

Higher education does this with resources somewhat different from those of religious communities, and in somewhat different ways. But if the two communities become foes, these differences are not what make them so. Rather, each can helpfully and appropriately take the other to task for its shortcomings and complement the other in the work of moral formation by means of virtues and resources each possesses. Furthermore, religious and academic communities of conviction need not be entirely separate. Each can—and in many cases, does—incorporate certain portions of the other into itself. Moral education and formation is difficult enough and requires what both at their best have to give.

Notes

1. Robert Morrill, *Teaching Values in College* (San Francisco: Jossey-Bass, 1980), 2–3.
2. Ibid., 4.
3. Glenn Tinder, "Can We Be Good without God?" *Atlantic Monthly* 264/12, December 1989, 69–85. See also Tinder's recent book from which this essay is drawn, *The Political Meaning of Christianity* (Baton Rouge: Louisiana State University Press, 1989).
4. Ibid., 69–70
5. Stanley Hauerwas, "How Universities Contribute to the Corruption of Youth," *Katallagete* 9 (summer 1986): 24.
6. Ibid.
7. Ibid.
8. See Craig Dykstra, *Vision and Character* (New York: Paulist Press, 1981).
9. Iris Murdoch, "Vision and Choice in Morality," in *Christian Ethics and*

Contemporary Philosophy, ed. T. Ramsey (New York: Macmillan, 1966), 208.

10. Iris Murdoch, "Against Dryness: A Polemical Sketch," *Encounter* 16 (1961): 20.

11. Edward Farley, *Ecclesial Man: A Social Phenomenology of Faith and Reality* (Philadelphia: Fortress Press, 1975), 102–5.

12. Hauerwas, "How Universities Contribute," 28.

13. Ibid.

14. Wayne C. Booth, "The Idea of a University as Seen by a Rhetorician," *University of Chicago Record*, Vol. 23, No. 1 (October 13, 1988), 2.

15. Ibid., 4.

16. See Parker Palmer, *To Know as We Are Known: Education as a Spiritual Journey* (San Francisco: Harper & Row, 1983) and *The Courage to Teach: Exploring the Inner Landscape of a Teacher's Life* (San Francisco: Jossey-Bass, 1998), for two excellent examples of a religious vision of education that speaks directly to contemporary secular college and university teachers.

17. Quoted in Scott Heller, "'Traveling Teacher' Inspires Professors with Talk of Truth, Love," *Chronicle of Higher Education*, Vol. 36, No. 24 (February 28, 1990): A3.

18. Simone Weil, *Waiting for God*, trans. E. Crawford (New York: Harper & Row, 1973), 109.

19. Ibid., 108.

20. Ibid.

21. Ibid.

22. Stanley Hauerwas, *The Peaceable Kingdom* (Notre Dame, Ind.: University of Notre Dame Press, 1983), 99.

Chapter 10

Love's Knowledge and Theological Education

"Love's knowledge" is a phrase borrowed from Professor Martha Nussbaum of the University of Chicago. It is the title of a book of her essays and of one of the chapters in that volume.[1]

I have borrowed Nussbaum's title partly because the phrase itself has been ringing in my ears as—what shall I say—a true phrase, ever since I first came upon it. The phrase points to a reality that lies at the very heart of theological education—and, indeed, at the heart of Christian faith and life. This unapologetic Presbyterian is reminded immediately by this phrase of the opening sentence of Calvin's *Institutes*, which goes as follows: "Nearly all wisdom we possess, that is to say, true and sound wisdom, consists of two parts: the knowledge of God and of ourselves."[2] And as Calvin's *pietatis summa* goes on to elaborate in great detail, to know God truly is to know God as the magnificent, inexhaustible Love that lies at the heart of everything and as the One who knows us in love by name before we know anything at all. Hence, also, to know ourselves at all rightly is to know ourselves as Love's creatures and heirs. Love's knowledge, then, is, in its most fundamental sense, *God's* knowledge—the knowing that belongs to the One who is love. But insofar as our knowledge conforms at all to God's own love and wisdom, love's knowledge is also *our* knowledge—of God and of God's creation, including ourselves.

That is part of what rings in my ears when I hear the phrase "love's knowledge." And it is part of what makes love's knowledge important for theological education. If theological education is truly theological—in the sense that David Kelsey, for example, has suggested (namely, that it has somehow to do with understanding God truly)[3]—then Love's knowledge is central to theological education. Love's knowledge is both the presupposition for and the fundamental content and substance of theological education. If there is no knowledge of *God*, the educational endeavor we are involved in is not *theological*. If there is no *knowledge* of God, any claims that what we are about is *educational* in any true and rigorous sense is simply false.

Nussbaum does not develop in her book or essay—indeed, she would not share—the Christian theological way of understanding the phrase "love's knowledge" that I have laid out here. But I am indebted to Nussbaum for more than just this mellifluous and evocative combination of words. The main point of her essay—and of much of her philosophical work—is also very important for those of us engaged in theological education to pay attention to. She has a clue for us. For her, the notion of "love's knowledge" suggests "the idea that knowledge might be something other than intellectual grasping—might be an emotional response, or [as she concludes as she develops her argument more fully] even a complex form of life."[4]

Knowledge might be something other than intellectual grasping. It might be a complex form of life. In saying this, Nussbaum is by no means collapsing into anti-intellectualism. She is saying, first, that knowledge cannot be gained through intellectual *grasping*—through the greedy, controlling, manipulative employment of intellectual force, no matter how highly skillful and impressive. Knowledge—or at least, some forms of knowledge—comes rather through intellectual vulnerability and receptiveness. It is received as if it were a gift, rather than grasped as an acquisition. Second, she is saying that knowledge as a complex form of life means that intellectual work finds its place and efficacy only in a larger context. Knowledge cannot be *merely* intellectual. Intelligence cannot "know" apart from feeling and commitment and ways of being that are consistent with what is known.

In a more recent book, *Poetic Justice*, Nussbaum presents a rather thorough critique of what she regards as some overly defensive and rationalistic legal practices and structures that have been emerging in our society in recent decades. She believes that in some influential quarters these practices are being enlarged into a more general way of seeing and being in the world. Her critique of our contemporary system of justice is focused not first on its results but on the way of life and of mind that breeds those results: a "Gradgrind-ish" refusal to regard persons in their fullness, inwardness, and difference; a reduction of them to enumeratable and aggregatable "facts"; and, above all, a studied incapacity to exercise what she calls "seeing-in"—"the great charity in the heart [that] nourishes a generous construal of the world."[5]

There are ways of life, in Nussbaum's view, that are false. It is not just that they are unhealthy or unfulfilling. While perhaps in some ways quite sophisticated, they are, nonetheless, ignorant, unknowing, out of touch with reality and truth. Likewise, some ways of life are ways of real knowing. In describing what she means by "love's knowledge," Nussbaum turns to a short story by Ann Beattie, "Learning to Fall." It is the story of a woman who, once badly hurt in a failed marriage, learns to love again—partly through the friendship of a neighbor, in whose own way of life and love she perceives a knowledge she wants for herself but finds she cannot grasp by grasping. She finds she must come to that knowledge in some other way. She must learn to fall. In her dance class she is learning how to fall bodily, which, "like prayer, it's something done yet, once you do it, fundamentally uncontrolled; no accident, yet a yielding; an aiming, but for grace. You can't aim for grace really. It has so little connection, if any, with your efforts and actions. Yet what else can you do? How else are you supposed to pray? You open yourself to the possibility."[6]

There are ways of life, apparently, that are suffused with love's knowledge. Several years ago a colleague of mine, Sister Jeanne Knoerle, and I had a visit from some people who are involved in an organization in Winston-Salem, North Carolina, called Human Service Alliance. Human Service Alliance is a very unusual organization. It is made up entirely of volunteers. More than two hundred people work together to sustain a hospice for terminally ill "guests," as they call them—twenty-four hours a day, year in and year out. They also run a conflict mediation service, a respite-care program for families with severely retarded children, and a wellness program for the community. All these services are provided at absolutely no cost to those who need them. As they say, "All services are gifts—an expression of love, compassion, good will, charity."[7] And everything that is done is volunteered. There are no paid staff—none. Some of the volunteers work only for a few hours per week or per month. Some volunteer several days or more each week. And some people move to Winston-Salem for a year or more, just so they can volunteer a portion of their lives caring for the dying, the retarded, the conflicted, and the sick and their families. The fact that these folks are all volunteers does not mean they are not skilled. In fact, they are highly skilled people—some doctors, some counselors, some just good organizers, and so forth. Nor does it mean that the services they provide are second-rate. Indeed, they are services of extraordinary quality.

Neither the quality of the services nor the unusual fact that this is an organization run without regard to personal compensation is, in and of itself, why I am talking here about Human Service Alliance. Rather, it is that these people believe the quality of their efforts is part and parcel of a distinctive way of knowing that they are experiencing, which they believe comes directly from the fact that their service is all a gift. They are discovering, they say, that in and through their practices of hospitality and healing, through their relentless focus on the care of others freely given, they come to *know* things they never knew before. They know the people they care for, and in a way that seems to them qualitatively different from anything they had experienced before. The doctors say this. They say that in this place they know the people as persons—they even, in some respects, know their illnesses—in ways their medical training never made possible (had even, perhaps, prohibited). They know each other, their fellow volunteers, in ways they find quite remarkable. They know how to get things done together. And they are astonished that it all seems to happen so easily. Their board meetings, they say, don't last very long; sometimes ten or fifteen minutes is all they need. When all is a gift—given and received— and when the gift is service to people in real need, a lot of problems get solved just in the course of things. They know death, intimately. They spend time with death in the most personal ways, almost every day. And, astonishing to them, in the midst of that knowledge they know life. The most remarkable thing they have come to know, they say, is "meaning for life and a purpose for their own lives."[8] "Love's knowledge," I think. In and through a way of life formed in love, they know realities that cynicism cannot know and that grasping cannot reach.

Some years ago, Marianne Sawicki's book *Seeing the Lord*[9] was published. Subtitled *Resurrection and Early Christian Practices*, this book argues at length the same basic point Sawicki made in a stunning essay in *Theology Today*, "Recognizing the Risen Lord." Her claim is that the risen Lord is a present reality who can be truly known, but only under certain conditions: namely, in the context of certain practices that together constitute a particular way of life. Central among these practices are feeding the hungry and remembering Jesus. The two must go together. Through a close reading of both Matthew and Luke, Sawicki discerns in the texts a working knowledge of how the resurrection of Jesus Christ is taught. What she finds is that

> the possibility of understanding resurrection comes through hunger: either one's own hunger or the hunger of another which one is able to recognize and alleviate. . . . For Luke, recognition of the Risen Lord is possible only within a community that knows both how to be hungry and how to feed the hungry. Stories about empty tombs have no efficacy, except within such a community.[10]

Words are not enough, not even the words of scripture. Rather, it is these words in relation to a peculiar context. The biblical texts themselves assert, says Sawicki, that words cannot deliver understanding. Access to the risen Lord is opened through teaching that transpires within a community sensitive to the needs of the poor, and which indeed forms such a community. This teaching is rooted not only in formal theological reflection on the very possibility of gaining access to the risen Lord but also in action on behalf of the poor undertaken because the teacher wants to see Jesus.

In *Practicing Our Faith: A Way of Life for a Searching People,* a diverse group of theological educators describes twelve "Christian practices" fundamental to the Christian way of life. These authors understand Christian practices to be "things Christian people do together over time in response to and in the light of God's active presence for the life of the world."[11] The book includes portrayals of such practices as keeping Sabbath, giving testimony, forgiveness, healing, dying well, honoring the body, ordering community, hospitality to strangers and even to enemies. The practices of discernment, of saying yes and saying no (asceticism, actually), of sustaining just economic relations, and of rendering our lives in song are also included. Each of these practices is described in such a way as to enable the reader to see in it a way of being that addresses fundamental human needs and contemporary cultural conditions through practical human acts. The chapters show how each of these practices has been given a fundamental shape and order in the course of the history of the Christian faith and yet has been open to enormous adaptability to circumstances in a wide variety of cultural contexts. And each chapter tries to show how these patterns of action are tangled up with the things God is doing in the world in such a way that distinctive qualities of life and forms of knowledge become available to us as we participate in them. Again, Christian practices as modes and means of grace; Christian practices as contexts for love's knowledge.

THEOLOGICAL EDUCATION IN THE FUTURE OF THE CHURCH AND CULTURE

I have borrowed Martha Nussbaum's phrase "love's knowledge" and given it a theological turn. I have picked up her hunch that such knowledge might be something other than intellectual grasping, that it might instead be a complex form of life. And I have followed her hunch down a trail that leads to fundamental Christian practices that together may constitute a shared form of life in which love's knowledge in its richest theological sense may emerge. I started with a claim that love's knowledge in this sense is both the presupposition for and the substance of a truly theological education. Now I am in a position to begin to spell out some of what that might mean for us as theological educators.

The standards of the Association of Theological Schools say that "theological schools are communities of faith and learning guided by a theological vision."[12] This statement seems to me to be right on target as an orienting description of the whole enterprise. In a way, it seems so obvious that it is easy to slip quickly over this sentence. But we should not. We should pause to contemplate what this claim means—and does not mean. One thing it can easily be assumed to mean (but I think should not) is that theological education is an amalgam of religious life on the one hand and higher education on the other, as if the two were independent spheres pieced together for primarily functional or pragmatic reasons. It is certainly true that we are surrounded by and in many ways dependent on and part of a very large and complex world of higher education in the United States and Canada. Very little of it could legitimately describe itself as "communities of *faith* and learning"—or would want to. Likewise, we are awash in a sea of faith made up of communities small and large, both liberal and conservative, that have learned well the modern polarization between faith and learning and that therefore, in too many cases, have come to regard learning as irrelevant, if not downright hostile, to faith.

The idea of love's knowledge will not allow this polarization. We are not and cannot be communities of faith plus communities of learning—as if by means of addition, that is, as if we could be one without the other but just happen not to. No; we must be communities-of-faith-and-learning.

Communities oriented by love's knowledge will and must be *intrinsically* communities-of-faith-and-learning.

This feature of the theological school is what gives it its deepest significance for the church and the culture. Something about the very nature of these schools is fully as significant as their capacity to train competent and informed leaders for the churches or to produce new knowledge of value to religious and secular society. The single most important thing about theological education in the future of the church and culture is that these schools actually *be* communities-of-faith-and-learning, guided by a theological vision in which faith and learning are bound inextricably together in something like the essential intimacy of love's knowledge. In a culture that has shorn them apart in so profound a way as ours has, so that the churches themselves are almost unaware of the loss, the very existence of places where faith and learning are fundamentally at one with each other is of utmost significance.

Here, too, is where the issue of quality must ultimately be pressed. We can and should ask how good our schools' faculties are, how substantial the financial and material resources are, how well equipped and staffed the libraries are, how coherent the curriculum is, and so forth. But the basic question about quality is not "How good are we?" but "What is the fundamental good upon which the whole enterprise is built?" The basic question is not "How do we measure up against various standards of excellence?" but "By what standard of excellence do we seek to be measured?"

An institution that takes love's knowledge as its standard is a rare one in our society, one that by its very nature presents a qualitative (could we say prophetic?) challenge to every other. Theological schools should not be—and, thankfully, are not—the only communities of faith and learning in our society. Every congregation should be, and so should every other religious institution. Indeed, I would hope that love's knowledge could characterize and permeate schools of every kind—as well as every other place of life and work. But insofar as theological schools are among the very few institutions in our society that are, by their own standards, calling themselves explicitly to be communities-of-faith-and-learning, I hope they will take that calling with full seriousness to its deepest levels and understand that the very quality of its existence in these terms is, in and of itself, among its most important contributions to the future of the church and culture.

Notes

1. Martha C. Nussbaum, *Love's Knowledge: Essays on Philosophy and Literature* (New York: Oxford University Press, 1990); see esp. chap. 11, which bears the same title.

2. John Calvin, *Institutes of the Christian Religion*, ed. John T. McNeill (Philadelphia: Westminster Press, 1960), 1.1.1.

3. See David H. Kelsey, *To Understand God Truly: What's Theological about a Theological School* (Louisville, Ky.: Westminster/John Knox Press, 1992).

4. Nussbaum, *Love's Knowledge*, 283.

5. Martha C. Nussbaum, *Poetic Justice: The Literary Imagination and Public Life* (Boston: Beacon Press, 1995), 38.

6. In Nussbaum, *Love's Knowledge*, 278.

7. Private communication from Joseph Kilpatrick.

8. Joseph Kilpatrick and Sanford Danziger, comps., *Better Than Money Can Buy: The New Volunteers* (Winston-Salem, N.C.: Innersearch Publishing, 1996), 142.

9. Marianne Sawicki, *Seeing the Lord: Resurrection and Early Christian Practices* (Minneapolis: Fortress Press, 1994).

10. Marianne Sawicki, "Recognizing the Risen Lord," *Theology Today* 44 (1988): 448.

11. Dorothy Bass, ed., *Practicing Our Faith: A Way of Life for a Searching People* (San Francisco: Jossey-Bass, 1997), 5.

12. "Quality and Accreditation: Final Report on the Redeveloped Accrediting Standards," *Theological Education* 32/2 (1996): 23.

Signs

Chapter 11

When the Bible Happens

It makes all the difference in the world: What do we think is happening when we study and teach the Bible? The poet Ntozake Shange writes:

> quite simply a poem shd fill you up with something cd make
> you swoon, stop in yr tracks, change yr mind, or make it up,
> a poem shd happen to you like cold water or a kiss.[1]

So, too, with the Bible. The Bible should happen to you.

Too often, I think, we regard the Bible as an inanimate object. We assume that it is lifeless, that it cannot itself do anything. If anything is to happen when we study and teach the Bible, we must be the ones to do it. We are the active ones. The Bible is passive. The Bible does not do anything to us. We must do something to it. We must make it relevant. We must discover what it meant when it was first written and decide what it means for us today. We are the interpreters. The Bible is the object of interpretation. We do something while the Bible itself lies still and dumb before us.

Interpretation, relevance, and the discovery of meaning in the Bible are essential in Bible study. But it is also crucial that we see the Bible as a living force and active agent, rather than as a dead relic or historic fossil, at least if we are to study and teach it correctly. If, after all, a poem can do something to us, how much more so can the Bible! We must approach the Bible with a sense of expectancy, a sense that in coming into its presence we risk having something done to us.

Hans-Ruedi Weber opens his book *Experiments with Bible Study* by relating a story from East Africa:

> A simple woman always walked around with a bulky Bible. Never would she part from it. Soon the villagers began to tease her: "Why

always the Bible? There are so many books you could read!" Yet the woman kept on living with her Bible, neither disturbed nor angered by all the teasing. Finally, one day she knelt down in the midst of those who laughed at her. Holding the Bible high above her head, she said with a big smile: "Yes, of course there are many books which I could read. But there is only one book which reads me!"[2]

This, Weber goes on to say, "is the whole secret of Bible study. People start out by listening to an old message, by analyzing ancient texts, by reading—naively or critically—the biblical documents of antiquity. They experience this exercise as dull or instructive, as something Christians ought to do or something they have been led to do by their own . . . interests. Yet a mysterious change of roles can then occur. Listening, analyzing, and reading, students of the Bible meet a living reality which begins to challenge them. . . . This divine presence starts to question, judge, and guide us. Perhaps gradually, perhaps quite suddenly, the book which was the object of our reading and study becomes a subject which reads us."[3]

Effective Bible study is, I think, Bible study in which this kind of role reversal happens. What we hope for is not just that people will come to know what is in the Bible but that the Bible itself will get under their skin to the point that it will not let them go. If Bible study is effective, it will stop people in their tracks from time to time, change their minds about things, or help them make their minds up. It may even fill them up with something and make them swoon.

But can this really happen through adult Bible study? Adult Bible study seems such a tame thing to do. A half dozen people are sitting around a table with their Bibles open, talking about what they hear when they listen to the Bible and about what they see when they read it. Perhaps a teacher is pointing out how the first four verses of Luke provide some important clues as to what the whole book is about. Can the Bible really *happen* to us when we are doing these sorts of things? Besides, we, as leaders of adult Bible study, may well wonder whether we are even close to being capable of bringing about anything like this.

Fortunately, we do not have to worry about that. It is not we who make the Bible happen. The Bible itself does that. Or more accurately, God does that through the Bible. Weber makes this clear when he says that the change of role that takes place when the Bible starts to read and shape us "does not come from the power of human scholarship or clever teaching and know-how."[4] It cannot be guaranteed by any methods. It happens, when it happens, by God's grace, and not by anything we do.

What, then, does all this have to do with how we teach? What difference does it make? The difference it makes is that it changes what we focus on, what we concentrate on when we plan for and carry out our teaching. And that, in turn, may suggest to us ways of teaching that are more in tune with what happens when the Bible "happens" to people.

Let us take a look at how this works. A teacher is a person who is concerned about and seeks to facilitate the learning of other people. A teacher is one who consciously focuses on, and tries to discern and affect, the learning going on in others. On the face of it, this concern for the learning of others does not seem a terribly novel or important idea. But its importance shows up in actual, everyday teaching-learning situations.

It is very difficult to lead people in the study of the Bible while paying serious and sustained attention to their learning. What is easier, and much more natural, is to become absorbed in our own activity of teaching. Leading adult Bible study is not easy. Therefore, it is not surprising that we find ourselves concentrating on what we, as teachers, should be saying, doing, suggesting, thinking, and feeling—especially if we feel a little nervous, uneasy, or conspicuous in our role. What shall I say? What resources should I use? How much material should I try to cover? What methods should be used? How am I coming across? These are all legitimate concerns. The problem arises when they become our first and only concerns—which they should not, since teaching is about concern for the learning of others. Good teaching begins not with teaching but with learning; and a good teacher begins not with his or her own perspective but with the learner's perspective.

I have found it helpful when planning for teaching to ask three questions. Doing this helps me keep the learner's perspective in view, both while I am planning for teaching and while I am actually doing it. The three questions are:

1. What changes do we hope for in the learners? What kinds of transformation do we believe the Bible is calling us into?

2. What do the learners need to do so that such changes may take place?

3. What do I, as teacher, need to do so that the learners can do what they need to do, so that these changes may take place?

The answer to the last question involves the teacher's plans, brought to life by the teacher. We, as teachers, often ask only this last question. But the answer to this question is derived from our answer to the second question. And this, in turn, depends on our answer to the first. So one must answer the first two questions before tackling the third.

Note how closely related the first question listed here is to our question of what goes on when the Bible happens to us. The two are virtually the same. But what is happening when we read and study the Bible? Are we gaining information about biblical characters and events? Are we learning moral rules and guidelines? Are we finding out what the people of Israel and of the early church had to say about their lives, about God, and about their relationships to God? The answer we give makes a difference in what we think is important for the learners to do and, hence, in what we will do as teachers.

Suppose we think that what primarily goes on when the Bible happens to us is that we are gaining information about biblical characters and events. Then the changes we will hope for in the learners will be changes in what they know factually from the Bible. What do they need to do to gain this information? Perhaps they need first to ask some questions—the kind that ask: Who did what with whom? Where, when, how, and with what result? Who was Jeremiah? Where and when did he live? What was he so upset about? What did he say and do? What effect did all this have on the people of Judah? The learners can find out the answers to these questions by reading certain passages of the Bible, perhaps, or by reading appropriate commentaries, or by listening to someone else answer these questions orally. And if this is what the learners are to be doing, then the teacher's task is to help them to do it—by giving them worksheets that tell them what passages to read in the Bible, by pointing them to the appropriate commentaries, by asking members of the class to do some research and report their findings to everyone else, or by giving a lecture that provides the pertinent information.

Similarly, if we think that what the Bible does is provide moral rules and guidelines, then the change we are striving for is that our learners will discover what these rules and guidelines are and how to apply them to their own lives. To do this, they will need to read in the Bible to see whether people in biblical times followed or did not follow these rules and guidelines and discuss whether and in what ways they can be applied to our situations today. The teacher would be responsible for choosing what would be read from the Bible and, perhaps, other sources. He or she may want to bring in some case studies of difficult ethical situations and ask the class to try to apply biblical ethical principles to them. A panel discussion might be set up in which various members of the class, the congregation, or the larger community discuss a current moral problem in light of their exploration of the Bible. The options are many.

A similar line of thought could be followed if we concluded that finding out what the people of Israel and the early church had to say is what is happening when the Bible happens to us. Then we might ask questions about what the characters and writers of the Bible said and meant. What might that mean for us now? The point here is not to trace through all the possibilities. It is to show the kind of thinking that we may engage in if we start with the first question first. It is a kind of thinking that can give direction and order and significance to our teaching of the Bible and can stimulate us to discover (and even create) methods of teaching for learning that are consistent with what happens when the Bible happens to us.

So far, our suggestions as to what the Bible does have been fairly limited. But if you look at them carefully, they all imply that what the Bible does is inform us somehow. It says things. It tells us what happened, it tells us what ethical guidelines we might live by, and it tells us what the people of the Bible had to say about their lives and their relationships to God.

Theologian David Kelsey suggests that the Bible does much more than inform us. It acts on us in other ways, too. God's activity is not limited to speaking. The Bible is not limited to being "a means by which God is asserting or proposing something."[5] In other words, God may be using the Bible for something beyond informing us. If so, how else is God making the Bible happen—in us and for our sake? And what might that mean for our teaching and learning?

I have a hunch that God is using the Bible for many more things than just to inform us. God is using the Bible, I would say, to give us courage, to set us free of whatever enslaves us, to seduce us (if that is not too strong a word) into the love God has for us, to call us to account, to turn us around from whatever paths of destruction we may be following, to humble us where we need to be humbled, to lift us up when we are heavily burdened, to forgive us, to redeem us, to make us holy. God is using the Bible not only to inform us but to form us and re-form us, to shape us into God's own.

What if this kind of thing occurs when the Bible happens to us? How in our teaching and learning do we cooperate with that?

Several years ago, I was teaching a seminary course on "Leading Adult Bible Study." In that course we talked about the ideas I have been trying to articulate in this chapter. When we had finished talking about those ideas, we turned ourselves into an adult Bible study group. We studied the book of Jeremiah for eight sessions, and the students in the course took turns leading the sessions. In the last session, the leaders concluded that the change they hoped for was what Jeremiah had hoped for: that we, like the people of Judah, might still sense hope even if we, too, were undergoing some form of exile.

The leaders did several things so that we could become informed about hope and exile and what these meant to Jeremiah. We read certain passages of Jeremiah. We did a word study of the meaning of *exile*. We were asked to find answers to questions of fact and meaning in the biblical story. But we were also asked to do more. A basket of good figs and a basket of bad figs were set before us. We smelled them, touched them, tasted them. We were asked to choose a phrase of hope from Jeremiah 24. (Look it up, you will find a number of them.) We all memorized the ones we had chosen. Then we all stood up and walked around the room and, looking one another in the eye, sometimes clasping hands, we said those words of hope to one another. Then we sat back and asked ourselves, "Who are people in exile today?" After we talked about all sorts of people, from political refugees to youth estranged from their families, we all tried to think of particular people we knew who were in some sort of exile. And each of us, using words from Jeremiah or some words of our own that were now shaped by our encounter with Jeremiah, wrote a message of hope to the person. I found out later that some of us actually sent those messages. Finally, we listened to some music that our leaders had picked out, and we prayed.

We left having been changed a bit, I think—encouraged, given hope, humbled, too. The Bible had done it. But the teachers cooperated with what the Bible was doing by asking us to do more than just find out what it said. They asked us, in some small way, to taste it, to touch it, to feel it, to memorize it, to speak it ourselves, and to pray it.

All of this does not provide new methods for Bible study. But new methods are not the most important things we need. Good methods are available from many sources, and they are built into the curriculum materials we use. What we most need is a way to think—a way to think about the Bible and a way to think through our planning and teaching—that can help us see how active a thing the Bible really is and how, by cooperating with it, Bible study becomes hardly a tame thing to do at all.

Notes

1. From Alicia Ostriker, "American Poetry, Now Shaped by Women," *New York Times Book Review,* March 9, 1986.
2. Hans-Ruedi Weber, *Experiments with Bible Study* (Philadelphia: Westminster Press, 1983), vii.
3. Ibid.
4. Ibid.
5. David H. Kelsey, *Uses of Scripture in Recent Theology* (Philadelphia: Fortress Press, 1975), 213.

Chapter 12

Learning to Be Sent

It's an interesting thing about those people who became apostles. They were in business for themselves—fishing, collecting taxes, holding households together—doing the things ordinary folk do to keep their heads above water and their hands out of trouble. Then something happened.

They were called by someone and sent somewhere. And when that happened, everything changed. They saw themselves differently, went places they never thought of going before, thought thoughts that never in a hundred years would have come into their heads, and did things they never in their wildest imaginations would have seen themselves doing.

Their world was turned upside down, too. They saw evil in what once had been business as usual, beauty and goodness in people and things they had scoffed at, scorned, or just plain ignored. Strangers became friends and enemies became neighbors. Called and sent—and everything was rearranged.

We see it not only in the Gospels. Here is Abraham—called and sent. Here are Moses, Deborah, Samuel, Amos, Mary, Paul, Timothy, Ambrose, Augustine, Luther, Winthrop, Whitefield, Moffatt, Livingstone, King, Teresa, Romero, Wojtyla—you name them—all called and sent. You? And me?

And of course, the one who calls and sends us all, himself sent by God. All, in one way or another, called to and sent into mission.

Albert Curry Winn wrote an exciting little book, *A Sense of Mission*, in which he says that "a sense of mission is precisely a sense of having been sent." And this, he explains, is the key to understanding the church, ourselves as individual Christians, and Jesus Christ. If we want to know who the church is, we must see it not as the people who know God best, who love God most, or who have God's greatest blessing but as the "sent people" of God—the people sent by God through Christ. And if we want to know who we are as individuals, we must not look to our good works or our sense of security in God, much less to our feelings of wholeness and fullness. Rather, we must see where it is Christ sends us. Then we come to know who it is we are.

Most of us, when we think about mission, conjure up images of missionaries who are sent into foreign places to give the message that has come to us. There is something right about thinking this way. Mission is being sent, and we are sent into what is foreign. But "foreign" does not necessarily mean a foreign country—although it might. And the foreign is not so much what is foreign to us as what is foreign to God's kingdom. Foreign territory, in this sense, may be found smack-dab in the middle of our own cities and towns, our own churches and families, even our own personalities. We are sent, in other words, by Christ into whatever betrays God's purpose and love—wherever that might be. And we are sent not to bring a message of our own but to be the sent people of God there, to be signs of the presence of God there.

To be a missionary—an apostle, a disciple, a Christian—means to be wherever you are and to go wherever you go with a sense not of just being there for God knows what reason but of having been sent there precisely for God's reason.

Now, I want to make two claims about Christian education and Christian nurture. First, all Christian nurture and education are for the sake of mission. That's why we do it. That's its purpose. Second, nurture and education are themselves forms of mission.

An old and widely used statement of the purpose of Christian education is "to help persons be aware of God's self-disclosure and seeking love in Jesus Christ, and to respond in faith and love—to the end that they may know who they are and what their human situation means, grow as [children] of God rooted in Christian community, live in the Spirit of God in every relationship, fulfill their common discipleship in the world, and abide in Christian hope." This fairly comprehensive statement of what it means to be a "sent one" was published in 1958 by the National Council of Churches in *The Objective of Christian Education for Senior High Young People*.[1] To be one sent by Christ means to be one who is aware of the God who sends us—to be one who responds by being sent to grow, live, fulfill and abide. We are this and we do this, not for our own sakes but for the sake of the One who sends us.

This does not happen naturally. All who have found their lives turned around and their worlds turned upside down *learned* that they were sent and were guided where they went. The educational mission of the church is to teach people that Christ sends them into all the foreign places of this world and of our lives, where justice is not done, where mercy's name is not known, where despair sickens unto death, where love is a stranger, and where the hunger for bread and for righteousness is not being fed. The educational mission of the church is to send people and guide people as they struggle to find ways to be living reminders of the presence of God where they go.

What does this mean for how we do nurture and education? It suggests that we learn by going and teach by sending. Going is more important than knowing or feeling or even doing. We come to know new things, feel in new ways, do things differently when we find ourselves in a new place. When we stay in the places we are used to, our minds filter out ideas and facts that might disturb the status quo. Our emotions become controlled and routine. We act habitually. But in new situations the habits are disturbed, the routines upset, and the filters readjusted. We become vulnerable to being changed.

To be sent is to become vulnerable. Vulnerability is the key to education. Children learn so quickly because they are vulnerable—ready to receive. Adults often learn slowly because we have, over a long period of time, built up our defenses against anything that might be different from and threaten the way in which we understand things and react to things.

Vulnerability is the key to mission also. Jesus came, above all, to be with us. That is the meaning of the incarnation: God with us. But he could not really be with us unless he was vulnerable to our pain, our limitations, our suffering, our death. In his vulnerability—which we see so plainly in his birth, in his washing of feet, and in the cross—we see the way in which God sent him to us.

Likewise, we cannot be sent ones unless we are willing to be vulnerable to the ones to whom we are sent. To be in mission means to be in the position of being vulnerable to what others are vulnerable to. It means to be willing to suffer what another suffers and to go with another in his or her own suffering. The words *equality* and *justice* take on their deepest meaning in this context. Mission demands equality and justice. It renounces self-protection against the powers that threaten the ones to whom we are sent.

We learn to be sent ones, then, by going into places where we are vulnerable. And once this happens, we begin to need the presence of God. We begin to see and understand the meaning of his Word. We come to know who we are and what we are to say and do. The stories of the Bible, the history of the church, discussion of current theological and social issues, the experience of Christian fellowship, participation in worship mean nothing to people who are not going into the world vulnerable. But when we are vulnerable, these things mean everything. We must educate in this context, or we cannot really educate at all.

A group of young people was sent by its congregation to work at a health fair in eastern Kentucky. The youth had studied poverty and hunger and the call of the gospel to care for the ill. But it wasn't until they were sent into a situation—one quite foreign to them—where they had a chance to meet, be with, talk with, come to know people whose lives were lived so differently from their own that any of this came alive. They came home hungry for more knowledge. They wanted to work to change things. They began to read the scriptures with fresh eyes. They had made friends with strangers whom they had once ridiculed. Because of this, their values had to be realigned and their faith appropriated in a new way.

Christian education is the mission of sending people into mission and going with them. The most important teachers for this group of young people were the adults who were there with them in Kentucky. They were vulnerable to what the youth were vulnerable to and in that context could teach and nurture them. To teach and nurture others, we must be with them in their vulnerability. Then they can hear us, will want to learn from us, will want us to go with them into the places they are being sent. Their lives and their worlds may even change because of us.

The place of education and nurture in the mission of the church is central, because it is through education that we learn who we are as sent ones of God and are sent into mission ourselves. But this is so only if mission is at the same time the center of education and nurture; because education that aims anywhere else and goes about it in any other way is not really Christian education at all.

Notes

1. *The Objective of Christian Education for Senior High Young People* (New York: National Council of the Churches of Christ in the U.S.A., 1958), 14–15.

Chapter 13

"My Teacher, We Made Bread . . ."

One Sunday many years ago, on returning home from church, I was having the typical what-did-you-do-in-Sunday-school-today conversation with my two sons. The younger, who was six, came up with this: "My teacher, we made bread together and I ate mine already and it was good." I didn't pay much attention at the time, but the line stuck with me. As I thought about it, it occurred to me that he had said something both simple and deep about what good teaching in the church is like.

"Made bread together." The word *bread*, the image of bread: "This is my body broken for you." "I am the bread of life. He who comes to me will never be hungry." "Is there one among you who would hand his son a stone when he asked for bread?" To make bread together in Christ's name is to make life together. And this is exactly what my son and his teacher were doing. I think they both knew it, in some mostly unsuspecting way.

We make bread together—make life together—in an infinite variety of ways. By telling stories: those strange stories from the Bible that have so many levels of meaning and such rich veins of truth to mine that once we hear them, we cannot resist hearing them again; and the unpretentious yet somehow no less mystery-filled stories of our own lives. By sharing and caring: holding one another in our arms and in our imaginations. By listening: really paying attention to one another, and to what is being said behind the others' words and faces. By giving praise: singing hymns we hardly know the meaning of, praying prayers that barely give shape to the unutterable things we know so deep within us.

Is this the Sunday school? Is this what really happens there? It is, though it is not what we usually notice, not what we could make happen if we tried. It is just what often seems to happen when we forget ourselves and become absorbed in some simple thing with another child of God—such as sticking dough in the oven to watch it brown and grow and learn texture and taste.

"I ate it," he said. This is important, too. To make bread together and then not to eat it is to fail to let it do its silent work in us. We are nourished in so many ways, and we don't remember 2 percent of them. Yet if we take food in, we are changed. The children in our church school classes take more in from us than we realize—certainly more than they ever tell us or give evidence of. Thinking back, though, we who were there as children can all recall certain faces, certain very particular places and days and things we did. Our memories are proof that we, too, ate the bread, and that it is still working in us.

My son finished his sentence with "and it was good." God said that once. James Weldon Johnson, in the rhythm and flow of the black preacher, put it this way:

> Then God smiled,
> And the light broke,
> And the darkness rolled up on one side
> And the light stood shining on the other,
> And God said: That's good![1]

We don't make life from nothing, as God did. We make it from the things God gave us: flour and salt and milk and one another. But when we do, for us it is the same. The light breaks, and the darkness rolls up on one side, and we say, "That's good!" We know it and God knows it. And God's blessing on us is that we can say it together.

What are they doing, these teachers? They come, each with his or her own piece of life, in fear and trembling, most of the time feeling they've got little to give and almost nothing to say. Probably somebody asked them to do it, almost twisted their arms to do it. But the reason many keep on doing it, I think, is that they are compelled to do it, from within, maybe even by a sometimes painful, sometimes satisfying grace that works in and through them. They search through the curriculum materials for something to teach and in the how-to manuals for ways to teach it. But what they do more than anything is bring themselves to another person, to a group of children they hardly know. And there they make bread together, and eat it, and know from time to time that it is good.

My son introduced his message with the ungrammatical phrase "My teacher, we . . . " He used to use that construction when he meant someone close to him. It was as natural for him to say "My teacher, we" as it was for him to say "I"—more natural, perhaps, since his "I," like the "I" of all children, was so bound up in the others around him whom he needs. To be the teacher in "My teacher, we . . . " is to have received a gift. Like all God's graces, that is the only way it comes. We can neither grab it nor earn it for ourselves.

Teaching in church school is nine parts getting a weary body out of bed early on Sunday mornings, cutting out construction-paper patterns, cleaning hardened glue from tables too low to bend over gracefully, matching the right snow boot with the right foot, and keeping noise levels within moderate bounds. But those nine parts are the things that make one part possible. And if you, as a teacher, are ever fortunate enough to overhear one of the children in your class say, "My teacher, we made bread together and I ate it and it was good," you will know what that one part is.

Notes

1. James Weldon Johnson, *God's Trombones: Seven Negro Sermons in Verse* (New York: Penguin Books, 1976), 17.

Study Guide

A Guide for Study and Conversation
Syd Hielema

INTRODUCTION TO THIS STUDY GUIDE

Even before I opened Craig Dykstra's book for the first time, its title—*Growing in the Life of Faith*—had stirred up questions that are at the heart of my work as a Christian teacher and at the center of my identity as a Christian. How can one describe faith growth? Have you ever pondered how *you* are growing in *your* faith? I do from time to time, and I must confess I find it somewhat unnerving. I find myself wondering if I *am* growing in my faith. I have to remind myself that *growth* is not synonymous with *progress*. Progress aims to become bigger and better; faith growth has a hundred different manifestations, many of which look as weak and helpless as the stunned Pharisee Saul sitting blind in Damascus (Acts 9:9). How can one write a book about such a seemingly illogical reality?

Plus, the complexities of personal faith growth do not present the only difficulty. Do you ever wonder how you affect the faith growth of others? It's a given that every Christian believer does make an impact. We do it *explicitly* as we live out the roles of teachers, leaders, preachers, parents, or friends. We also do it *implicitly* whenever we are with others; the child behind us in the pew notes our demeanor as we worship, and the teenaged driver observes how we respond when someone cuts us off at an intersection. How are all such hopelessly intricate dynamics to be analyzed?

When I first read *Growing in the Life of Faith* several years ago, I found words that gave expression to thoughts I had long held but had never been able to articulate. I also found thoughts that were new, which deepened and provided a big-picture context for my own thoughts. Frequently, I would read a paragraph and stare out the window for some time, allowing its ideas to percolate through my system and resonate with my experience. I knew I had found a book that allowed mysteries to remain mysteries and named words inside them that opened these mysteries up for deeper understanding and concrete steps of action. I had found a jewel.

The first year after I read the book, I gave a copy to anyone I thought might read it. Eventually, I realized that many of these readers were able to understand the book more fully when I helped them unpack some of Dykstra's challenging ideas and drew them into conversation about the issues he was raising. That realization became the catalyst for this study guide. Since Dykstra's original volume was first published in 1999, I have encouraged pastors, church education and congregational youth ministry leaders, school teachers, college and seminary students, parents, and grandparents to study this book; and I have kept each of these roles in mind as I wrote this study guide.

The guide follows a simple structure. Each session begins with a brief synopsis of the chapter, which seeks to bring its themes into clear focus. The synopsis assumes that the chapter has been read and, therefore, functions as a brief review. If there are confusions, the group should address these first, working from the hope that several heads are better than one and the group will clarify the confusing thought(s). Naming helpful points provides an easy way to establish common ground between the group and the chapter, which can serve as a foundation for the ensuing discussion. Identifying unsettling issues is also important; those ideas that question our own assumptions or practices are often the ones that challenge us to grow most intensely.

> Each chapter's synopsis is followed by an invitation to "CHU" on its insights by inviting each participant to identify one thought from the reading that was particularly Confusing, Helpful, or Unsettling (CHU).

Each group needs to negotiate the best way to correlate "CHU-ing" with the discussion questions that follow. I believe that working through the points of confusion is essential for every group. I can imagine four different strategies for dealing with the "HU" items:

1. They can be stated and simply remain undeveloped, forming a context for the discussion questions.
2. They can lead the group to focus on certain discussion questions that flow naturally from them.
3. They can lead the group to ignore the discussion questions and allow the HU comments to establish the flow of the discussion.
4. The "HU" step can be skipped entirely.

Perhaps it would work best if one of the four is chosen as the default strategy, while reserving the freedom to choose one of the other three when a change is clearly appropriate.

The discussion questions are almost always grouped in clusters, with the expectation that each cluster will take some time to be worked through properly. I would recommend spending quality time on selected question clusters rather than covering them all.

In addition, the discussion question sections (except for the first and last) are organized under four headings. Questions under the heading titled "Observe" encourage us to compare Dykstra's ideas to our own understandings: to what extent do his perceptions match ours? Questions under "Reflect" invite us to use the chapter as a mirror that evokes self-examination. These are followed by "Implications for Faith Education" questions, and each chapter ends with "Areas for Deeper Exploration." I find so many challenging insights in *Growing in the Life of Faith* that I'm sure one could list a dozen or more areas for further exploration in each chapter. I trust that each group will dig further on its own as the Spirit leads. My only prayer is that many others will be enriched by the insights of this book as I continue to be.

My experience has been that small group discussions are enhanced when they are concluded with a time of prayer and singing. Not only are these activities wonderful ways to grow together in community before the face of God, they also reinforce the central themes of the book (i.e., the group will practice what Dykstra preaches).

Introduction: Mystery and Manners

Perhaps you will ask yourself whether a book's introduction is essential to grasping the book or whether it is simply a verbal sigh of relief exhaled by the author after completing his or her work. The introduction in *Growing in the Life of Faith* clearly belongs to the essential category. Furthermore, Dykstra's moments of self-reflection in these pages provide a wonderful invitation to readers to engage in similar self-reflection, thereby establishing a solid personal context for reading the book.

Flannery O'Connor's distinction between mystery and manners is not only the central distinction of this chapter but also

> The introduction and chapter 1 are both quite short. If the group you are part of may have difficulty completing a study of the entire book, it may be wise to use only parts of the study guide for these two sections and cover them both in one session.

a fundamental thesis for *Growing in the Life of Faith*. What O'Connor calls "manners" bears great similarity to what Dykstra later calls "Christian practices" and "habitations of the Spirit." In this distinction, we see that the thousands of mundane, ordinary regularities of life (manners) are a central means by which we experience the mystery of the faithfulness of God. Christian educators are called to pay attention to the presence of God so that we may guide others in glimpsing that presence.

The chapter includes one other important distinction: "education is not the same as experience" though it is "a form of experience" (pp. xx–xxi.).

Experience just happens in daily life, but "education is the work of bringing to consciousness the hidden dimensions embedded in and through our actions and relations and institutions, giving these dimensions names, and then helping each other take notice and live in their light" (p. xx). In other words, education *names* experience and thereby provides a way of *seeing or interpreting* that experience. Education is somewhat like the focus knob on an old-fashioned slide projector, bringing greater clarity to the jumble of our everyday experience.

> **CHU on the chapter**
>
> What was:
>
> • confusing
> • helpful
> • unsettling?

Questions for Discussion

(Note: The following Questions for Discussion do not follow the four-part format that is used for each subsequent chapter.)

Dykstra begins by remembering the manners that have shaped him, beginning in his childhood home and continuing to the present. These manners were experienced in the contexts of family, educational institutions, the workplace, church communities, and national and global events. List some of the manners that are part of your history (including the present), describing both the activities and the relational contexts in which they were formed. It will be helpful for group chemistry if everyone present contributes to this discussion, but the memories of some spin faster than others. So, rather than going around the circle, consider inviting the one who is ready to remember first to do so, and then invite others, taking care that everyone participates.

How can the mystery be glimpsed inside these manners? How has the faithful presence of God been present through the life histories that were spoken? (This is more of an "I wonder . . ." question, requiring the freedom to ponder out loud.)

Dykstra writes, "I have been fortunate to have teachers who used words with such care that I have been able to see beneath the manners into the mystery" (p. xx). Those who have taught us include not only teachers but also parents, pastors, friends, colleagues, spouses, children, authors (and one could go on). Identify one person who has helped you "to see beneath the manners into the mystery" and describe what it was that enabled this person to do so: gifts of articulation, relationality, wisdom, discernment, vulnerability, empathy, or others.

One final important thread in the introduction concerns the place of community in the Christian life, "what Christians call the fellowship of the Holy Spirit" (p. xix). I recall vividly a moment during a small group get-together (that had met biweekly for eight years) when I received the revelation that I had seen the face of Christ in every person in the room at one time or another. How have you seen the face of Christ in others? What difference has this seeing made in your life?

PART I: HUNGER

Chapter 1: The Hunger for Daily Bread

In this opening chapter, Dykstra describes the cultural context for faith education in our time and introduces several concepts that are developed in more detail later in the book. We are hungry for God, but often we do not have the vocabulary and practices required to digest the food that we receive, Dykstra argues. The history of the Christian faith reveals that disciplined piety encourages the growth of strong digestive muscles which deepen life in the Spirit, life in the presence of God. Today, however, we live with this paradox: a deep hunger for the presence of God is coupled with a "nasty suspicion" (p. 9, quoting the theologian Edward Farley) that there is no presence of God to be found inside our practices, that there is no mystery behind our manners. In this chapter, Dykstra introduces the concept of practices, which he later develops much more extensively (especially in chapters 3–5).

The hunger that Dykstra describes resonates with the prophecy of Amos that declares:

> The time is surely coming, says the Lord GOD,
>   when I will send a famine on the land;
> not a famine of bread, or a thirst for water,
>   but of hearing the words of the LORD.

They shall wander from sea to sea,
   and from north to east;
they shall run to and fro, seeking the word of the LORD,
   but they shall not find it.

(Amos 8:11–12)

It also calls to mind one of Augustine's most famous statements: "You have made our hearts restless, O Lord, until they find their rest in Thee." Though this hunger and restlessness are part of our human wiring, food and rest are not easily found. "We can turn everything from computer chips and laser beams to legal briefs and leveraged buyouts into daily bread. The bread that we feed on is the bread of business and busyness and boredom" (p. 11). Dykstra's lament echoes the words of an earlier prophet: "Why do you spend your money for that which is not bread, and your labor for that which does not satisfy? Listen carefully to me, and eat what is good, and delight yourselves in rich food" (Isa. 55:2).

> **CHU on the chapter**
>
> What was:
>
> • confusing
> • helpful
> • unsettling?

Dykstra recommends we focus this hunger on "texts and practices through which the grace and presence of God have been experienced" (p. 6). Can the church lead the hungry to find nourishment in these places? Yes, if it functions as a path instead of a tomb. "If the church is a path, a place to walk and to practice the faith, we may be surprised along the way by the living God and recognize and know that Christ is present—to us, in our own lives" (p. 10). This challenge sets the stage for the book as a whole to serve as an encouragement to the church of Christ to feed the hungry in his name.

Questions for Discussion

Observe

What evidences do you see of our culture's hunger for God? Spiritual hunger wears many different masks. Recently an observer called this the "whatever" culture: it is hungry for God but chooses to cover up that hunger with a "whatever" shrug. Do you agree? What might that particular mask reveal? What other masks have you discerned?

"Our society is no longer scripturally literate," writes Dykstra (p. 6), an observation which assumes that an earlier era had greater scriptural literacy. Have you noticed this loss of literacy? In what specific ways? What effects does this loss have upon our life together as a society?

Reflect

Jesus teaches, "Blessed are those who hunger and thirst for righteousness, for they will be filled" (Matt. 5:6). Describe the condition of your own hunger for righteousness, for daily bread. What specific shape does this hunger take—that is, what do you long for? What activities or dynamics in your life allow this hunger to be deeply felt? Conversely, what activities or dynamics serve to mask this hunger, to hide its existence?

Edward Farley describes a "nasty suspicion" that there is no God providing daily bread to meet our hungers, which, Dykstra suggests, drives us to "a kind of practical atheism" (p. 9). A common pattern in the Christian life is that practical atheism takes hold especially in particular areas of our lives. Do you see it in your life? In what areas? What feeds that dynamic, and what serves to heal that dynamic?

Implications for Faith Education

One of the great challenges of faith education lies in teaching those who show next to no outward signs of hunger for the bread of the Lord. I frequently hear college students say, "I wish I had taken faith education more seriously during my high school years, now that I realize how wonderful it actually is." Where have you encountered this challenge? Does such apparent lack of hunger contradict this chapter, or is it a masked hunger? To what extent should one accept this phenomenon as normal, developmental behavior? How does such acceptance affect one's teaching?

Faith education often begins by searching for and appropriately connecting with the hunger Dykstra describes. This searching usually takes the shape of patient, persevering listening and noticing. In what ways have you sought to do this? Recount stories that tell what you have learned from such listening and noticing.

Areas for Deeper Exploration

Which movies, plays, songs, novels, or other expressions have you seen or heard which express a hunger for God (perhaps without naming it as such)? In what ways have they helped you to understand this hunger? If a particular one resonates with your group, perhaps it would be fruitful to experience it together.

PART 2: LIFE

Chapter 2: The Faithful Life

Throughout his career, Craig Dykstra has resisted attempts to articulate neat formulas about the character of faith or simple stages that describe faith maturation. This resistance comes from his deep conviction that "the word *faith* refuses to be defined simply" (p. 17). Faith is not its own starting point, but rather is a *response* to the activity of God who is known through the story of God's actions. Dykstra distinguishes "faith" from the "life of faith." To describe the former, he follows John Calvin's lead and provides a Trinitarian understanding: "Christian faith . . . is the knowledge of God in Jesus Christ through the Holy Spirit" (p. 22). The entire story of the actions of God are held together in Jesus Christ (2 Cor. 1:20–22; Col. 1:15–20), and through the Holy Spirit we are grafted into the story (Eph. 1:13–14).

Emphasizing knowledge as the central dimension of faith can be misleading, because knowledge often connotes that which is abstract, impersonal, and objective. Instead, here it resonates with the older English we find in the King James Bible: "Adam *knew* Eve his wife; and she conceived, and bare Cain" (Gen. 4:1). "Knowing" in this sense is intensely and intimately relational, but it is not merely subjective. In the context of the God-person relation, it is a "firm and certain knowledge" that "is couched in the recital of a story about this God. The story is the one told in the Bible" (p. 18). It is knowledge in which "the attitudes and the knowing come together; they are parts of one another" (p. 22).

Faith flows to the life of faith because knowing God and being known by God are utterly transformational. Just as Eve gave birth after she was known by Adam, so new life is born in us when we are known by God. "The 'life of faith' is the way of living that is organized by faith and flows out of faith" (p. 19). This is not to say that faith is prior and the life of faith is subsequent to it. Rather, the life of faith of the community provides a context for faith to grow, and faith in turn comes to expression in the life of faith. Every dimension of our being comes to reflect and participate in new life more fully. On the one hand, there is no recipe or formula for such participation. On the other hand, "the life of faith . . . must be patterned, structured, kept in place and on course over the long haul through the development of disciplines and habits, both personal and corporate" (p. 29).

We find a second distinction in this chapter that is also central to the book: the distinction between life according to the Spirit and life according to the flesh (see especially pp. 23–24). Every part of our faith and life of faith experiences the contrary pulls of the Spirit and of the powers and principalities that war against the Spirit. At its deepest level, sin is not about doing bad things; rather, it distorts our ways of seeing, our sense of identity, the priorities that orient our lives, how we experience reality. In other words, just as faith and the life of faith are all-encompassing and embrace all that we do and are, so the struggle between life in the Spirit and life in the flesh is also all-encompassing.

> **CHU on the chapter**
>
> What was:
>
> • confusing
> • helpful
> • unsettling?

Questions for Discussion

Observe

I would guess that this was one of the most difficult chapters to write, because it seeks to provide words and concrete concepts that do justice to the mystery of faith. Describe in your own words the distinction between "faith" and the "life of faith." (It may be helpful to read Dykstra's additional thoughts in n. 11, pp. 31–32.) In our age, the phrase "firm and certain knowledge" (pp. 18, 20) seems like an oxymoron when applied to faith. In what ways do you experience faith's knowledge as "firm and certain"? On page 23 Dykstra lists several Scripture passages that describe the newness of the life of faith. Read some of these together (I highly recommend excerpts from Romans 8). How does the "life of faith" described in these passages flow out of "faith"?

The distinction between life according to the Spirit and life according to the flesh (p. 23) can also be described as the struggle between nourishing one's hungers with the true bread of life or with false breads that do not satisfy (p. 24). Dykstra dares to say that these contrasting phrases "point to those things in the life of Christian faith so basic that everything else is derived from them" (p. 24). Do you agree? In what specific ways is this struggle "so basic"? Make your responses concrete by giving specific examples of the "everything else" that is derived from the struggle.

Reflect

The word "faith," while central to Christian thought and practice, is often used without careful examination of what is meant by it. As you read this chapter, how was your understanding of the word "faith" affirmed, challenged, and/or stretched? What might you have realized for the first time concerning your own understanding of the word "faith"?

I have studied this book with many college students and found that they resonated deeply with the assertion that "faith is not only knowing the message; it is knowing the Messenger" (p. 21). What is the difference between these two knowings? What difficulties arise when one of these is emphasized over the other? How well do you hold these two knowings together? What shapes the way you hold them together?

The chapter assumes that faith affects our entire being and, therefore, gradually transforms us so that "we actually experience our lives differently" (p. 24), "the very environment in which we live is both enlarged and transformed" (p. 26), and "our very hungers become transformed, so that to live in Christ is the only food we crave" (p. 30). Ponder your own life history; in what specific ways do any of these three statements describe your life (at least somewhat)?

Implications for Faith Education

The fact that there is so much mystery woven within faith can paralyze the faith educator. What difference could I possibly make? The task seems overwhelming and impossible. In what ways do you experience moments of paralysis in your role as a faith educator?

The preacher in Ecclesiastes writes, "Just as you do not know how the breath comes to the bones in the mother's womb, so you do not know the work of God, who makes everything. In the morning sow your seed, and at evening do not let your hands be idle; for you do not know which will prosper, this or that, or whether both alike will be good" (Eccl. 11:5–6). I have found that combining this teaching with the distinction between faith and the life of faith is powerfully liberating for me as a faith educator. I am not called to make a difference; I am not called to transform someone's faith. I am simply called to sow seeds in the soil of others' lives of faith and then to let go and wait for the mysterious presence of God to work on those seeds. How have you come to terms with the mysteries involved in faith education? What remains unresolved?

Areas for Deeper Exploration

This chapter involved many, many thoughts that are worthy of further study. (The chapter is so packed; the material here could easily have filled three chapters.) This material deals with faith couched within the story of God (p. 18); faith as trusting belief (pp. 19–20); faith as intellectual inquiry into the truth (p. 22); the corporate dimension of faith (pp. 24, 26–27); several aspects of the life of faith: seeing, struggling, serving, and hoping (pp. 26–29); and the distinction between faith and meaning (p. 30). Pursue any specific dimensions listed here that the group finds intriguing or fruitful.

Chapter 3: Growing in Faith

Dykstra builds on the distinctions of chapter 2 to focus directly on the central theme of the book: growing in faith. Because faith is somewhat elusive and always involves the struggle between Spirit and flesh, one cannot lay out precise guidelines for growing in faith that guarantee steady improvement. This growth is "God's gift"; and receiving it as such "frees us to allow the Spirit to work in our growing, rather than to struggle against the Spirit by trying to control it through our own powers" (p. 38).

Imagine that our faith/life of faith is a rainbow composed of many colors. Some of the colors are clear, vibrant, and alive. Others are pale, weak, almost sickly. We can see streaks, smudges, darknesses within the colors that do not belong there. Growing in the life of faith is like a cleansing and deepening of the colors, so that the full rainbow becomes just a bit more what it is meant to be. "Growth in the life of faith involves the penetration or infiltration of faith into ever-increasing dimensions of our existence" (p. 38).

Reading tip: Occasionally, Dykstra makes a major point in the chapter endnotes.

Dykstra then moves to the principal thesis of the book: Christian practices are central to growing in the life of faith. "A *practice* is an ongoing, shared activity of a community of people that partly defines and partly makes them who they are" (p. 48, n. 16). *Community* indicates that the body of Christ plays an absolutely indispensable role in personal faith growth, which is a radical claim in a highly individualistic culture that often focuses primarily on "my personal relationship with Jesus Christ." *Activity* points to what Dykstra calls "participation in the means of grace" (pp. 40–41). I am not a passive observer or absorber; I grow in the life of faith as an active participant.

The last half of the chapter (pp. 41–46) introduces the concept of Christian practices. Many of the thoughts here are developed in more detail in the next two chapters and, therefore, do not need to be discussed in detail yet. Just as faith encompasses every dimension of our lives, so do the practices. Just as faith shapes our identities, so "these practices become the fundamental habits of life around which identity and character are formed" (p. 45). Just as the Spirit/flesh struggle is interwoven throughout faith, so it is possible "to engage in the practices 'according to the flesh' rather than 'in the Spirit'" (p. 45).

CHU on the chapter

What was:

- confusing
- helpful
- unsettling?

Questions for Discussion

Observe

One of the central theses of the entire book lies in Dykstra's assertion that "practices . . . place people in touch with God's redemptive activity" (p. 43). This statement is radical because our experience-centered culture assumes that *feelings of closeness to God* or *feeling God within* most fundamentally put us in touch with God. In addition to feelings, there are several other common candidates for what places us in touch with God: doctrinal purity, moral uprightness, clarity of meaning. Before reading this chapter, how might you have completed this sentence: "The dimension of life that places me most closely in touch with God's presence is _____ ." How—if at all—has reading the chapter affected the way you complete the sentence? (If you find it difficult to agree with Dykstra at this point, remember that the next two chapters develop this thesis in much more detail.)

Reflect

Look over the list of practices on pp. 42–43; invite everyone to name two or three that are central to each one's life, and describe why each is central. In what ways do these practices place you in touch with God's redemptive activity? This list is by no means intended to be exhaustive (for example, Dykstra names several others on p. 145); what other practices come to mind?

Implications for Faith Education

Perhaps faith education and practices seem to be two crucial but very separate areas of the Christian life. The former involves working with curricula, lesson plans, classroom management, and teaching techniques; the latter refers to regular habits of worship, hospitality, seeking justice, and so on. Explore the connection between these two by discussing this question: what practices are woven within the activities of faith education? For example, the manner in which a teacher begins each class (and thereby sets its tone), the acts of hospitality that transform a class from a gathering of cliques and loners into a community, and the telling of personal stories to illustrate points in the curriculum are all practices woven within the activities of teaching. What other practices come to mind? In what ways do you practice them or see them practiced in your community? What effects do these have upon faith education?

Areas for Deeper Exploration

During the past few years, a significant body of literature concerning the practices has been published, led by *Practicing Our Faith* (ed. D. Bass [San Francisco: Jossey-Bass, 1997]). A great deal of helpful information is available at www.practicingourfaith.org. You may find it beneficial to explore these materials to deepen and expand Dykstra's work with practices.

PART 3: PRACTICES

Chapter 4: The Power of Christian Practices

"Work out your own salvation with fear and trembling; for it is God who is at work in you, enabling you both to will and to work for his good pleasure" (Phil. 2:12–13).

"Let the word of Christ dwell in you richly; teach and admonish one another in all wisdom; and with gratitude in your hearts sing psalms, hymns, and spiritual songs to God" (Col. 3:16).

These two teachings from the apostle Paul point to a central thesis of not only chapter 4 but the entire book: when we live out Christian practices, we discover that our actions have become a means through which God acts within us and through us, and "the suspicion that theology is really about nothing more than human subjectivity—simply loses its power" (p. 53). Just as the Word of Christ (one of many biblical ways of naming the presence of the Holy Spirit) dwells within in increasing richness as the practices of teaching, admonishing, and singing are carried out, so there are *depths* inside the practices. As they are practiced in greater depth (multiple layers) and breadth (multiple practices in varied contexts), "they become arenas in which something is done to us, in us, and through us that we could not of ourselves do, that is beyond what we do" (p. 56).

The practices of reading and hearing Scripture and allowing enemies and strangers to be transformed into neighbors illustrate these dynamics. Through the former "the community comes to know a story; and by knowing the story it finds itself in a new world, on an adventure, and in relation to the Agent who makes the dependable promises that initiate and sustain it all" (p. 60). At the heart of the story stands the proclamation that "you are no longer strangers and aliens, but you are citizens with the saints and also members of the household of God, . . . in whom you also are built together spiritually into a dwelling place for God" (Eph. 2:19, 22). The body of Christ has been transformed from enemies and strangers to fellow citizens; as it lives out the story of God, it reenacts that story by continuing this transformation of enemies and strangers into friends and neighbors.

So understood and lived out, practices become "habitations of the Spirit." One might put it this way: the Spirit *inhabits* the body of Christ as that body practices *habits* that participate in God's work of redemption. Or, to paraphrase Paul's words from Colossians 3 quoted above, "let the word of Christ dwell in you richly as you [*insert several Christian practices here*]." This inhabitation is particularly fostered when "multiple practices are engaged in in relation to one another" (p. 63) for "the power of these practices . . . comes only when they are in interrelation to one another" (p. 56).

CHU on the chapter

What was:

• confusing
• helpful
• unsettling?

For example, the practice of reading Scripture may evoke a passion for seeking justice; practices that seek justice will in turn likely deepen one's reading of Scripture, build community, and further hospitality; and the cyclical rhythm of interwoven practices continues to deepen.

Questions for Discussion

Observe

The previous chapter provided a long list of practices; this chapter focuses primarily on two from that list. Almost all Christians agree that the practice of reading and hearing Scripture is central. Do you agree? Why or why not? In what ways do you (personally) and your community honor that centrality? It may be helpful to list every way in which the Scriptures are read and heard in your community (remember, for example, that many hymns are Scripture-based).

Dykstra names the transforming of enemies and strangers to fellow creatures and neighbors as a fundamental Christian practice. Do you agree? In what ways does this practice resonate with the central heart of the Christian faith, and in what ways might it be more peripheral? In what ways is this practice carried out in your community? To what extent do these expressions of this practice reflect the importance you perceive it to have in the Christian life?

Reflect

Dykstra observes that practices are ordinary activities that we do all the time, but "on second thought . . . we may begin to realize how rarely most of us *really* do many of [them]" (p. 54, emphasis added). Take one practice that has been present in your life for quite some time, and mentally trace its history. Do you see variations in the depth and intensity with which you have carried out this practice? What factors have caused these variations? What steps have you taken and could you take to strengthen its depth and intensity?

Implications for Faith Education

Dykstra describes four things God uses the Bible to do (pp. 58–60). Review these four together, and use them to examine the faith education you have received and are part of delivering. What assumptions about the purpose of the Bible are implicit in the faith education you have experienced? Recall and describe examples of Bible teaching that illustrate aspects of these four purposes. What did they look like?

Areas for Deeper Exploration

Dykstra refers to several classic writings on Christian piety and living in this chapter, including Eugene Peterson's *Working the Angles*, Dietrich Bonhoeffer's *Life Together*, and Philip Haillie's *Lest Innocent Blood Be Shed*. If anyone in the group has read any of the books Dykstra has mentioned, it would be encouraging to hear a favorite passage or two read aloud. *Weapons of the Spirit* (1989) is a wonderful documentary film about Le Chambon and would provide a good group viewing experience. Pierre Sauvage—the film's writer, producer, and director—was born in this unique Christian oasis but did not learn until the age of eighteen that he and his family were Jewish and survivors of the Holocaust.

Chapter 5: Education in Christian Practices

Several dimensions of Christian practices are woven throughout this chapter, and this complex interweaving can obscure its most important thread: *practices are teachable*. One cannot *give* faith to another through teaching, one cannot *transform* another's life of faith through teaching, but one can *teach* another how to grow in living out Christian practices, and this teaching, in turn, may transform another's life of faith and faith.

Dykstra's short paragraph on p. 71 that outlines three ways in which a practice is learned holds the entire chapter together. These three ways—doing, watching, and being coached—flow from the conviction that practices are *skill-based*, that is, they are (among other things) abilities that one learns how to do and works toward improving. A common assumption about education is that one first learns theory and then puts it into practice. Here that sequence is not operative; doing, watching models, and being coached are like three moments on a wheel that never stops turning. The "doing" helps one recognize what to look for in watching others; both of these awaken an awareness of the need for coaching; coaching provides encouragement and guidance for continued "doing," and so the wheel goes round. As the skills develop, the depth of the practice also expands.

In the book's introduction, Craig Dykstra describes the relation between experience and education. "Education is our attempt to help one another understand our experience of this Mystery [of God] in its breadth and depth and in its implications for ourselves and for the world" (p. xii). Education in the practices also fits this pattern of education that clarifies and deepens experience. Because many practices are communal in character, learning the practices involves the *experience* of growing in relationship with others who function as teachers. Their teaching, in turn, deepens as our relationship with them deepens, as our teachers become "personally significant to us" (p. 73). Dykstra's six conditions for learning the practices (p. 73) illustrate the mutual deepening that takes place within a healthy intertwining of education and experience.

> **CHU on the chapter**
>
> What was:
>
> • confusing
> • helpful
> • unsettling?

Questions for Discussion

Observe

A common assumption in our compartmentalized society is that "professional" activities require intensive training in specific skills, but "faith" activities are simply done automatically and naturally. Dykstra's description of learning the skills that are inherent in the practices belies that assumption. To what extent has that societal assumption been your assumption? Do you agree with Dykstra's account of skills, which treats Christian practices as analogous to baseball (pp. 68–72)? Why or why not?

Brainstorm together a "skills analysis" of any one practice. For example, the practice of encouraging others requires skills in (1) noticing where encouragement is needed, (2) determining if I am the right person to provide encouragement, and (3) finding the right words to say (and not to say) to provide encouragement. What specific skill set is required for any other practice (for example, Sunday worship)?

Reflect

Recall how the three ways of learning a practice—doing, watching, and being coached—have been present in your life, remembering that they occur in many different kinds of combinations. The doing may have been voluntary or required; the watching may have been deliberate or completely unintended and not appreciated until years later; the coaching may have been actively sought out, or dispensed unasked (and, perhaps, without being appreciated at the time). The watching may have occurred in person or through reading biographical accounts; similarly, the coaching may have been live or provided through books. Watching may have inspired doing, or doing may have awakened the need for coaching and watching. Frequently, I hear others say that they were determined to do something well after watching it being done poorly. Provide an anecdotal learning history of any practice that is part of your life.

Implications for Faith Education

Most teachers of faith education are fairly comfortable in the coaching role (after all, that's central to teaching), but the thought of serving as a role model can be terrifying. What I find reassuring is the research that shows that very few people are seeking *perfect* models; rather, *genuine* models who are honest about their confusions and weaknesses and obviously care about their students are deeply appreciated. Think of those whom you perceive as models; has this *perfect vs. genuine* distinction been true for you? How do you function as a role model for others? In what ways is this terrifying, stimulating, and/or encouraging?

Areas for Deeper Exploration

Many dimensions to this chapter have been bypassed in order to focus on the process of teaching habits. These two questions address other topics from the chapter.

Dykstra writes, "Christian educators need to think about how to lead people beyond a reliance on 'random acts of kindness' into shared patterns of life that are informed by the deepest insights of our traditions, and about how to lead people beyond privatized spiritualities into more thoughtful participation in God's activity in the world" (p. 67). What pictures or experiences does this assertion bring to your mind? Imagine the two extremes that Dykstra names here as points on a continuum. In what ways have you seen a community shift on this continuum, and what factors contributed to this shift?

Developing the practices involves the paradox of growing in skill while remembering that "faith is not a human achievement; it is a gift. . . . Our basic task is not mastery and control. It is instead trust and grateful receptivity" (pp. 75–76). How do you experience that tension in your life? Without the paradox, the practices can quickly degenerate into salvation by works, empty ritualism, or judgmental legalism. In what ways do you encounter shades of any of these or other temptations?

PART 4: PLACES

Chapter 6: The Formative Power of the Congregation

Part 4 of *Growing in the Life of Faith*, titled "Places," applies the material presented in parts 1–3 to five different arenas of life: the congregation, the family, the faith education of children and adolescents, the college or university, and the theological school. Dykstra takes us to these faith communities because "the beliefs, values, attitudes, stories, rituals, and moral practices of a faith community are the human forces most powerful in shaping a person's spiritual journey" (p. 83). These five—with the addition of one's circle of fellow believers—are the places where the vast majority of faith growth occurs. Each of these communal settings is also a place where the struggle between life according to the Spirit and life according to the flesh (described in chapter 2) is very active.

Dykstra begins with the congregation, and he identifies "the achievement-oriented lifestyle"—a desperate attempt to earn the loving attention of others—as the fundamental idolatry that infects the Christian church (p. 86). He dares to say "that virtually every personal and social evil has its roots in our need to manipulate the world into paying attention to us" (p. 90). This particular evil is very crafty, for when we come to understand it more clearly or "win" a small victory over it, that understanding or victory in turn becomes an achievement that reinforces rather than undermines the evil and thus continues a cyclical pattern of mutual self-destruction.

But there are practices that address this idolatry, especially worship shaped by the rhythms of confession and repentance (p. 91). The term "worship" has two overlapping meanings for Dykstra: It refers to the specific *event* of believers gathered for praise, prayer, and instruction, and it refers to one's *entire life* lived as a prayer of dependent adoration before the face of God. As the rhythm of confession and repentance is woven into the worship event, the worshipers' entire lives are freed to be lived more honestly and vulnerably, and self-destructive patterns *begin* to be broken. That is why worship is the central practice of the congregation. It frees the communal body to be renewed by its Lord, rather than anxiously seeking to justify itself through its own achievements. Perhaps the clearest sign that the seeds of such freedom are present is humor, a lightheartedness that does not need to take oneself so seriously (p. 95).

> **CHU on the chapter**
>
> What was:
>
> - confusing
> - helpful
> - unsettling?

Questions for Discussion

Observe

Dykstra's assertion that virtually every evil has its roots in seeking attention is a dramatic claim (p. 90). One could use his vocabulary to paraphrase the serpent's temptation in Genesis 3 to say, "God isn't actually paying loving attention to you. God wants to keep you out of the way, inferior, by forbidding you from eating that fruit. If you really want to get God's attention, go ahead and eat some" (see Gen. 3:5). Identify ways in which you see the connection between seeking attention and specific evils.

Are there specific evils that have nothing whatsoever to do with seeking attention? In what ways is the "seeking attention" hypothesis important for the themes of this chapter?

Understanding worship as both event and lifestyle flows directly from New Testament teaching (read, for example, Col. 3:16–17). In our society it is commonly assumed that worship is limited to a Sunday event and is completely separate from the rest of life. How do the Carl Phillips et al. and Harvey Cox stories summarized in this chapter illustrate these two over-lapping definitions? How do you understand and experience the inter-twining of these two definitions of worship? What factors help you to integrate them, and what factors contribute to pulling them apart?

Reflect

Read the parable of the Prodigal Son (Luke 15:11–32) out loud together. Notice that *both* sons are trapped in the achievement-oriented lifestyle; the younger one assumes that his sinful achievements define his identity, and therefore, he is only worthy to be called a servant (i.e., one whose rela-tionship to the master is defined by achievement). The older son assumes that his good achievements define him. The father rejects both assump-tions and treats both sons as children, not servants. How do these conflict-ing identities of child and servant play out in your life? What dynamics reinforce or undermine each of these identities? (Remember, the struggle between these two is present in every believer's life; the purpose of this discussion is not to berate ourselves for noting this struggle, but to encourage one another in growing through it.)

Someone once said that "being too busy is the socially acceptable sin in Christian community." To what extent is this true of your congrega-tion? What factors contribute to or provide antidotes for the "too busy" syndrome?

Several years ago I asked an out-of-town friend of mine what her con-gregation was like, and I'll never forget her reply. After hesitating, she looked somewhat embarrassed and then replied, "I'm not sure what to say, except that it's a forgiving place." Her observation resonates very well with Dykstra's emphasis on confession and repentance in this chapter. Ponder the character or climate of your congregation. What words or phrases come to mind? What dynamics contribute to this character or cli-mate? How central is confession and repentance? How prevalent is com-munal forgiveness?

Implications for Faith Education

A dilemma at the heart of faith education is this: achievement is a significant motivator in education; when the goal of education is to rest in grace more deeply, the *means* of achievement easily undermine the *end* of grace. In what ways does your congregation's faith education provide healing for the achievement compulsion, and in what ways might it unwittingly reinforce it?

Seeker-sensitive congregations constitute a significant movement in contemporary church culture. A common assumption in this movement states that "confession of sin" is not seeker-friendly and, therefore, should not be a part of such worship. Do you agree with this assumption? How does that assumption fit with this chapter? Adolescents also do a great deal of seeking. What is the place (if any) for confession of sin in adolescent faith education?

Areas for Deeper Exploration

Are there any Lake Wobegon fans in the group? (Lake Wobegon is the fictional Minnesota town whose ongoing sagas are reported weekly by Garrison Keillor on his public radio show *A Prairie Home Companion*.) Very often Keillor describes congregational life with the "lightness of touch" that Dykstra says is a sign of freedom (p. 95). Find an appropriate segment (www.prairiehome.org, link to "program archives") and listen to it as a group.

Transforming Congregational Culture by Anthony Robinson (Grand Rapids: Eerdmans, 2003) explores in concrete detail and with sensitivity and wisdom the struggle between Spirit and flesh within the congregation. I recommend this book highly to all in positions of congregational leadership who wish to work out the themes of this chapter.

Those who desire to explore the achievement compulsion more deeply in a personal, devotional way may enjoy reading Henri Nouwen's *The Return of the Prodigal Son: A Story of Homecoming* (New York: Image Books, 1994).

Chapter 7: Family Promises

One might be tempted to look at this chapter's title and assume that it is a *niche* chapter: helpful for those dealing with marital or parenting issues, but not essential to the faith-educating life of the church as a whole. Dykstra's assertion that families are most fundamentally about promise-making debunks that assumption, for the Christian faith is all about (as the old hymn declares) "standing on the promises of God." Both marital and baptismal promises are spoken and heard in liturgical settings, which are "contexts that secure promises" (p. 102). Our family-oriented promise-making takes place inside the promise-making and -keeping of God and is sustained by the promise-making of an entire community. Family promises are one (albeit central) dimension of discipleship; there is a logical sequence to examining faith growth in the family *after* discussing its presence in the context of the congregation.

Dykstra makes an important distinction between family promise-making and promise-keeping (pp. 100–101). It must be the former—and not the latter—that constitutes families, because the heart of the matter is not *success* but *commitment*. This distinction resonates with the themes of the previous chapter: like congregations, families are driven not by a dynamic of achievement, but by a rhythm of confession and repentance that frees one to recommit to the promises in spite of past failures, weaknesses, and just plain mediocrities.

Dykstra links family promise-making to the whole of the Christian life under the umbrella of "the vocation of discipleship," which is "the response that believes and accepts God's promises and in turn promises simply to participate in that new way of life" (p. 107). In his Gospel, Mark records a similar link: after a particularly poignant scene in which Jesus' own family concludes that he is "out of his mind," Jesus declares, "Who are my mother and my brothers? . . . Here are my mother and my brothers! Whoever does the will of God is my brother and sister and mother" (Mark 3:21, 33–35). One liberating implication of setting family within the context of discipleship is "that the particular sociological shape of one's own family now has no primacy" (p. 108). Narrow definitions of family cannot be ultimate, because the definition of family flows from the "being-discipled" family of God.

> **CHU on the chapter**
>
> What was:
>
> - confusing
> - helpful
> - unsettling?

Questions for Discussion

Observe

Dykstra stresses that it must be promise-making rather than promise-keeping that constitutes family. What are the implications of stressing that distinction? Do you agree? If we accept that promise-making constitutes family, what is the role of promise-keeping in relation to promise-making?

What difference does it make that family promises are made in liturgical settings? Or, to put it another way, what contrasts can you see between family promises made in liturgical contexts and the promise-making vacuum of our culture? What settings other than liturgical are available in our culture for family promise-making?

In my experience, the ways a congregation enfolds nontraditional families reveal a great deal about its character. This enfolding (or lack thereof) takes place in many ways, including relationships, small group structures (e.g., the "couples Bible study"), appointments to leadership positions, and language used to describe the membership. In what ways have you seen congregations encourage *all* families to grow in discipleship?

Reflect

A generation ago, *Love Story*, a blockbuster movie, declared that "love means never having to say you're sorry," a motto that reflects the cultural promise-making vacuum that Dykstra describes (pp. 102–3). I can recall times of trudging up the stairs to a child's bedroom to say "I'm sorry, I became angry and said things that I didn't mean." Ponder the role that both speaking and hearing the phrase "I'm sorry" has played in your own experience of family promise-making and promise-keeping. What differences does this phrase—by its presence or its absence —make?

"We have a responsibility now for one another's family promises" (p. 109). That's easy to say, but anyone who has observed poor parenting or one spouse treating a partner with disrespect knows how delicate it *always* is to carry out such a responsibility. In addition, a congregation trapped in the grip of the achievement compulsion can wreak havoc on family life by adding layer upon layer of activities for individual family members to participate in, often straining its promise-keeping abilities. Perhaps the best way to fulfill our responsibility for one another's family promises is by developing practices that nourish promise-making and promise-keeping. For example, in our home we deliberately resist the fast-food syndrome and schedule our lives around sit-down family mealtimes. What practices are (or could be) part of your home and community life that strengthen and support the promise-making fabric of family life?

Implications for Faith Education

When a child is baptized or dedicated in your congregation, does the entire congregation make a promise to that child similar to the one Dykstra describes (p. 108)? If yes, read the promise that is made out loud together. In what ways does the congregation carry out this promise?

Family promise-making and -keeping are skills that need to be learned through doing, watching, and being coached. How are these skills learned in your church community? What suggestions do you have for strengthening this learning?

One way to strengthen the complementary relationship between congregational discipleship and family life is to seek ways to involve the family appropriately in its members' faith education. For example, curricula can include suggestions for follow-up during family devotions. These attempts can backfire, however, and alienate children who come from homes where family devotions are simply impossible (for whatever reason). How can the discipleship links between congregation and home be strengthened, and what dangers lurk behind efforts to strengthen these links?

Areas for Deeper Exploration

Many movies and novels explore the dynamics of the promissory character of family life. A favorite of mine is the movie *Babette's Feast*, because it weaves together the dynamics of a family (a pastor and his two daughters), the dynamics of their little congregation, and several unusual expressions of the practice of hospitality. What favorites come to your mind? If possible, watch an appropriate video together as a group.

Chapter 8: Youth and the Language of Faith

I must confess that I wish this chapter was the first one of a sequel to *Growing in the Life of Faith*, with the rest of the sequel expanding and making concrete the concepts of this chapter. As a professor of youth ministry, I recognize that Dykstra's account of the role of language in faith education is absolutely critical. In raising this subject, he has taken us into the heart of the paradox that is woven throughout this book: the more central a concept is in faith education, the deeper its elusiveness, and the greater the weight of its mystery. Trying to speak the truths that are most important to us reminds us of just how ambiguous human language can be, and really hearing what others are saying requires great sensitivity.

We are creatures wired in such a way that we must give words to our experience in order to truly experience it. As young children, we don't really give words to our experience; rather, we are given words by the communities that nurture us. Because faith lies at the center of our experience and gives it coherence, faith, language, and experience are inextricably woven together. This jumble is further complicated by the struggle between Spirit and flesh that can be discerned in every thread of the weave. Words interpret experience, but "so many diverse patterns of interpretation are available" (p. 121), many of which subtly (or blatantly) celebrate the idolatries prevalent in the culture.

Furthermore, using the right words may have very little to do with using words rightly. See, for example, the powerful Halbfas quote on pp. 119–20, which I encourage you to read out loud together. The distinction Halbfas makes resonates with the two meanings of worship introduced in chapter 7. Just as worship is both an event and an entire way of life, so one's language of faith is not compartmentalized, limited to "God-talk," but is seen most clearly in the way one speaks about all matters of life. "Some people just speak about children, their house and garden, supper and bed, and yet their discourse is full of faith and hope, thanks and prayer" (p. 120).

The adolescent hunger for identity and meaning occurs within the language that is available. How one uses language fits the pattern of practices that Dykstra has discussed earlier in the book. It is a learned skill, and the learning takes place as one does it, observes others using language, and is coached in its use. The words that one employs are able to become a habitation of the Spirit, able to become "discourse . . . full of faith and hope, thanks and prayer" (p. 120). Because language learning follows this pattern, adolescents learn to use it well when they belong to communities that use it well. For this reason, such learning "is not simply a task for youth leaders, teachers, and ministers with youth. It is a task for the whole religious community" (p. 125).

> **CHU on the chapter**
>
> What was:
>
> - confusing
> - helpful
> - unsettling?

Questions for Discussion

Observe

I began the synopsis by pointing out how elusive and mysterious our words about faith can be. Attempt to become a little more clear about the role of language in your own life of faith by describing, with the help of specific examples, what the following sentence means to you: My everyday language reveals a great deal about my faith and my life of faith, giving expression to how I see the world (p. 114), my distinct way of life (p. 115), and the dynamics of my faith community (p. 116).

The excerpt from the trial of Daniel Berrigan (pp. 117–18) illustrates how the language of one faith is incomprehensible to the language system of another. Have you ever experienced or observed this type of confusion? Tell the story, and observe what about the language of faith was misunderstood.

Reflect

Dykstra wonders if "we ourselves, as parents, friends, teachers, and pastors of youth, do not really know and use the language of faith in any meaningful way" (pp. 123–24). One possible way to think about this is to see our language as "humble truth-telling," that is, naming realities for what they truly are in the light of God as clearly as we are able by the light we have received: naming blessings as blessings, sin as sin, and a fourteen-year-old girl as a temple of the Holy Ghost (p. 113). Humility is essential if it is not to be spoken "rigidly and in an authoritarian manner" (p. 126). Identify a person who uses the language of faith well, and describe the qualities and characteristics that combine to form this skill. In what specific ways has this person served as a model for you?

Frequently short phrases or sentences function as "touchstones" for our language of faith, serving as a prism through which our language flows. For example, Anne Lamott writes that all her prayers boil down to "help me, help me, help me" and "thank you, thank you, thank you" (*Traveling Mercies* [New York: Anchor Books, 1999], p. 82). I find that Jehoshaphat's prayer, "We do not know what to do, but our eyes are on you" (2 Chron. 20:12), shapes the language of my faith, especially in difficult situations. Are there such phrases or sentences that are (or have been in the past) central for you? What are they? Why are/were they so central? If certain phrases were once central but are no longer, what changed?

Merton Strommen observes that religion "is almost a taboo subject in the home" (p. 123). To what extent is his research confirmed by your experience? Why is it almost taboo? What practices might we cultivate to ease this anxiety? For example, some families read age-appropriate devotional material at dinnertime, pray with their children at bedtime, or conduct various rituals that correlate with the Christian year. What are the benefits and potential dangers of such practices?

Implications for Faith Education

Theodore A. Turnau III, a professor in the Czech Republic, responded to the tragic events of 9/11 by writing, "Repeatedly I heard friends say, 'It looked just like a Hollywood movie.' That means, quite simply, that popular culture . . . teaches us how to understand the world. It teaches us how to see" ("Equipping Students to Engage Popular Culture," in *The Word of God for the Academy in Contemporary Culture(s)* (ed. John B. Hulst and Peter Balla [Budapest: Karoli Gaspar Reformed University Publishing House, 2003], p. 135). A great deal of adolescent identity-searching is shaped by the language-world of popular culture. This shaping affects faith education in both positive and negative ways. For example, popular expressions of the hunger Dykstra described in chapter 1 can help a teacher connect with students' hunger for God. In what specific ways do you notice the effects of popular culture? What do you see as its positive and negative effects?

Dykstra's assertion that religious language "makes possible historical continuity" (p. 118) brings to mind a well-known quote from Jaroslav Pelikan: "Tradition is the living faith of those now dead; traditionalism is the dead faith of those still living" (*The Vindication of Tradition* [New Haven, CT: Yale University Press, 1984], p. 65). One of the results of popular culture's antihistorical tendencies is that all things historical are denigrated, and all that is traditional is perceived as dead traditionalism. How do these tendencies affect your work in faith education? In what ways do you accommodate these tendencies, and in what ways do you challenge them?

One response I have every time I read this chapter is what Dykstra calls "the problem of the too big" (pp. 66–67). I think that shaping the faith language of adolescents and even strengthening my own involves "learning a whole way of life" and is "too large, too grand, too big" (p. 67); in other words, it easily feels hopelessly overwhelming. But I've also learned that little steps can make significant inroads; for example, in my own faith teaching, I quickly introduce students to the Hebrew word *shalom* and then use it in many ways. I find it functions as a firm stepping-stone in a joyfully tumultuous mountain stream. Are there words or phrases that you use in your teaching, or that others used in teaching you, that serve this function? What are they, and how are they helpful?

Areas for Deeper Exploration

Dykstra writes, "a major task for adolescents is to find . . . a way of life that they can make their own" (p. 121). A recent publication, *Way to Live: Christian Practices for Teens* (ed. Dorothy C. Bass and Don C. Richter [Nashville: Upper Room Books, 2002]), provides a great deal of concrete wisdom and guidance for adolescents concerning finding this way of life and develops the central themes of *Growing in the Life of Faith* very well. A related Web site, *www.waytolive.org*, offers many resources that encourage young people in their growth in the life of faith.

Chapter 9: Communities of Conviction in Religion and Higher Education

Chapter 10: Love's Knowledge and Theological Education

Perhaps you found chapter 9 to be one of the more difficult chapters to follow (if so, I hope you found the last paragraph on p. 134 to provide a helpful summary of the first half of the chapter). I have combined chapter 9 with chapter 10 in this guide because the latter expands upon and clarifies the central themes of the former (and both are relatively short). Both deal with higher education, although chapter 10 focuses on *theological* higher education. These themes are crucial for faith education: when a young adult leaves her home community to attend college or university, the faith education baton is passed on to what may feel to us like a black hole of secularism. How are we to understand this important life transition and help others navigate it well?

Dykstra quickly penetrates to the heart of the matter. Many assume that the primary faith challenges a young adult faces in a university concern the temptations of heavy drinking and casual sex. One's morality, however, flows from one's perception of reality. Therefore, Dykstra is more concerned in these chapters with how we are trained to see the world, and this seeing flows from assumptions concerning the nature of higher education. He notes that ethicist Stanley Hauerwas claims that "even Christian higher education is . . . largely corrupting, since secular assumptions govern the structure of the curriculum, contemporary methods of inquiry, and virtually every other important dimension of the educational environment and process" (p. 135). The language of inquiry in the university often becomes highly specialized, and it tends to assume that criticism and analysis are the only legitimate ways of growing in knowledge. The all-too-frequent result of these assumptions is "an overall sense of fragmentation in thought and work" (p. 130). One might say that the previous chapter's emphasis on the language of faith is now applied to the university context. A common assumption in higher education is that there is only one road to true knowledge, one right way to see reality, one proper language to speak: that which was given to us by the Enlightenment. Dykstra suggests that the struggle between Spirit and flesh also runs through our assumptions about knowing, and therefore, all such assumptions are to be examined carefully.

Religious communities, counters Dykstra, are often able to give "unity to every level and dimension of human existence as well as to the mystery beyond its horizons" (p. 134). A fundamental task of the university is to encourage its students to pay attention to reality as it is, and religious communities have a contribution to make to that process: "in some flawed but still potent ways [they] form people in ways that give us some freedom from neurotic fears and egocentric compulsions to control and distort, and thus they can help us develop the capacity to love reality itself" (p. 134). Through true seeking of knowledge, we become (paraphrasing Simone Weil) "people capable of paying attention, which itself is the substance of prayer, which in turn is the substance of love" (p. 138).

That brings us back to the place of practices in faith education. Acquiring knowledge is not limited to criticism and analysis. The practices of prayer, prophetic speech, hospitality, and love of the enemy (p. 138) are in themselves ways of knowing. While chapter 9 provides hints in this area, in chapter 10 this theme becomes more explicit. "Knowledge might be something other than intellectual grasping. It might be a complex form of life" (p. 142). Volunteers with the Human Service Alliance confirm Dykstra's hypothesis. "They are discovering . . . that in and through their practices of hospitality and healing, through their relentless focus on the care of others freely given, they come to *know* things they never knew before" (p. 144, emphasis his). Understanding knowledge in such a holistic, complex manner frees one to see reality more deeply. These two chapters suggest slightly different strategies: Christian communities can seek to make an *impact* upon *all* institutions of higher education; theological schools, however, can strive to *"be* communities-of-faith-and-learning" (p. 147, emphasis his).

> **CHU on the chapter**
>
> What was:
>
> • confusing
> • helpful
> • unsettling?

Questions for Discussion

Observe

Remember your own school education through the light of this chapter. In what ways did it serve to aid you in paying attention to reality and forming godly character and vision? In what ways did it contribute to fragmentation and/or intellectual pride? What dynamics or assumptions or practices in these schools allowed these contributions to be made? A small but growing number of colleges and universities are recognizing the limitations of Enlightenment-based curricular structures and are experimenting with alternatives. Are you aware of any such experiments? How do they relate to the themes of this chapter?

Reflect

Frequently one hears first-person accounts from scientists who, after discovering something new, experienced a prayerful awe and wonder in delighting in something greater than themselves. Perhaps such accounts answer Dykstra's question, "Is prayer a way of knowing that a university can possibly consider?" (p. 138). How have you experienced prayerful ways of knowing? How does this way of knowing intertwine with other ways of knowing?

Implications for Faith Education

I spoke once with a fifty-something youth group volunteer who hosted the dozen high school seniors in his church for breakfast at a local restaurant every Friday at 7 a.m. He said, "It's our last year with them; I want them to know that we love them before they leave." After forty-five minutes of food and conversation, the students went to school while he and the other leaders went to work. His story helped to convince me that the church needs transition practices, that is, practices that serve to pass the baton of faith education from the church to the next place that is part of a young adult's life (most frequently, the university or college). Are you aware of other transition practices? Do you believe that they are necessary, or do they undermine maturation by providing too much hand-holding?

Areas for Deeper Exploration

The central themes of these two chapters take us into deep and profoundly intriguing epistemological waters. There is a growing body of literature that explores these waters, often in the following manner: our universities are rooted in an Enlightenment epistemology, which itself is rooted in ancient Greek epistemology. This epistemology gives an exalted place to the objective knower who functions as a detached subject analyzing objects. The biblical worldview assumes a Hebraic epistemology, which sees knowing relationally and holistically. As the knower, I am never detached from what I am seeking to know, and my intellectual analysis is completely intertwined with all other aspects of my being. For further exploration, I recommend three books that Dykstra refers to (cf. p. 140, nn. 16, 18). An essay that I have found particularly helpful is Marvin R. Wilson's "The Contour of Hebrew Thought," in *Our Father Abraham: Jewish Roots of the Christian Faith* (Grand Rapids: Eerdmans, 1989, pp. 135–65). For an unusual and thought-provoking (though less direct) treatment of these themes, see Brian D. McLaren's *A New Kind of Christian* (San Francisco: Jossey-Bass, 2001) and its sequel, *The Story We Find Ourselves In* (San Francisco: Jossey-Bass, 2003).

PART 5: SIGNS

Chapter 11: When the Bible Happens

Chapter 12: Learning to Be Sent

Chapter 13: "My Teacher, We Made Bread . . ."

These three final "chapter-ettes" cull various threads from the whole of *Growing in the Life of Faith* and weave them into inspiring anecdotes and advice that relate directly to the teacher involved in faith education. Every teacher resonates with Dykstra's description of the nine parts of teaching: "getting a weary body out of bed on Sunday mornings, cutting out construction-paper patterns, cleaning hardened glue from tables . . ." and all the rest (p. 164). Dykstra calls these chapters "signs"; signs are tangible pointers to realities deeper than themselves. Signs provide bits of hope and encouragement that the real thing actually exists and that one is traveling in the right direction.

Faith education involves paying attention to the presence of God in the Bible and in our own lives. We may teach the Bible with many different goals in mind, says Dykstra, but ultimately "God is using the Bible . . . to give us courage, to set us free of whatever enslaves us, to seduce us . . . into the love God has for us . . . to form us and re-form us, to shape us into God's own" (p. 155). We are not called to squeeze the Bible into our lesson plans; we are called to cooperate with what God is doing in and through the Bible.

> **CHU on the chapter**
>
> What was:
>
> • confusing
> • helpful
> • unsettling?

To teach the Bible, to cooperate with it, is to allow it to read us. Then we are situated inside the mission of God; we are the sent ones who have become "vulnerable to being changed" (p. 160). Faith education is being sent into foreign territory, which "may be found smack-dab in the middle of our own cities and towns, our own churches and families, even our own personalities" (p. 159). In such foreign territory we come home, for there our lives become habitations of the Spirit, the place where God is.

Questions for Discussion

(Note: This final section does not follow the four-part rhythm of previous Questions for Discussion.)

Dykstra observes that teachers "search through curriculum materials for something to teach and in the how-to manuals for ways to teach it. But what they do more than anything is bring *themselves* to another person" (p. 163, emphasis added). This observation resonates with the apostle Paul's warm letter to the Thessalonians, where he says, "So deeply do we care for you that we are determined to share with you not only the gospel of God but also our own selves, because you have become very dear to us" (1 Thess. 2:8). How have teachers shared themselves with you? What effect did this sharing have? How do you share yourself with others? In what ways does this come easily, and in what ways is this a tremendous challenge?

Dykstra suggests three questions to ask when planning for teaching (p. 153). Read these out loud together. One way to look at these questions is to see that they begin by asking what God will do, then how the learners can cooperate with what God will do, and then how the teacher can help the learner cooperate with what God will do. What do each of these questions assume about the character of faith education? Change the word "us" in the first question to "them"; how does that change the meaning of the question? If any in the group have been involved in leading faith education during the past year, invite each one to take a specific lesson that has been taught and brainstorm together how working with these questions might have shaped that lesson.

Concerning our own faith education, Dykstra suggests that "we are nourished in so many ways, and we don't remember 2 percent of them" (p. 163). Many of the reflection questions in this study guide were designed to encourage such remembering. Now that you have completed the book, how has your remembering deepened and expanded? What are you thankful for as you remember? What implications does your remembering have for your involvements in faith education?

Invite the group to spend five minutes in silence, paging through the entire book with this question in mind: identify one central insight or conviction that *Growing in the Life of Faith* has rooted or strengthened in you. Describe why it is so central, addressing how it has affected your own faith, your life of faith, and/or your involvements in leading faith education.

INDEX

Christian education (*continued*)
 field of, xix
 fundamental aim of, 71
 as mission, 159–61
 planning for teaching, 153–54
 and Sunday School, 162–64
 of youth, 123–27, 159
Christian practices:
 educational significance of, 7–8,
  67
 as habitations of the Spirit, 63–64,
  66
 list of historic, 7–8, 42–43, 70,
  144–46
 as means of grace, 40–46
 as ordinary and mundane, 53–54
 as participation in the work of
  God, 11–13
 peculiarity of, 75–78
 as physical and intelligible action,
  71–72
 and power, 56
 practice defined, 67–70
 teaching and learning of, 44–46,
  71–74
congregation, limits and power of,
  83–84, 88, 90–95
Cox, H., 93–94
creeds and confessions:
 Apostles' Creed, 106
 Brief Statement of Belief, 42
 Confession of 1967, 23, 40, 42
 Declaration of Faith, 18, 29
 Didache, 115
 Heidelberg Catechism, 20–21
 Larger Catechism, 41–42
 Small Catechism (Luther), 11
 Theological Declaration of Barmen,
  42
  summary of, 18
 Westminster Confession, 23
Cyril of Jerusalem, 115

death:
 by bread alone, 11
 knowledge of, 144
 power of, 26–27, 29
Dowey, E., 27

Edgerton, R., 137
education:
 defined, xx
 in faith, xx–xxi
  See also Christian education,
   higher education, theological
   education
enemies, as fellow creatures, 60–63
Erikson, E., 120–21

faith:
 and belief, 19–20
 Calvin's definition of, 18
 as communal, 39–46, 117–17
 defined, 18–19, 22
 education in, xx–xxi
 growth in, 38–39
 and human development, 36–38
 as meaning-making, 17, 30
 and metaphors for growth,
  34–36
 and personal knowing, 20
 as reality apprehension, 92–93
 as regeneration, 34
 as response to divine gift, 17
 as trust in God, 89
 and truth, 22
 as a way of life, 17–19, 22–30,
  115–20
  See also hope, love
family:
 and adoption, 98–99
 and baptism, 105–8
 as constituted by promises,
  97–101
 and marriage vows, 98, 102–5

Construal p. 143
mellifluous p. 142

Book: "A sense of Mission"
Abert Curry

Printed in the United States
142474LV00006B/15/P

Made in the USA
San Bernardino, CA
27 July 2018